Life After Cars

THESIS

Life After Cars

Freeing Ourselves from the
Tyranny of the Automobile

Sarah Goodyear, Doug Gordon,
and Aaron Naparstek

THESIS

THESIS

An imprint of Penguin Random House LLC
1745 Broadway, New York, NY 10019
penguinrandomhouse.com

Most Thesis books are available at a discount when purchased in quantity for sales promotions or corporate use. Special editions, which include personalized covers, excerpts, and corporate imprints, can be created when purchased in large quantities. For more information, please call (212) 572-2232 or e-mail specialmarkets@penguinrandomhouse.com. Your local bookstore can also assist with discounted bulk purchases using the Penguin Random House corporate Business-to-Business program. For assistance in locating a participating retailer, e-mail B2B@penguinrandomhouse.com.

Book design by Alissa Rose Theodor

LIBRARY OF CONGRESS CONTROL NUMBER: 2025005061
ISBN 9780593850725 (hardcover)
ISBN 9780593850732 (ebook)

Printed in the United States of America
2nd Printing

The authorized representative in the EU for product safety and compliance is Penguin Random House Ireland, Morrison Chambers, 32 Nassau Street, Dublin D02 YH68, Ireland, https://eu-contact.penguin.ie.

For our children

The car has made the big city uninhabitable. It has made it stinking, noisy, suffocating, dusty, so congested that nobody wants to go out in the evening anymore.

André Gorz, "The Social Ideology of the Motorcar," 1973, translated by Chris Turner

Contents

Part III

How We Get Free

Introduction

Cars ruin everything.

That's not the message we've been getting our whole lives. Since the beginning, the auto industry (along with its best friend, the fossil fuel industry) has assured us that car ownership is a magic portal to ease, comfort, and personal freedom. Car companies and their allies have gotten away with peddling that rose-colored vision because there's a superficial truth to it: Automobiles do provide mobility to countless people, and they've become the backbone of the global economy. What the industry doesn't want you to think about—ever—is what cars have cost us.

Far from serving as a figurative and literal vehicle for freedom and independence, cars exclude vast numbers of people from full enfranchisement in society—children, older people who have lost the ability to drive, people with disabilities that prevent them from driving, people who can't afford to buy or operate a car. Automobiles have produced far more collective damage to the world, in terms of death, illness, and environmental destruction, than nearly any other invention in human history.

This rarely acknowledged reality—the true face of cars—is the exact opposite of the image the US automobile industry spends billions on advertising every year (GM alone shelled out more than $3 billion on ads in 2022). You know, the ads that show drivers roaring through empty cities and racing along deserted coastal roads or through sensitive desert habitats in hulking SUVs and sleek sedans. The industry isn't just selling cars with those images. What they're really hawking is a fantasy veiled in chrome and steel, the fantasy of power and control and independence. The American dream on wheels, no matter where in the world one lives.

A hundred years later, that dream is running on empty. Instead of unbounded freedom and rugged self-reliance, the never-ending proliferation of automobiles has delivered a host of costs and burdens. Among them are the demolition of our neighborhoods, towns, and cities to make way for expensive car infrastructure like freeways. Sprawling surface parking lots sit empty much of the time, forming millions of acres of desolate asphalt wastelands that amplify the heat of ever-more-brutal summers and generate toxic runoff during increasingly violent rainstorms. Car dependence enforces grinding financial servitude for tens of millions; an epidemic of violent death; a broad range of chronic, often fatal illnesses; countless hours lost in traffic; isolation from our fellow human beings, resulting in loneliness, alienation, and societal polarization; and the ongoing destruction of the natural world.

You could say it's the opposite of freedom. At this point, we are not driving cars. Cars are driving us. And we're headed for an existential crash.

That's why we've written the book you're holding in your hands. We want to illuminate the scale of the damage that cars cause, the forces that have created this situation and that are invested in perpetuating it, and the way that the fight for better transportation is deeply linked to the fight for a more equitable, sustainable, and just society. Most important, we want to arm you with the tools you need to implement real transformative change.

And who are we? To put it simply, we're ordinary people who have been passionate about the need for safe, clean, and sustainable transportation for a long time. Doug, a TV producer and writer, was also a neighborhood safe streets advocate, better known online as *Brooklyn Spoke*. Aaron was the founding editor of *Streetsblog*, a news site that launched in 2006 and was dedicated to what was then called New York's "livable streets" renaissance. Sarah, a journalist and author, joined the *Streetsblog* reporting team soon after the launch and later went on to cover cities and transportation for publications such as *Grist* and *CityLab*. We started making *The War on Cars* podcast in 2018 because we felt a sense of urgency about communicating one fundamental message: It's way past time to radically rethink—and shrink—society's collective relationship with the automobile.

We knew that we could create a podcast that covered cars the way they ought to be covered, from all angles. We wanted to highlight the ways in which people around the world, from elected officials to ordinary citizens, were rising up with solutions to the problem of automobile dominance. We also knew that our podcast wouldn't just be about policy solutions or advocacy surrounding traffic safety and livable streets. We wanted the name of the podcast to reflect the idea that cars are, without exaggeration, one of the most significant and negative environmental, political, social, and cultural forces in the history of humanity. As we tossed around one idea after another, Sarah blurted out that what we were trying to do was create "a podcast for the 'war on cars.'"

We had our title.

But *The War on Cars*? Really? Before we even recorded our first episode, we could already hear people asking, "Isn't that title too harsh? Doesn't it turn people off? Why can't it be something that brings people along and encourages them to be open to your message? Does it have to be a war?"

But the title didn't come out of thin air. The phrase has been kicking around for a long time. Paul Fairie, a researcher and instructor at the University of Calgary, unearthed a trove of early news stories with references to a "war on cars" or some variation. One, from 1904, is headlined "Farmers Declare War Against Automobiles," and describes how a group of rural Wisconsinites placed heaps of gravel on the road to block the incursion of motor clubs from Chicago. Another, from 1907, is headlined "War on Motorists" and reports that "the opening gun in the fight between Glen Echo [Maryland] and the automobilists of Washington" was a move to reduce the speed limit to six miles per hour.

Eventually, references to a "war on cars" would change their meaning. In 2002, *The Economist* published a story titled "The War Against the Car" and asked if the then-mayor of London, Ken Livingstone, was purposely making traffic worse so that he could enact congestion pricing the next year. No longer did the stories about a "war on cars" describe put-upon small-town folk fighting back against the scourge of urban joyriders. Instead, the phrase came to encapsulate the way drivers feel downright attacked by any policy or design solution that gives space to pedestrians, cyclists, and transit users—or otherwise addresses the many negative externalities of cars.

It's a story from Canada, though, that's the true inspiration for the podcast's title. In 2010, a bombastic Toronto city councillor named Rob Ford ran for mayor on a platform that included ending what he called the city's "war on cars." The city had already invested in a plan to build a comprehensive light-rail network as well as hundreds of miles of bike lanes. Ford had long been an opponent of these efforts. Roads, he declared, were "built for buses, cars, and trucks, not for people on bikes." The issue loomed so large over the election that when Ford eventually won, he declared during his very first press conference as mayor, "Ladies and gentlemen, the war on the car stops today."

Rob Ford's (admittedly masterful) deployment of the phrase *war on cars* was catnip for a news media hungry for clicks and desperate for eyeballs. It was also a perfect example of how conservative elected officials and their partners in the press hijack our attention and political narratives with wedge issues and culture war nonsense. Think of how a company asking its employees to say "Happy holidays" gets filtered through the outrage machines of cable news and is transformed into the "war on Christmas," or how an all-female reboot of a beloved 1980s movie gets spun into a "war on men." That's how taking a few parking spaces to install a bike lane equals a "war on cars." To paraphrase a popular saying, when you're accustomed to driving, sharing the road feels like oppression.

Today, any effort to reclaim streets for people is met with claims of a war on cars. "Paris Mayor's War on Cars Moves Up a Gear with Ban in the Heart of the City" was how France 24 described Mayor Anne Hidalgo's efforts to limit cars on the Rue de Rivoli and otherwise make the city friendlier for cycling in 2017. The *New York Post* published a 2019 story about transformation of curbside car storage into Citi Bike stations, loading zones, public seating, and bike lanes under the headline "NYC's War on Cars Has Eliminated 6,100

Parking Spots in Two Years." The story even lamented that one hundred spots would soon be turned into charging stations for electric cars. How turning parking spaces for one kind of car into parking for another kind of car equals a "war on cars" is puzzling, but once things become fodder for the culture wars, they don't always make sense.

The three of us think it's worth fighting to take back the streets of our cities and towns from the automobile. That's why we decided to take the phrase *The War on Cars* back for ourselves, and in the process transform it into a weapon in the struggle that we've been part of for decades.

As it was at the beginning of the automotive era, today's war on cars is really about fighting for people.

When we launched, our quest to bring attention to the destructive aspects of car culture felt quixotic. Something profound has happened in the past few years, though, a shift in consciousness sparked by the converging crises of climate change and COVID and bolstered by the hard work of progressive transportation planners, activists, and elected officials around the world.

Increasingly, activists are noting the intersection of the broken transportation system with other inequitable systems. The housing affordability crisis is fueled by land-use regulations that favor single-family homes in sprawl environments. Months of working from home during the pandemic made long, expensive car commutes on congested highways seem ever more punishing and ridiculous. Traffic enforcement takes a disproportionate toll on Black and brown communities. Women bear the burden of navigating a transport network that is still geared toward traditional male commuting patterns. And the climate crisis is now affecting daily life on every continent in every season, from catastrophic floods to wildfires that leave millions of people choking on smoke from our planet's burning forests. Name an issue affecting society right now, and there's a good bet it is caused or at least exacerbated by society's overreliance on cars.

The time has come for a reckoning with the destructive and inefficient mobility system we have built. Our climate and our own health can no longer withstand the assault of the automobile. This reckoning won't be easy, though.

Cars are everywhere. That's part of why they can be so hard to see—and why envisioning a world with fewer cars is such a challenge. The pervasive hegemony of auto infrastructure can make it seem like cars are an inevitable part of a "circle of life" that begins with nervous parents driving a newborn baby home from the hospital to mourners escorting a hearse in a highway funeral procession. And because no one alive today has ever experienced the world without cars, some people may find it hard to imagine how we ever did without them.

The cost of our chronic car denialism is steep. Global carbon emissions from SUVs reached nearly 1 billion tons in 2022, which would rank them among the top-ten most-polluting nations. Nearly 43,000 people were killed by cars in the US in 2022, when pedestrian fatalities were the highest they had been since 1981, up 77 percent between 2010 and 2021. In 1969, 42 percent of American children walked or biked to school. In 2017, that number was 11 percent.

The good news is that people around the world are waking up to the fact that the water we swim in is not fine. An international movement to push back against car dominance is gaining ground. Cities including Paris, Bogotá, Montréal, Oslo, and New York are redesigning their streets, putting the needs of pedestrians, people on bikes and other mobility devices, and transit riders over drivers. Gen Z has been slower to embrace driving than previous generations. Positive coverage of bikes, pedestrian safety, parking policy, and related issues has been booming at major news outlets.

Cars as we know them today are unsustainable, and people must take the world back from cars if we are to survive the current existential threats to our society and the environment. We believe that together, we can seize this era in history to reimagine the autocentric landscapes where we live and rethink our own personal relationships with the car.

Maybe you've never thought much about it before, other than feeling an underlying sense that automobile dependence is somehow an immutable fact of life, like the laws of physics. Sure, you might say to yourself every now and then, cars suck in a lot of ways, but this is just the modern world and there isn't anything or anybody who can change it.

This book is for you.

Or maybe you *have* thought about it, while sitting in traffic. You may have looked around yourself at the wider and wider highways, the taller and fatter SUVs, the choking brown haze on the horizon, the miles of vehicles idling in traffic, and the shimmering heat rising off acres of asphalt and thought, "This system is crazy."

This book is for you.

Maybe you remember the thrill of getting your driver's license, the freedom you felt the first time you got behind the wheel, only to discover before too long just how expensive and stressful driving can be. You'd like some options, but it seems too intimidating to think about and you don't know how to begin.

This book is for you.

Or maybe you are already trying to reduce car dependence where you live, organizing your neighbors to get a bike lane, or some better bus service, or sidewalks that kids can walk on safely to get to school. Maybe you want information and examples to help you convince people in your community and your family that things could be different, and better, and cheaper without so many cars. Maybe you want some moral support in fighting what can seem like an unwinnable battle.

This book is for you, too. Because you're not alone. Others are fighting back.

In part 1 of this book, we'll look at the history of how we got to this automotive impasse and dig deep into the psychology of car culture. In part 2, we'll explore the surprising damage cars do in our world—some of it deeper and more consequential than you might realize—and talk to researchers and activists who are trying to shed a light on those harms, raise the alarm, and rally forces for change. In part 3, we'll dive into all the ways that people around the globe are fighting back against the tyranny of the car, with tactics ranging from DIY guerrilla street improvements to major government infrastructure projects like freeway teardowns. And we'll offer insight on how to exert influence on those in power, from the public meeting to the street demonstration to the ballot box.

Life After Cars will tell you everything you always wanted to know about how we got to this point—and most important, about how we can make the transition to a better world, a world that flourishes after cars no longer dominate, and how you can be a part of it.

We don't have to live like this, and we don't have to wait for permission to initiate change.

Welcome to the war on cars.

Part I

How We Got Here

1

A Brief History of the War on Cars

In the first panel of *Action Comics* number 12, published in May 1939, mild-mannered reporter Clark Kent is outside the offices of the *Daily Star*, a precursor to the more famous *Daily Planet*. A small crowd has gathered, and when Kent asks someone what has happened, he is shocked to learn that a friend of his has been hit and killed by a reckless driver.

Enraged, Kent calls the city's mayor and asks why Metropolis has "one of the worst traffic situations in the country." The mayor's response will likely be familiar to anyone who has tried to get an elected official to take traffic violence seriously. "It's really too bad," the mayor says. "But—what can anyone do about it?"

Kent vows to do something about it himself. He changes into Superman's iconic blue-and-red uniform and, in a single bound, takes to the skies, smashing through the window of a radio station and commandeering the live broadcast. "The auto accident death rate of this community is one that should shame us all," he tells listeners. "More people have been killed needlessly by autos than died during the world war!" Then, in a panel that shows the superhero in close-up for emphasis, Superman proclaims into the microphone, "From this moment on, I declare war on reckless drivers—henceforth, homicidal drivers answer to me!"

The subsequent pages and panels flow by in a cinematic montage of vengeance against automotive carnage. Superman descends upon a county tow pound where the cars of traffic violators are stored and proceeds to "smash and tear them to a pulp," gleefully stating, "I think I'm going to enjoy this private little war!" He confronts a used car dealer who knowingly sells dangerous lemons and destroys his inventory. He picks up a car with a drunk driver and admonishes him to "leave the liquor alone." At one point, Superman himself is mowed down by a "hit-skip" (or hit-and-run) driver. Pretending to be a ghost, he then jumps in the motorist's back seat and threatens to haunt him if he continues to drive recklessly. He targets traffic enforcement, stopping a police officer from taking a ten-dollar bribe from a driver who wants to get out of a speeding ticket. He redesigns roads, using his incredible strength to eliminate a dangerous curve through a mountain pass. Superman even confronts a motor company executive about prioritizing "profits at the cost of human lives," before laying waste to the entire automobile factory.

Finally, Superman goes after the man he believes is most responsible for the crisis: the mayor of Metropolis. Superman carjacks the politician and terrorizes him by driving so fast that the mayor, a bit of a lead foot himself, fears that Superman is going to kill them both. Then our hero flies the hapless elected official to the city morgue, where he forces the mayor to look at the maimed bodies of "auto victims," people he says the mayor killed with his lackadaisical approach to enforcing traffic laws. Scared straight, the mayor swears he will do everything in his power to make sure all traffic rules are "rigidly enforced." (In the story's humorous coda, Clark Kent is about to get in his car to drive to city hall to cover an announcement about the mayor's traffic safety initiative only to discover that, thanks to the city's new zero-tolerance policy for traffic violations, he's received a parking ticket.)

To modern readers, Superman's violent "war" on cars might be a bit surprising, and not just because the image of the Man of Steel as a menacing vigilante stands in stark contrast with the heroic "Truth, Justice, and the American Way" version popularized by the 1950s TV series or the classic 1978 movie starring Christopher Reeve. (At one point in the 1939 comic, the mayor calls him a "hoodlum" and laments that not even hundreds of police officers can stop him.) It's probably not even that this Depression-era Superman is shown using his powers to right social wrongs instead of stopping some megalomaniacal villain from destroying the city. No. What is most shocking is that the biggest threat to the citizens of Metropolis in 1939 was not a monster or alien invader nor even Superman's famous archenemy Lex Luthor, who wouldn't appear in print until a year later. It was the car.

Almost eighty years before we started *The War on Cars* podcast, why did Superman announce via a radio broadcast (the podcasting of its day) that it was time to start a "war on reckless drivers"?

In 1914—the year Jerry Siegel and Joe Shuster, the creators of Superman, were both born—approximately 4,700 people in the United States were killed in motor vehicle crashes, a rate of 4.8 per 100,000 population. In 1939, the year *Action Comics* number 12 was published, 32,386 people in the United States were killed in motor vehicle crashes, a rate of 24.7 per 100,000 population. (For comparison, as bad as traffic fatalities are today, they occurred at a rate of "only" 13.8 per 100,000 population in 2022, the most recent year for which comparable figures are available.)

Siegel and Shuster, like a lot of people living in the United States in 1939, would have known their share of people who had lost their lives or suffered life-altering injuries because of reckless driving. Only a few decades into the mass automobilization of North American cities, the duo also would have had recent experience living in cities before cars really took over. The problems caused by automobiles would have only grown over the course of their lifetimes, as would a culture of complacency as the death toll continued to rise. To Siegel and Shuster, it must have seemed like only a superhero could stop the carnage.

Cars and the War on People

The only reason anyone knows the name Henry Bliss today is that he holds the macabre distinction of being the first person in the United States killed by a car. According to a report in *The New York Times*, on the evening of September 13, 1899, Bliss stepped off a downtown streetcar on Central Park West and Seventy-Fourth Street, when he was suddenly struck by a taxi (an electric taxi, interestingly enough). Eyewitnesses said that Bliss was flung to the pavement, his head and chest crushed by the impact. He was rushed to Roosevelt Hospital, but his injuries were too severe to treat, and he died the next morning. Henry Bliss was sixty-nine years old.

The taxi driver, Arthur Smith, was arrested, charged with manslaughter, and held on $1,000 bail—the equivalent of about $37,000 today. As the *Times* reported, Smith claimed "a large truck occupied the right side of the avenue," leaving him no choice but to drive extremely close to the streetcar and making it impossible for him to avoid striking Bliss. Smith was later acquitted, achieving another kind of distinction as the first in a long line of drivers to face zero criminal consequences for killing a pedestrian.

Most histories of automobiles in the United States begin in 1896 with Henry Ford and his Quadricycle, a two-cylinder, gas-powered vehicle made from bicycle wheels, a seat from a horse-drawn buggy, and other miscellaneous parts. Or they begin on October 1, 1908, with Ford's Model T "rolling off" (in every telling, it's always "rolling off") the assembly line at the Piquette Avenue Plant in Detroit. The seeds for the United States' status as *the* dominant economic superpower of the twentieth century were planted by Ford, the invention of cars, and the efficiencies he pioneered at his factories. The automobile industry built the American middle class, which in turn bought the cars and houses that created the postwar suburbs, entrenching what we now know as "car culture." The history of the United States in the twentieth and twenty-first centuries is, in a very real way, the history of cars—and vice versa.

As the saying goes, history is written by the victors. In many ways there's no bigger victor in American history than cars, especially when one considers how completely they have shaped the economy, pop culture, politics, the built environment, the natural landscape, and even the climate. That's why we at *The War on Cars* believe there's an alternate history of cars that must be told, one that includes a more honest reckoning with mass motoring's effects on all of the above. That history should begin not with the triumph of Henry Ford, but with the tragedy of Henry Bliss. Given his status as patient zero in what has been one of the biggest public health crises this nation and the world have ever known, he deserves to be remembered as the first victim of car culture instead of just the answer—or, sorry, question—in a *Jeopardy!* category. ("I'll take Famous Firsts for $400.")

At least twenty-five more people would be killed in auto-related fatalities in the United States through the end of 1899, a high number given that only around 2,500 motor vehicles were produced in the country that year. (As long as we're focused on an alternate history, there's an alternate *reality*, too, where the country looks at a new invention with an annual deaths-per-product ratio of about one to one hundred and stops it from ever being adopted at scale, or at least delays it until it can be made safe. Don't be surprised if our next book is a science fiction story about a team of time travelers who go back to stop the rise of the machines.)

In the nine years before the Model T hit the streets, more than 2,200 Americans were killed by cars. Things would only get worse from there. Much worse. In 1910 alone, nearly 1,600 people died in motor vehicle crashes. In 1920, it was 12,155 people. In 1924, twenty-five years after Henry Bliss was killed, the death toll was 18,400 people. The crisis was so obvious and widespread that *The New York Times* ran a story that same year headlined "Nation Roused Against Motor Killings" above an illustration of a caped figure with a skull for a face driving a massive, open-topped car over a crowd of terrified people, mostly women and children. The caption: "The Modern Juggernaut."

As University of Virginia historian Peter Norton describes in *Fighting Traffic: The Dawn of the Motor Age in the American City*, his indispensable and outstanding history of the reaction to the rise of cars during the 1910s and 1920s, the nation was indeed roused

The early reaction to cars and the deaths they caused was anything but subtle. *The New York Times*, November 23, 1924

against motor killings. In 1919, the Detroit Safety Council, seeking to draw attention to the epidemic, ran a campaign to ring bells at city hall, fire stations, churches, and schools "on any day in which a life was lost to a traffic accident." Many cities focused on the disproportionate number of child victims, putting the responsibility for their deaths, as Norton writes, "squarely on the shoulders of motorists and their cars."

Tributes to the victims of car crashes resembled the ceremonies and memorials to soldiers who had been killed in the Great War that had just ended. In 1922, the city of Baltimore erected a twenty-five-foot wood and plaster obelisk dedicated to the 130 children killed by drivers the previous year. Norton describes how 200 "White Star Mothers," each one of whom had lost a child to traffic violence, attended the march, their designation an echo of the honored "Gold Star" families whose loved ones have died in wars. Cities such as Pittsburgh (286 children killed in 1921), Washington (97 children killed in 1921), and St. Louis (32 children killed in 1923) memorialized their dead with similar monuments and solemn observances.

Comparing car deaths with war deaths was intentional. Cars were waging an all-out assault on urban residents. In 1926, automobiles killed 1,066 New Yorkers; 408 of them were children. Nationwide, 60 percent of automobile fatalities in the 1920s were kids under age nine. It was a horror almost without precedent in modern life, especially because it was the result of a relatively new technology that was hardly a necessity and was largely seen as a plaything for the rich.

Anger at drivers and their cars permeated the culture. To bring attention to this deadly scourge, public demonstrations and public thinkers did not shy away from using violent imagery and direct language. Pittsburgh's 1921 campaign included a safety parade featuring a float displaying "a little girl, crushed between two colliding automobiles." As Peter Norton describes, the base of a monument erected in Baltimore "had four plaster reliefs, each depicting lethal traffic disasters involving vehicles and children."

Newspapers frequently labeled motorists as "killers" and "remorseless murderers," and rarely questioned whether a driver was at fault for killing a pedestrian—the reverse of the prevailing journalistic assumptions these days. As the *St. Louis Post-Dispatch* put it in a 1923 editorial, any driver who claimed that he could not avoid hitting a child, even one "darting into the street," was committing "the perjury of a murderer." In reporting on the forty-five men, women, and children killed in 1922 in Louisville, the city's *Pioneer News* named two of the motorists responsible and described them as "death car drivers."

Such descriptions were not limited to the operators of cars; they were frequently used to describe automobiles themselves. In 1923, a year before *The New York Times* ran its haunting illustration of Death driving a car, an editorial cartoonist for *The St. Louis Star* depicted a man kneeling before an automobile, the car's headlights appearing like eyes and its grille illustrated to look like a gaping maw. The man, wearing a jacket labeled "reckless and vicious drivers," offers a plate of children's bodies as a ritual sacrifice to what is labeled as the "Modern Moloch." (Compare this with the more modern crisis of gun violence, a problem the writer Garry Wills described in a widely circulated 2012 essay as "Our Moloch.") In late 1920s Harlem nearly ten people were injured by car drivers every day on a single one-mile stretch of the neighborhood, a grim preview of the racial disparities that mark traffic safety to this day.

Brooklyn, the modern home base of *The War on Cars*, declared its own war against cars. On May 10, 1927, the Brooklyn Safety Council, along with a group of "leading Brooklynites and high police officials," dedicated a big display dubbed the "Death-O-Meter." It was strategically positioned near a major traffic circle "where hundreds of thousands of automobilists on their way to Coney Island can not help but see it." Like an old-fashioned ballpark scoreboard, it kept a running tally of the number of people injured or killed on the streets of Brooklyn: 2,232 injured and 54 killed by the time of its dedication just five months into the year. The Death-O-Meter admonished drivers to "Slow Up" and asked them "What's Your Hurry?" In neighboring Manhattan, the City Club of New York produced what it called "municipal murder maps" to keep track of the carnage wreaked by automobiles; the 1928 edition featured 154 black dots marking the spots where children had been killed by drivers the year before.

These days, the language used by mainstream media to describe traffic violence is emotionally detached and passive, as if to shield everyone from the reality of a system that kills tens of thousands of people annually and injures millions more. Outside of the most egregious cases, such as when an intoxicated driver kills several people in one crash, the news for the most part covers car wrecks as nothing more than an inconvenience for other folks behind the wheel. That crash on I-85 that's messing up the morning commute? The traffic reporter in the helicopter is never going to break down and acknowledge the horrific truth that someone has died, one of the approximately 110 people who are killed that way every single day in the United States.

Even the very people responsible for fixing this public health crisis resort to dry, academic-sounding jargon when talking about road deaths. Take the "killed or seriously injured" metric used by transportation officials to measure road safety; it is often abbreviated to KSI as if to obscure its meaning, which is the sudden and brutally violent loss or devastating alteration of individual life.

This is why we, along with other advocates for safe streets, prefer the word *crash* over *accident*. *Accident* implies that safety is a matter of individual responsibility, and that death and injury are just the cost of mobility in a modern society. "The reason the word 'accident' is such a harmful one is because it's kind of magic," said Jessie Singer, author of the book *There Are No Accidents*. "It is like a giant rug under which we can sweep massive amounts of tragedy to avoid having to look at it anymore, to avoid having to do anything, to tell a simple story." Using the word *crash*, on the other hand, leaves open the possibility that a driver did something wrong, or that better road design might have prevented tragedy, or that multiple factors—all of which could be addressed—stacked up to contribute to the outcome. The word *crash* also harks back to the 1910s and '20s, when the deaths caused by cars were still shocking and not just a thing that made people late to work.

Motordom Strikes Back

Long before Silicon Valley popularized the idea, cars were the original "move fast and break things." Quite literally, they moved faster and more unpredictably than anything that had been on streets before, and, the early history shows, they broke a lot of people.

Despite the use of graphic imagery like Brooklyn's Death-O-Meter, many of the early anti-car campaigns were, in essence, toothless emotional appeals to the drivers' better selves. This approach, which we still see in many modern traffic safety PSAs, is a bit like trying to get King Kong to come down from the Empire State Building by telling him he might break a few windows or hurt someone if he falls. Even a hundred years ago, some people realized that no amount of lecturing drivers could significantly affect motorist behavior. It would be far more effective to tame the machines by slowing them down. Again, Peter Norton's research is indispensable here. "If reasonable safety of life and limb can only be had by impairing the motor car's efficiency," read an editorial in the *St. Louis Post-Dispatch* in 1923, "the motor car will have to pay that price."

A pedestrian struck by a driver at sixteen miles per hour has only a 10 percent chance of being severely injured or killed, while a pedestrian struck at thirty-one miles per hour has a 50 percent chance. That jumps to a 75 percent chance of severe injury or death at thirty-nine miles per hour, and a 90 percent chance at forty-six miles per hour. Which means that being hit by a driver just doing the legal speed limit on most roads in the US equals almost certain death. And the increasing mass of modern vehicles means the equation is only getting less favorable for people outside the car.

Almost as soon as cars began taking over cities, people understood intuitively that slowing them down was the key to keeping pedestrians safe, and there was broad popular support for reducing speeds. In 1923, the public outcry against the automotive scourge came to a head: Some 42,000 people in Cincinnati signed petitions in favor of an ordinance requiring automobiles to be equipped with a mechanical governor that would limit cars to a top speed of twenty-five miles per hour. Supporters of this campaign did not mince words. "Which Shall It Be?" asked an ad in *The Cincinnati Post.* "A Limit of 25 Miles Per Hour and SAFETY or No Limit and the Lurking Danger of DEATH!"

The proposed Cincinnati ordinance was a real test for "motordom"—the name Norton uses to describe the consortium of automobile manufacturers, oil companies, road builders, parts suppliers, driving clubs, and other groups advocating for cars. Motordom knew that cars had a major image problem. But this coalition also saw that resistance to motor vehicles was slowly waning, as more cars hit the streets and more affordable models made it to the masses. Motordom understood that any effort to restrict the speed of cars would impede this growing acceptance and cut into one of their biggest selling points: the ability to go anywhere *fast.*

And so the industry and its allies seized on the Cincinnati ordinance as an opportunity, mounting a coordinated campaign that mobilized a growing and influential constituency: car drivers. The Cincinnati Automobile Dealers Association sent a letter to every car owner in the city, urging them to vote against the ordinance and donate to efforts to defeat it. That money was then used to mount an even bigger campaign, including get-out-the-vote efforts and ads in *The Cincinnati Post*. One notable ad compared the proposed speed-governor ordinance with a "Great Wall of China Against Progress" that would keep visitors out of the city and cause drivers to spend money in Columbus, Indianapolis, or Louisville instead. Arguing that "Present Laws are Adequate" to ensure safety, the ad beseeched the citizens of Cincinnati to vote no. By the time of the election in November of 1923, motoring interests had completely taken control of the debate. The safety effort that began with 42,000 petition signatures dwindled to just 14,000 votes in favor of the ordinance. More than six times that many people voted against it.

Had Cincinnati's speed-governor law succeeded, we might now be living in a world where a driver's speed is kept in check not just by police enforcement, signs, and polite public service campaigns, but by proven technologies such as GPS-based intelligent speed assistance, which could restrict cars and trucks to the posted limit. Instead, we are to date mostly applying that kind of innovation to vehicles like shared scooters and e-bikes.

Still, despite this early and decisive victory, motordom believed it had been granted only a temporary reprieve. The fear that other municipalities might have more success in limiting the speed and reach of cars spread across the industry and automobile enthusiasts. Norton, using his own militaristic analogy, writes that the various auto-related interests "never returned to a peacetime footing." While there is a growing movement around the world to lower speed limits—from Seattle's speed limit of twenty miles per hour on residential streets and twenty-five on larger arterials, to Amsterdam's victory in 2024 to lower the citywide speed limit to thirty kilometers per hour, or eighteen miles per hour—cars' war on cities has been going ever since.

Pesky Pedestrians

Before Henry Bliss stepped off that streetcar in 1899, he probably didn't give a thought to looking out for an oncoming car. It wouldn't have occurred to anyone. For all of human history, and well into the first two decades of the twentieth century, streets were public spaces like any other: places for transporting people and goods, sure, but also places for stopping, doing business, socializing, and playing. But with the rise of cars, all of that changed—or rather was changed, by carmakers and their allies.

Jaywalking, a word people use today without a second thought, was coined by automotive interests in the 1920s. Motordom sought to shame people into staying off the roadway by implying that they were "jays"—contemporary slang for country hicks—and that they simply didn't know how to walk properly in the big city. Later, campaigns such as "Cross at the Green, Not In Between" would solidify the message that people on foot belong on sidewalks and in crosswalks, and nowhere else. A nation that was once roused against motor killings would buy more and more cars, gradually but steadily turning its ire against pedestrians who impeded the progress of the new rightful owners of the street: motorists.

It wasn't just a territorial victory. When the focus was shifted from murderous motorists to pesky pedestrians, crashes resulting in death became simply individual tragedies and not symptoms of larger societal concerns. This understanding of the problem worked against the implementation of systemic solutions. If pedestrians were responsible for their own deaths and injuries, the government was off the hook. There was no need to fight messy political battles over speed governors, better designed streets, or other limits on where and how people could drive.

This philosophy of individual responsibility has permeated the safety conversation for a hundred years now, and it continues to inform many of the educational efforts to reduce traffic deaths. In 2019, for instance, the Colorado Department of Transportation launched a traffic safety campaign featuring people dressed as giant eyeballs. "This is to remind pedestrians to make eye contact before stepping into the road," said the agency's traffic safety manager.

Even when campaigns are targeted at drivers, it's all about personal responsibility. In 2024, the National Highway Traffic Safety Administration—a federal agency that could use its power to force car companies to install speed governors—launched a campaign called "Speeding Catches Up with You" which focused on "social norming" as a way of deterring people from speeding.

The car's early takeover of city streets was a success, at least for cars. The result was the undercurrent of death we ride with to this day.

We Have Always Been at War with Cars

Stories about the origins of the word *jaywalking* might go viral every now and then, but the larger history of the pushback and outrage that accompanied the arrival of cars in cities has mostly been forgotten, perhaps deliberately so. The Henry Ford Museum of American Innovation in Dearborn, Michigan, which grew out of its namesake's collection of objects from the Industrial Revolution, highlights the many automobiles that played a significant part in US history and culture, from the 1961 Lincoln Continental limousine in which President John F. Kennedy was riding when he was assassinated, to a 1952 Oscar Mayer Wienermobile. The Smithsonian Institution's National Museum of American History in Washington, DC, has a permanent exhibition, *America on the Move*, about the history of transportation in the United States from 1876 to 1999. The exhibition "examines how transportation . . . has shaped our American identity from a mostly rural nation into a major economic power, forged a sense of national unity, delivered consumer abundance, and encouraged a degree of social and economic mobility unlike that of any other nation in the world." It's located in the General Motors Hall of Transportation. As Peter Norton notes, "If there is an official history of the automobile in the United States, this is it."

But it doesn't take corporate whitewashing—carwashing?—to explain why the darker side of the early rise of automobiles has largely been forgotten. Outside of historians such as Norton, few have dedicated their careers to telling the story of the violence and outrage that accompanied the arrival of the motorcar in cities. Cars are now an essential, unquestioned part of most people's lives. Unlike Jerry Siegel and Joe Shuster in 1939, no person alive today has known a world that was not just full of cars, but also built expressly to accommodate them.

Even those who initially lamented the dangers of cars eventually accepted their inevitability. "The automobile has won out in fair competition, but it has much to answer for it, it seems to me, quite aside from its reputation as a killer," wrote E. B. White, the *New Yorker* writer and author of *Charlotte's Web*, in a 1942 essay.

But did cars really win out "in fair competition"? And did they forge "a sense of national unity" and encourage "social and economic mobility," as visitors to the Smithsonian are taught? This was certainly not the case in the first half of the twentieth century, when the well-funded forces of motordom came together to defeat the Cincinnati speed-governor ordinance, or when they launched the sophisticated public relations campaign that created the concept and crime of jaywalking.

It also wasn't true after World War II, the period when the US cemented its status as a car-based country. The construction of the Interstate Highway System is the largest public works project in American history; it's also one of the country's largest social engineering experiments. In addition to creating the modern car-dependent suburb, it displaced an estimated 475,000 households and more than a million people during the 1950s and 1960s.

In his great book *The Power Broker*, author Robert Caro writes about how the seven-mile-long Cross Bronx Expressway, "a huge trench gouged across a city," tore through the borough and displaced 60,000 people, many of them immigrants. In 1959, the construction of an elevated section of I-81 in Syracuse, New York, leveled the entire 15th Ward, which at the time was home to nearly 90 percent of the city's Black population. Approximately 1,300 families were displaced. It's unlikely that these residents felt "a sense of national unity" or that even those whose homes were spared experienced much in the way of "social and economic mobility" during or after the highway's construction.

In response to the expansion of automotive hegemony in this period, a new war on cars emerged. Famously, during a wave of protests in the 1950s and 1960s that came to be known as "highway revolts," communities across the country did what they could to stop the expansion of roads that they rightly believed would destroy cities. Urbanist and writer Jane Jacobs and other activists in Greenwich Village went head to head with New York's master builder Robert Moses, fighting his plan to demolish large swaths of Soho and Little Italy for his planned ten-lane Lower Manhattan Expressway. That project, intended to deal with traffic created by roads and bridges Moses had already pushed through, would have displaced nearly 2,000 families and 800 businesses. It was finally canceled for good in 1971.

Communities in other cities, from New Orleans to Oakland, also pushed back against highway construction, battles that united historic preservationists, Black community activists, and environmentalists. In Washington, DC, the proposed construction of the North Central Freeway brought together a diverse coalition that successfully fought against what it called "White Men's Roads Through Black Men's Homes," preserving multiple neighborhoods in the process.

Ultimately, though, the victories were few, and disproportionately benefited constituencies with a fair amount of wealth and privilege. Most communities could not combat the combined forces of federal and state governments working in service of the car's insatiable appetite for more space.

Today, despite what we've learned about the destructive effects of freeways in cities, the roadbuilding continues. As of this writing, Texas is expanding I-35 through Austin, a project that will cost $4.5 billion and displace more than 100 homes and businesses, all in the hope of speedier commutes for people who live outside of the city. Wisconsin will spend $1.2 billion to expand 3.5 miles of I-94 in Milwaukee from six to eight lanes. More than 20 percent of residents along the proposed expansion don't own a car. All these freeway projects are being done in the name of reducing congestion. As we'll discuss later, none of them will work.

As the saying goes, insanity is doing the same thing over and over again—and expecting less traffic.

A Love Affair or an Arranged Marriage?

For generations, automobiles have been promoted as an unmitigated technological marvel. If you question the role of cars in society, or politely suggest that cities invest in public transportation and protected bike lanes, you risk being called a Luddite. The auto-dominant paradigm rests on the idea that the problems cars create can be solved only with new and different cars. Electric cars, autonomous cars. Cars that fly.

Nothing could be further from the truth. Far from being anachronistic relics, nineteenth-century inventions such as trains and bikes are the best tools we have for solving twenty-first-century transportation problems. Organizing our entire transportation system around personal automobile ownership is a historical blip, one that was pushed on society by corporate and government interests and that does not truly represent societal and consumer preferences.

Sometimes, when we tell people we host a podcast called *The War on Cars*, we get a little pushback. That's to be expected when you take any position outside the dominant culture and point out its flaws. Sarah was once talking to a guy at a cocktail party who, after finding out what she did for a living, asked belligerently whether the podcast also covers "all the positive things about cars"—as if a hundred years of car culture, billions of dollars in annual highway spending, and the marketing departments of every major automobile company weren't already taking care of that.

Some critics dismiss us as out-of-touch urban elites. They point out that because we all live in New York—one of the few US cities with enough density, bike lanes, and good transit to enable a comfortable car-free lifestyle—we can't possibly understand the way "real" Americans live. "Besides," people will say, "Americans have a love affair with cars. Good luck trying to change that."

In response, we like to point out that Doug was raised in a town north of Boston on a cul-de-sac with no sidewalks. After college he lived in Atlanta—a poster city for car dependence, urban highways, and sprawl—and drove a Volkswagen Jetta to work. Sarah—a proud New York native—lived for several years in rural and small-town Maine, where she owned both an SUV *and* a 1973 Ford Mustang (cherry red, with a black vinyl top).

We understand American car dependence quite well because we have experienced it firsthand—and rejected it. We know that's not an option for most people, even the people who'd like to make a different choice. Being able to relate to other people while still explaining that car dependency didn't win in a "fair fight" is part of our mission.

Even the famous expression "America's love affair with cars" was a car industry creation, not some folksy saying that arose spontaneously. Peter Norton discovered that the phrase appeared in a 1957 Chevrolet ad before being popularized in a television special that aired on October 21, 1961, on NBC. Called *Merrily We Roll Along* and starring comedian Groucho Marx, the special was sponsored by DuPont, which at the time owned a 23 percent stake in General Motors. In the special, Groucho says that "our love affair with the automobile" started long ago, and that "it was a real love affair, one that changed our whole way of life." The phrase became part of the popular lexicon almost overnight. Produced the same year that Jane Jacobs published her seminal book *The Death and Life of Great American Cities*, and airing just as the highway revolts were gaining steam, Groucho's hyping of the "love affair" was a brilliant defensive ploy on the part of the automobile industry. For generations, that hype has successfully obscured the darker reality of a world built for cars.

People over Parking

On August 10, 2018, Madison Lyden, a twenty-three-year-old tourist from Australia, was riding a bicycle on Central Park West when an Uber driver suddenly pulled ahead of her into the painted bike lane. According to news reports, Lyden swerved into the adjacent car lane to avoid the Uber and was hit by a sanitation truck. In an eerie echo of what happened one hundred twenty years earlier, Lyden died just seven blocks from the spot where Henry Bliss had been killed.

Even though it's against the law to block a bike lane, the Uber driver who obstructed Lyden's path was not charged. (He wasn't even ordered to pay the fine for such an offense, which is $115.) The driver of the sanitation truck, Felipe Chairez, was allegedly drunk at the time of the crash; investigators found three beer bottles on the floor of his truck's cabin, and he was arrested and charged with driving while intoxicated, among other offenses. However, just as taxi driver Arthur Smith was acquitted after he claimed he could not avoid hitting Henry Bliss, the man who drove into Madison Lyden got off easy. Prosecutors ultimately dropped the main charge against Chairez, concluding that even had he been sober, it wouldn't have made any difference, because he was driving in his lane and obeying the speed limit at the time of the crash. He was released with just a $1,000 fine—the equivalent of about $27 in 1899.

Madison Lyden's death spurred a wave of activism in New York, supported by her family in Australia. A year after she was killed, the New York City Department of Transportation installed a protected bike lane on eighteen blocks of Central Park West. (The full stretch, running fifty-one blocks, or about 2.5 miles, was completed in 2020.) But for the most part, the story remained local, as most traffic deaths do.

Even the coverage the protected bike lane did receive in the local press showed the way pro-car bias has pervaded mainstream media. In 1924, *The New York Times* published that haunting image of the Grim Reaper driving over women and children under the bold headline "Nation Roused Against Motor Killings." This time, that same paper published a story headlined "The People of Central Park West Want Their Parking Spaces (Sorry, Cyclists)."

Increasingly, though, advocates for active transportation aren't accepting "sorry" as an answer anymore. Since Henry Bliss was hit by that taxi in 1899, cars and automobility have killed anywhere from sixty to eighty million people and injured at least two billion worldwide. After decades of weary acceptance, there's a growing global movement questioning the inevitability of the ongoing toll. More and more people are asking what the first warriors against cars asked: Why must we sacrifice our loved ones to appease the automotive gods? When will people matter more than parking? When will we say, "Enough"?

That people are asking these questions gives us hope, but it will take more than questions and hope to turn the tide. "Hope is a discipline . . . we have to practice it every day," says the American activist and organizer Mariame Kaba. All over the world, individuals and advocates are practicing the discipline of hope by changing their own relationship with driving, joining up with larger campaigns to fix streets where they live, and staging direct actions that challenge the dominance and alleged inevitability of cars. There's just one thing every advocate for a better, less car-dependent future always finds standing in their way—the culture.

2

Car Culture and Bikelash

In March 2018, a driver allegedly suffered a seizure, pressed the accelerator, and ran a red light at the intersection of Fifth Avenue and Ninth Street in Park Slope, Brooklyn. She killed two children, aged one and four, who were in the crosswalk with their mothers. The women were also injured; one of them, who was pregnant at the time, later lost her unborn child.

It was a horrific tragedy, but it most certainly was not an accident. Ninth Street's history of deadly crashes could be traced back to at least 2004, when two fifth-grade boys were killed by a truck driver as they crossed the street on their way home from school, a heartbreaking incident that resulted in only modest changes on the busy thoroughfare. In 2016, a forty-one-year-old man was killed by a hit-and-run driver. Motorists would frequently hit cyclists. Every now and then drivers plowed into stores, causing serious injuries and major property damage.

At the time of the March 2018 crash, Doug lived just a short walk from Ninth Street and his kids attended school a block away. As news of the tragedy spread around the neighborhood, Doug sprang into action. He put out the call on social media asking people to join him the next day outside of the Park Slope YMCA that was a favorite destination of the city's then-mayor, Bill de Blasio. The gym just happened to be right up the street from the crash site. More than a hundred local residents showed up, including many stroller-pushing parents. With them and a phalanx of reporters looking on, Doug told the mayor that the carnage had to stop. In response, the mayor promised that Ninth Street would finally get a major overhaul. Six months later the New York City Department of Transportation redesigned Ninth Street with narrower car lanes to prevent speeding, new pedestrian islands to shorten crossing distances, and a set of protected bike lanes on either side of the two-way street.

Not everyone was pleased. Drivers were upset that adding pedestrian islands had required the removal of about four to six parking spaces per intersection. They complained that narrowing the street had slowed traffic (even though slower speeds result in fewer crashes and, as we explained in the last chapter, they also result in less severe outcomes). Some business owners said the new design had made it difficult for customers to access their shops, even though Ninth Street has subway stations that serve several different lines, as well as multiple bus routes, and few in the neighborhood drive for their daily needs. Some people worried that the bike lanes would hinder emergency response vehicles, ignoring the ample space that the DOT had left in the middle of Ninth Street, which was wide enough for even the biggest fire trucks to get through. Others raised what they said were process-oriented objections: They weren't against bike lanes per se, just the ones on Ninth Street and the way they were designed. Still others said that there hadn't been enough notification, an odd assertion given the high-profile nature of the tragedy that prompted the redesign.

As time went on, the arguments against the bike lanes became increasingly hyperbolic and confusing. The owner of a funeral home said he could no longer load and unload caskets, even though the new design had increased the distance from the parking lane to the sidewalk by only about seven feet. According to some residents, the bike lanes were unnecessary, because so few cyclists used them. Other residents insisted the lanes were dangerous because there were so *many* cyclists using them.

More than a year after the terrible crash that had prompted the street redesign and after months of escalating complaints, a group called Citizens United for Safety came together for the express purpose of getting the Ninth Street bike lanes removed. They plastered flyers around Park Slope promoting a neighborhood meeting, asking in blazing red lettering, "What would you do if your house were on fire and the ambulances and fire trucks couldn't get to you in time because of narrowed streets caused by bike lanes?" The flyers promised that people from "all neighborhoods" were welcome and that "elected and city reps" would be at the meeting, to be held at a local church.

By the time the meeting rolled around, on an unseasonably hot Wednesday evening in September 2019, tensions were high. In front of a standing-room-only crowd of more than a hundred people in the unair-conditioned basement of the Church of Gethsemane, the head of Citizens United for Safety invited a climate activist, meditation instructor, and documentary filmmaker named John Halpern to kick things off. Things got weird fast.

Halpern claimed that the Ninth Street traffic calming project was part of a citywide conspiracy funded by a crony of Jeffrey Epstein, the infamous financier and sex offender. Each of Halpern's ridiculous claims was met by a chorus of laughter, which he dismissed by falsely claiming that at least 40 percent of the bike lane supporters at the meeting were "lobbyists or friends of lobbyists" who had been paid to attend by Transportation Alternatives, New York's main cycling and pedestrian advocacy organization. The meeting's organizers had promised that people from all over the city were welcome, but Halpern complained that "the majority of the people in the room don't live here." When it was pointed out that Halpern lived in Upper Manhattan, about fifteen miles from Park Slope, the jeers grew even louder. Halpern, a practicing Buddhist, stood on a chair and yelled at the crowd, "You wanna clown around with me?"

Things only deteriorated from there. When one pro–bike lane attendee decried Halpern's presentation as "propaganda," a burly man pointed at the bike advocate and said, "I'll beat your ass." That prompted even more shouting and chaos. It was at this point that Doug quietly moved from where he had been standing in the crowd, stood next to Halpern, and pulled a piece of paper from his pocket. What happened next went by in a flash, but a local reporter later offered this play-by-play:

> Amid the commotion, Doug Gordon, a safe streets advocate and co-host of The War on Cars podcast, walked to the front of the room and began reading the names of the five people killed by drivers on Ninth Street since 2004. As he was doing so, Halpern reached out and pushed him, then flipped off the crowd.

Fortunately, Doug was not hurt. He did not push Halpern back, instead calmly returning to the back of the room. Interestingly, the sudden burst of violence seemed to lower the temperature, and the meeting continued in a much calmer fashion before fizzling out. The Ninth

Street bike lanes remain in place to this day, but the outrage that greeted their installation was an example par excellence of what can happen when anything comes along to challenge car culture.

It Almost Plays Out Like Mad Libs

Resistance to any design or policy solution that deprioritizes cars is almost always fierce. The phenomenon is by no means limited to bike infrastructure; it can be triggered by anything from the installation of an expanded sidewalk to an express bus lane. Even the mere suggestion that people consider driving less can cause tempers to flare. But there's something about bicycles in particular that routinely engenders a level of emotion and resistance that goes far beyond the usual knee-jerk reaction to change. The response is so over-the-top and specific it demanded a new word: *bikelash.*

You won't find it in the dictionary, but we define bikelash as "the negative and outsized reaction of car culture to change." While it's rare for things to get physical, it's not unusual for policies that favor people on bikes over people in cars to provoke angry, hyperbolic, illogical, and absurd responses. What is it about bicycles that transmutes more typical resistance to change into full-on bikelash?

One of the earliest uses of the term was in a 2010 story in *The New Republic* headlined "Bike-Lash!" It describes the negative reaction that frothed up when then US Transportation Secretary Ray LaHood told a conference of bicycle advocates that walking and cycling should be considered equals with other forms of transportation. Critics accused LaHood of pandering to cyclists and reminded him that bicycles would never be as important to the economy as cars.

The following year, *New York* magazine used the term—this time without a hyphen—to headline a cover story about the blowback against the New York City Department of Transportation's efforts to install bike lanes, an initiative helmed by then–DOT Commissioner Janette Sadik-Khan. The biggest of these fights centered on a lane along Brooklyn's Prospect Park West, something we were deeply involved in as journalists and advocates. In that project, what had been a three-lane speedway with parking on both sides and no dedicated space for bikes was reconfigured into a safer and more pleasant street by removing one lane for cars and installing a two-way, parking-protected bike lane. The resulting design kept more drivers within the speed limit, shortened crossing distances for people on foot or in wheelchairs, and got people on bikes off sidewalks—where they risked harming pedestrians—and out of mixed traffic, where they could get hit by cars. By every conceivable metric, from safety stats to the counts of people on bikes using the new protected bike lane, the project was a smashing success.

Foreshadowing some of the wild claims that would fill the church basement the night Doug was shoved, opponents of the Prospect Park West bike lane sued the city, alleging that the DOT and "radical bike lane lobbyists" colluded to suppress dissent about the project. They accused Sadik-Khan and her team of relying on "misleading, selective, and unsound data to support false conclusions" about the bike lane's safety and utility. Their attorney assured people that the group was not opposed to *all* bike lanes, just the one that happened to have been installed on the street where the majority of its members lived. "People feel there is a larger policy, which looks good on paper, and everyone can get behind in a general manner, but has been implemented in such a rash way, with not just a lack of information but misinformation being conveyed to communities," said the plaintiffs' attorney, Jim Walden. Walden, who had made a name for himself as an assistant US district attorney prosecuting international heroin traffickers and investigating organized crime, told a TV interviewer, "As a former federal prosecutor I've never really seen something like this." The lawsuit, originally filed on behalf of groups calling themselves Neighbors for Better Bike Lanes and Seniors for Safety, wound its way through the courts for years before the plaintiffs gave up in 2016. Today, the Prospect Park West bike lane is a fixture of the neighborhood and one of the most pleasant and safest bike lanes in New York.

Walden's hyperbole was a textbook example of bikelash. The phenomenon is so common and the stages of it are so predictable that it almost plays out like Mad Libs, with the local players left to fill in blanks labeled "city" or "street name."

"This Isn't Amsterdam"

One of the top arguments you hear about reducing car dependence in North America, the UK, and Australia is that in those places, cities were built for driving—so they could never be anything like the cities we think of as epitomizing bike and pedestrian friendliness. This fallacy is typically expressed with some variation of the phrase "This isn't Amsterdam," although any place with a lot of bikes, good transit, and pleasant, walkable neighborhoods will do as a stand-in. The online version of *New York* magazine's "Bikelash" story, for example, is headlined "Not Quite Copenhagen" and quotes a Prospect Park West bike lane opponent as saying of the Big Apple, "We will never be Amsterdam, never be Copenhagen."

This common assertion reveals the ignorance of the bikelasher.

Copenhagen, for example, wasn't always the Copenhagen most people think of today. In the 1950s, following the lead of their American counterparts, planners in the Danish capital recommended constructing a twelve-lane road that would have paved over the city's lakes and demolished some of its most historic neighborhoods. Thankfully, the plan never came to fruition, but that didn't stop cars from infesting the city. Copenhagen faced a choice: accommodate the cars and lose the city, or keep the city and lose the cars. This idea came to a head in 1962, when officials argued that the cars clogging Strøget, a main shopping street, were creating all sorts of problems, including danger, noise, and pollution. They announced a plan to pedestrianize the area, which was initially met with heavy resistance from local shopkeepers, who feared a lack of parking for customers would lead to a decline in sales. Many business owners insisted that Scandinavia's cold and gloomy winter months made cars a necessity for daily activities such as shopping, and that it was ludicrous to think Strøget could ever become sufficiently attractive to people on foot and on bikes. Copenhageners, the argument went, were simply not built like other Europeans, especially those from warmer climates. According to the famous architect and urban planner Jan Gehl, the shopkeepers sang a now-familiar refrain: "We're not Italians, we're Danes; we need our cars."

To help soften the resistance, city officials presented the pedestrianization as a two-year experiment, telling shopkeepers that if it didn't work out, the cars could return. That's not what happened, though, because the experiment was an immediate success. In the first year alone, pedestrian volumes increased by 35 percent. In 1964, Strøget was permanently pedestrianized, this time to the general delight of area shopkeepers, who welcomed the extra foot traffic and all the business it brought. Over time, the area became even more attractive to locals and tourists alike, with "stopping and staying activities" such as grabbing a bite to eat or browsing in a store increasing by 400 percent. Today, of the approximately eighty thousand people who visit the 1.1-kilometer shopping street each day, only a small minority would be old enough to remember how controversial it was to ban cars so many decades ago. In fact, the only thing that would ignite a controversy now would be proposing to reopen the street to automobiles.

Copenhagen's experience reveals a fundamental truth about social change: People will almost always resist what they haven't experienced firsthand. That's why advocates for sustainable transportation and more pleasant streetscapes must never assume that just because things work well elsewhere, similar plans will be immediately accepted in their hometowns. Pippa Coom, a former member of the Auckland Council in New Zealand, knows this well. An enthusiastic supporter of safe streets, she watched as many bike lane projects she championed became the subject of local outrage, even if she knew full well that such changes would work and be popular with time. "If you're in New Zealand saying, 'I was in Paris and I saw these amazing cycling streets,' no one wants to hear about the experience of other places. They just want what applies to their hometown. And in Auckland you hear the same things: 'We're never going to be like Amsterdam, we're not going to be like cities in Europe, we're not going to be like Copenhagen.'"

"I Like Bikes, But . . ."

Another common rhetorical tactic is for bike lane opponents to say they "actually like cycling." Some might even go so far as to describe themselves as "avid cyclists." But let them finish their thought and it will always be followed by a big pause and an equally big "but."

During a 2019 episode of *The View*, the popular daytime talk show host Whoopi Goldberg used similar language when confronting Bill de Blasio about something she said was really pissing her off. "You've built eighty-three miles of protected bike lanes, OK," Whoopi told the mayor. "And I like bikes, I like people who ride, but I don't think you understand the impact of taking something like Tenth Avenue, which is six lanes, down to two and a half." She went on to complain that these changes had made it impossible for trucks to make necessary food deliveries, especially during winter snowstorms. "Nothing flows," said Whoopi.

There were more than a few problems with Whoopi's rant. Chief among them was the fact that *there was no bike lane on Tenth Avenue.* Still, getting things right is not as important to the bikelasher as giving the impression that they've arrived at their opposition to bike lanes in good faith. "I like bikes" is the spoonful of sugar that makes the anti-bike medicine go down.

Fake News

Whoopi Goldberg's detailed critique of an imaginary bike lane revealed another key feature of bikelash, which is that there's something about bicycles that makes otherwise intelligent people say completely unintelligent things. At the height of New York City's Prospect Park West–related bikelash, *New Yorker* staff writer John Cassidy—who covers economics and politics and who was educated at Oxford, Columbia, and Harvard—wrote a column criticizing the city's increasing investment in cycling infrastructure. "I don't have anything against bikes," Cassidy began (see if you can already spot a bikelash trope). "As a student, I lived in the middle of Oxford, where cycling is the predominant mode of transport, and I cycled everywhere." Employing another classic bikelash trope, he wrote that city hall "sometimes seems intent on turning New York into Amsterdam, or perhaps Beijing." Moving on to our final bikelash trope, Cassidy also claimed that when he drove up and down Brooklyn's Fourth Avenue, what he usually saw were "cars and trucks inching along in single file (it's a two-way street) with an empty bike lane next to them." Just as with Whoopi Goldberg, the problem for Cassidy was that Fourth Avenue didn't have a bike lane. And instead of just a "single file," at the time Cassidy wrote his screed, the avenue had six lanes for cars and trucks with parking on either side of the street. Oops.

These basic errors aside, what made Cassidy's column the perfect example of how bikelash can trip up even the smartest people was his claim that investing in cycling infrastructure didn't make sense "from an economic perspective.

> I also question whether the blanketing of the city with bike lanes . . . meets an objective cost-benefit criterion. Beyond a certain point, given the limited number of bicyclists in the city, the benefits of extra bike lanes must run into diminishing returns, and the costs to motorists (and pedestrians) of implementing the policies must increase. Have we reached that point? I would say so.

In response, plenty of equally intelligent people pointed out that Cassidy's argument was the thing that didn't make sense, *especially* from an economic perspective. Financial journalist Felix Salmon wrote that Cassidy's claim that adding bike lanes to the city must "run into diminishing returns" was simply incorrect, as evidenced by the fact that "the number of cyclists in New York has been growing just as fast as the city can create new lanes for them." Ezra Klein, writing in *The Washington Post*, said that Cassidy's logic defied not just economics but geometry: "There's no further room for roads in Manhattan or its environs, but given the city's comfort with tall buildings, there is room for more people. If each and every one of them decides to buy a car, as Cassidy has, the streets will become essentially impassable." The *New York Times* columnist and Nobel Prize–winning economist Paul Krugman was more direct, calling Cassidy's column "awesomely self-centered." *The Economist* magazine dismantled Cassidy's argument, suggesting he re-familiarize himself with the economic concept of negative externalities:

> As things stand, given that cyclists help alleviate some of these externalities (a cyclist takes up dramatically less road space than a car, doesn't use on-street parking, does not emit ozone, and does not contribute to climate change) it seems quite sensible to allocate a larger share of New York's roadways to lanes for cyclists. From an economic perspective.

Moral Panic!

In 2016, New York City proposed a law that would help people on bikes avoid conflicts with drivers by allowing them to treat the pedestrian signal as a green light. This practice, which uses something called a leading pedestrian interval (LPI) to give people who aren't in cars a head start of a few seconds through intersections, is common in bike-friendly cities in Europe and has been in place in Washington, DC, since 2013. New York's proposal, however, attracted the ire of Alan Dershowitz, the famous (infamous?) attorney and Harvard law professor. "People who love to ride bikes in New York often hold up Europe as a model," Dershowitz wrote in an editorial on the subject. "Well, my experience in Europe has been different. Bike riders—and there are many more of them in most European cities— seem to be more respectful of red lights." Dershowitz's editorial lambasted New York City cyclists for their culture of "rampant running of red lights" and suggested that until bike riders changed their behavior, any talk of rewriting laws for them was premature. A story in *Grist* made a similar argument against laws favoring cyclists, saying that "bikers should live by the same laws as everyone else." (It's a standard no one ever applies to drivers. When's the last time anyone said that if drivers want lower gas prices or potholes to be fixed, they need to stop killing people first?)

It's simple to say cyclists should obey traffic laws just like "everyone else," but it's sometimes hard to notice that nobody else obeys traffic laws. In a car-centric system where so few people bike, lawbreaking cyclists stand out, making them easy to condemn. That same car-centric system makes lawbreaking drivers hard to see but easy to condone, or at least excuse.

Michael Hobbes, a journalist and a podcaster, said that this is what makes bikelash similar to other moral panics, which he defines as "a majoritarian backlash to social progress that benefits minority groups." Such panics typically involve demonizing a perceived "other" for their transgressions, most of which are exaggerated or even imaginary, and either ignore or even actively distract from much larger and very real societal problems, especially when solving those problems might require tweaking the status quo. "A lot of people . . . find cyclists annoying on a visceral gut level in a way that they don't find drivers annoying because all of the infrastructure is designed around cars," said Hobbes. Even pedestrians, who also exist in a world where cars have always been part of the landscape, tend to be much more focused on cyclist behavior than the thing they really should be afraid of: getting hit by a driver. According to Hobbes, "You really have to zoom out to see . . . the problem is actually cars, but on a day-to-day, minute-to-minute level, it doesn't seem that way."

Moral panics often use extreme examples to prove the potential destructive force of even the slightest change to the established order. But as Hobbes said, "The only evidence of this grave societal threat is . . . these weird random anecdotes that don't actually hold up to any scrutiny." Take Dershowitz's claim that New York City cyclists appear to have an inherent disregard for the law. According to a study conducted by researchers at the University of South Florida, cyclists are just about as law-abiding as drivers. The researchers recruited one hundred bike riders from the Tampa region and equipped their bicycles with sensors, cameras, and GPS trackers. After recording the cyclists' movements for two thousand hours and analyzing the data, the study found that the cyclists obeyed traffic laws 88 percent of the time, while similar observations of drivers showed that they obeyed the law 85 percent of the time.

Sure, these cyclists weren't on the mean streets of New York City, but a similar study in London showed nearly the same results: A 2007 study by Transport for London looked into the "anecdotal evidence regarding the proportion of cyclists jumping red lights at junctions" and found that, despite common perceptions that the majority of cyclists disobey traffic signals, 84 percent of people on bikes followed them. Given these studies, we think it's safe to assume that New York City cyclists are likely falling somewhere in the same range.

None of this is to say that cyclists don't run red lights or otherwise break traffic laws. But finding a solution requires understanding *why*. A study by researchers at the University of Colorado and the University of Nebraska–Lincoln attempted to unpack this dynamic. Observing that "nearly everyone has jaywalked, rolled through a stop sign, or driven a few miles per hour over the speed limit," the researchers noted that such infractions, while "unmistakably illegal," are generally accepted as inconsequential. Bicyclists, however, "seem to attract a higher level of scorn and scrutiny" for their illegal behavior. The researchers wanted to get to the bottom of why people break traffic laws and find out whether cyclists really are as reckless and dangerous as conventional wisdom would have it.

After surveying nearly eighteen thousand people in seventy-three countries, they found that 100 percent of respondents admitted to breaking the law while driving, walking, or cycling. Where things differed was in the reasons various road users gave for flouting the rules. Drivers and pedestrians said they typically broke laws to save time. Cyclists, however, said they typically broke laws to stay safe, doing things like riding on the sidewalk to avoid mixing it up on a dangerous road with cars and trucks. Cyclists also said they broke laws to save energy—rolling through a stop sign, for instance, to avoid having to start pedaling again from a dead standstill. The researchers said that while such behavior was technically illegal, "most bicyclists can generally be described as rational individuals trying to function safely and efficiently given the context and norms of where they live and the transportation system put in front of them."

An analysis of Brooklyn's Prospect Park West bike lane bears this out. Before it was installed, about half of all cyclists rode on the sidewalk. After it was installed, only 3 percent rode on the sidewalk. That's a massive behavioral shift that occurred almost overnight, all because of the availability of a safe bike lane. It's also an excellent data point that should steer cities toward a solution for the problem of scofflaw cycling. As former New York City DOT policy director Jon Orcutt observed, "If your policy changes infrastructure, it will change culture."

If a lot of people in your city are stealing bread, that probably says more about bread prices than it does about people who like sandwiches. The same logic applies to cyclists (which is itself an arbitrary term for a group that doesn't have much in common other than the particular mode they're using at any given moment). If most people on bikes in your city are breaking the law, that says more about the laws than the people riding bikes. That's why New York legalized its "LPI rule" in 2019 and why, as of this writing, eleven states plus the District of Columbia let people on bikes treat stop signs as yields, a practice commonly referred to as the "Idaho stop" after the first state to legalize it in 1982. Contraflow bike lanes, which allow cyclists to safely ride in the opposite direction as cars on one-way streets, are increasingly common in cities from Montreal to Minneapolis and are a much more rational response to the "problem" of wrong-way cycling than finger wagging. (Don't worry, we'll get to street design and its impact on safety and behavior in chapter 8.)

Embrace the Bikelash

The installation of infrastructure is often enough to change cyclist behavior, but it isn't always enough to end bikelash. That's because bikelash, like other moral panics, taps into something much deeper than simple questions of how people get around. Cars have been at the top of the transportation food chain for a long time. If they're taken down a peg in favor of cycling—or walking and transit—it sends a message to drivers that perhaps they're not as important as the slick car commercials that air during the Super Bowl and everything around them has led them to believe. As a 2017 paper by a team of New Zealand researchers who examined opposition to bike lanes around the world put it, "cycle lanes present fundamental challenges to existing power relationships within cities."

Bikelash is not something to resist or be afraid of, but rather to embrace. It might not seem like it when you're being shouted down by a group of angry neighbors at a community meeting—or even being shoved by one of them—but if people are freaking out about bike lanes, it's a sign your city is doing something right, or at least starting to rethink the primacy of cars. Knowing that bike lane opponents tend to resort to the same tired complaints against providing safe alternatives to driving should also be comforting. After all, while the reasons to make your city less car dependent are many, with new ones arising every day, in our experience no one has been able to come up with an original or convincing argument against it.

Bikelash can be thought of as car culture's version of the Kübler-Ross model of the five stages of grief. There's *denial*, as people state, "We will never be Amsterdam," or claim that nobody's using the bike lanes that are too dangerous because of all the people who are using the bike lanes. *Anger* comes in many flavors, from the general demonization of cyclists as reckless scofflaws to a famous TV host yelling at a mayor that all the bike lanes in the city—real or imagined—have pissed her off. *Bargaining* occurs when people resort to lawsuits or other last-ditch efforts to cancel or water down bike lane projects so they don't take parking or otherwise upset the car-centric status quo. *Depression* is probably the shortest lived of these stages, and leads rapidly to *acceptance*, neither of which can be measured at the individual level. That's because while some people will always remain depressed, angry, or in denial about turning car lanes into bike lanes, the real sign of acceptance is the people who, thanks to new infrastructure, seem to appear out of nowhere and start biking to school, work, and wherever they please.

Here's the other oddly comforting thing about bikelash: It's just another piece of our culture-war-driven media landscape. Whether it's on local TV news or in social media posts, outrage drives ratings and engagement—and it's trivially easy to find people who are outraged by bikes. The reality is often quite different. In the waning months of Michael Bloomberg's time as mayor of New York, a *New York Times* poll showed 64 percent approval for bike lanes and a whopping 73 percent approval for Citi Bike. (Bloomberg's approval rating at the time was 49 percent; if a bike lane had run for mayor, it would have won in a landslide.) Even as far back as August 2011, the very same month *New York* magazine ran its "Bikelash!" cover story, a Marist Poll showed 66 percent of New Yorkers supported bike lanes. The media wanted people to believe that the more the city invested in cycling, the more people hated it. The truth was that the more people saw the city's investments in cycling, the more they liked what they saw. Unfortunately, "Most People OK with Change, Want More" doesn't make for good headlines. That's the catch-22 of moving beyond bikelash. When a city starts to change, the people who have the most to lose (such as parking spaces) tend to speak up immediately, while the people who don't yet know what they have to gain (such as safer commutes, cleaner air, and healthier, happier life-styles) tend not to speak up until they see that change is possible, as we saw happen in Copenhagen.

Unless you're well versed in transportation planning—or host a podcast about taking on car dependency—you can be forgiven for not knowing the many ways in which the world can be better with fewer cars. It's even OK and perfectly natural to be skeptical that a world with fewer cars is possible. The American economist Lant Pritchett says that all changes to social norms generate four reactions in successive order: They're first perceived as silly, then controversial, then progressive, before finally being seen as obvious.

Rethinking our relationship with cars is one of the biggest social norm changes of all, up there with smoking bans or other public health initiatives that were first greeted with resistance. Seat belts are essentially as old as cars themselves, with Volvo patenting an early restraint system in 1889. But it took until 1968 for the US to require that seat belts come standard in all new vehicles, with many car owners so outraged over even the perception of being told how to behave that they cut them out of their cars. In 1980, when Michigan state representative David Hollister introduced a proposal to fine motorists for not wearing a seat belt, he received hate mail comparing him with Hitler. It wasn't until 1984 that New York became the first state to enact a mandatory seat belt law. Today, more than 91 percent of Americans buckle up when in a car. We have no way to prove it, but our guess is that about the same percentage of Americans have no idea that something that now seems so obvious was once so controversial.

Perhaps you live in a town where support for bike lanes and safer streets seems almost nonexistent. You might have been dismissed by neighbors or elected officials as a naive utopian idealist. Maybe you've even been shouted down at a community meeting. (We're hoping no one shoved you.) Take heart: Every city that pushes back against car dependency experiences something resembling bikelash, even if bikes have nothing to do with it. It's a normal part of the process of imagining a life after cars. There's more support out there than you might think. Find your people, and together you can make it through.

Part II

How Cars Ruin Everything

3

Cars Ruin Childhood

It's about eight fifteen on a Friday morning in June, and half a dozen third and fourth graders are standing at the end of a driveway on a quiet, leafy street in Montclair, New Jersey, waiting to get picked up for school. But they're not waiting for a parent to pull up in a minivan or for a big yellow school bus to stop and open its doors. They're waiting to ride with the bike bus.

The Montclair Bike Bus works just like a regular school bus, only with kids riding their own bikes together under adult supervision along established routes with scheduled stops—although the bike bus doesn't stop so much as it slows down for a moment. If kids want to participate, all they have to do is wait at one of those designated spots at the appointed time and, as soon as they see the bike bus coming, hop on their bicycles and start pedaling. One of the busiest bike bus routes begins with just a handful of children and gradually picks up enough riders that it grows to include more than three hundred kids and adults, like a giant game of blob tag on wheels.

Each bike bus is shepherded by a small cadre of adult volunteers—some are literally called "sheepdogs" and are tasked with riding alongside the pack to keep it together. These volunteers include parents accompanying their own kids, teachers who combine the bike bus with their work commute, and even empty nesters who, after raising their own children in Montclair, want to participate in something that keeps them connected to the community.

The Montclair Bike Bus was founded in 2023 by five families who wanted their kids to be able to bike to school, but who understood that the township didn't have the kind of bike infrastructure that enabled it. Montclair's charming downtown and proximity to Manhattan via commuter rail has led some people to call it "the Brooklyn of New Jersey," but cars still dominate. Households own an average of two cars, and it can be all too easy even for people who enjoyed walking, biking, and taking transit when they lived in the city to fall into the suburban trap of defaulting to driving for most trips. While many streets have sidewalks, there are still plenty of streets designed to move traffic as fast as possible. Bike lanes are essentially nonexistent.

Still, as the success of the bike bus shows, what Montclair lacks in bike infrastructure, it makes up for in social infrastructure. Today, ten schools participate, with friends from different schools often able to ride together before splitting off to their final destinations. Sometimes the proliferation of these bike buses results in delightful scenes where one large group of kids on bikes will be ringing their bells and yelling hello to another large group of kids riding in the opposite direction, who are ringing their bells and yelling hello right back. You can't help but smile.

The Montclair Bike Bus also has an effect that lingers long after the last bike pulls into the schoolyard: It gets young students ready for a day of learning. "[When] they come to school, they're *energized*," said Drury Thorp, a teacher at the Watchung School in

Montclair and a bike bus leader. Some of the kids use that same word to describe why they love participating in the bike bus. "I feel more energized . . . and . . . ready to learn when I ride my bike to school," said Abby, a fourth grader. The bike bus happens weekly on Fridays, but Abby wishes it would also happen on other days, especially Mondays. "Everyone's tired and everything from the weekend, so I feel like biking would help them get a bit more energy and be ready for the day," she reasoned. Tiago, a first grader whose mom accompanies him on the bike bus, loves the chance to ride in the street, which beats the experience most seven-year-olds have of being limited to riding in playgrounds, on sidewalks, or on sleepy cul-de-sacs. "I really enjoy riding on my bike, and I never usually get to ride a mile," said Tiago. "You have a lot more space than on the sidewalk, and I don't like the sidewalk." When Ollie, a third grader, was asked why he liked the bike bus, he stated simply, "Because it's fun."

The world's first organized bike bus was formed in 1998 by a small group of parents in Brecht, Belgium. It was followed by bike buses in other cities in Europe, South America, and Australia.

But it wasn't until 2021 that a combination of factors—including the global-pandemic-related "bike boom," a greater focus on livable cities, growing concerns about climate change, and the ubiquitous nature of social media—turned the bike bus concept from a scattered handful of independent efforts into a worldwide phenomenon.

That year, inspired by a "bicibús" started in the Catalan city of Vic, five families in the Eixample district of Barcelona began riding bikes to school. Soon more than 120 students were participating, and new routes were added to serve multiple schools. To make the routes as safe as possible, volunteers worked with local police, who blocked traffic to allow groups of kids to pedal through busy inter-

Parents and kids ride to school in safety as part of a Barcelona bicibús.
Sarah Goodyear

sections. The spectacle of hundreds of children, some as young as five, riding their bicycles through the streets of a dense city was a moment made for social media. Videos of the Barcelona Bicibús went viral.

Halfway around the world, Sam Balto, a physical education teacher at Alameda Elementary School in Portland, Oregon, saw a video of the action in Barcelona and was immediately blown away. "When you see the children in the scale of a city like Barcelona, it's like these kids are really taking up a lot of space," said Balto. He started his own version on Earth Day in April 2022, attracting an impressive seventy-five students in the first outing. By the following school year, the Alameda Bike Bus had more than doubled in size, with approximately one hundred seventy students riding behind "Coach" Balto on his Dutch-style cargo bike.

Balto posted a video of his bike bus to TikTok and, just like the Barcelona Bicibús video, it also went viral. The online attention resulted in stories in *The Washington Post*, *USA Today*, *People*, and *NBC Nightly News*. Balto was interviewed on the *Today* show and by Kelly Clarkson for her daytime talk show. The coverage kicked off a positive feedback loop, inspiring parents and educators to organize bike buses in San Francisco, Chicago, Boston, a host of small

"People are seeing how important mobility is for children," says Sam Balto, who organizes a bike bus in Portland, Oregon. Jonathan Maus/*Bike Portland*

towns, and even in more car-dependent cities like Atlanta and Los Angeles.

According to Coach Balto, the bike bus movement has tapped into something deeper than just the typical reaction people have to feel-good news stories involving adorable kids. "There's a tremendous unmet demand for walking and biking in the US and around the world," said Balto. "I think that really people are seeing how important mobility is for children—their independence, joy, and freedom. The bike bus is a tool and a mechanism to create that."

Guille Lopez, a Barcelona parent, agrees, especially because kids are so often left out of conversations about the design and use of public space. "The powerful thing of bike bus is . . . it's their streets, it's their city, it's going to their school," said Lopez. "So the fact that for once they are not on the sidewalks and on the margins and they can own their street, that's very powerful."

There's a slightly less positive but still radicalizing way to see each bike bus, and that's as a symbol of what a world built for cars has done to children. After all, in places where kids can get to school safely on their own, organized bike buses aren't novel or even necessary. "That's the goal of the bike bus," said Sam Balto. "We want to send a message that all of this effort and all of these volunteers are only needed because the streets aren't safe enough for kids to ride on their own."

Letting Kids Be Kids

Cars have stolen a fundamental part of childhood from children: their ability to experience the world independently. In 1969, more than 40 percent of kids in the US between the ages of five and fourteen walked or biked to school. Today, it's around 11 percent. A similar story has unfolded in countries around the world, but it's not because kids have changed. In the 1970s and 1980s, the American psychologist Louise Bates Ames published a series of books on the stages of child development from age one through age fourteen. In *Your Six-Year-Old: Loving and Defiant*, published in 1979, Ames included a list of milestones parents should look for in kids entering first grade. Some were purely physical, such as whether they had lost any baby teeth. Others were cognitive, such as being able to "tell left hand from right" or "count eight to ten pennies correctly." But included on the list was a question that speaks volumes about societal views of childhood independence then as compared with now. Ames asked parents about their child, "Can he travel alone in the neighborhood (four to eight blocks) to the store, school, playground or to a friend's home?"

Ames's books are still immensely popular, although not every part of them has aged well. Most notably, child psychologists today have a better understanding of neurodivergent kids whose development doesn't follow easily categorizable milestones. Still, Ames's perspective reflected what was then a widely held belief, that young children are perfectly capable of walking places independently. (That their parents would let them do so was an even more deeply held assumption.) It's a different story today. Many modern American parents and their counterparts in other developed parts of the world would not allow even the most fiercely independent, confident, and responsible older child to walk to the store, school, or playground, alone or with friends.

We can't argue this is entirely the fault of cars. Modern parenting happens in a complex system of social pressures, economic structures, and racial disparities that influence the amount of independence parents allow children, sometimes to the point of not allowing them much at all. Fears about "stranger danger" are a factor, even though these fears are largely debunked by statistics showing that a relatively small number of children are kidnapped by people unknown to them or their families. (According to the FBI, 296 children were abducted by a stranger in 2022. In contrast, 1,129 children aged fourteen or younger were killed in car crashes in the US in 2022, and more than 156,000 were injured.)

There have also been dramatic changes over the past few decades in how children spend nonschool hours, and it's not unusual for kids who might otherwise be allowed to walk home by themselves to instead be rushed straight from school to an endless array of extracurricular activities, almost always in a car. Working parents might drive their kids to school on the way to work simply because it's one of the few times of the day harried families get to be together. It's complicated.

Still, building a world where children can get around without needing someone to drive them would go a long way toward restoring at least some of the autonomy and freedom they've lost over the generations. It would also save parents a lot of time and worry.

In 2017, researchers with the Centers for Disease Control and Prevention in Atlanta asked parents of school-aged kids what made it difficult for their youngest child to walk or bike to school. Parents could choose multiple reasons, which were then ranked by prevalence. According to the findings, the most frequently cited obstacle was living too far away (51.3 percent), followed by traffic danger (46.2 percent). Weather (16.6 percent) was a distant third, while "other" (14.7 percent) beat out crime (11.3 percent) and school policy (4.7 percent). Some responses varied according to the child's age or the parents' demographic background, education level, or income. But the relative ranking of barriers did not change.

Using evidence from pediatricians and child development specialists, the Safe Routes Partnership, a national nonprofit that advocates for safe walking and biking to and from schools, believes that most kindergartners without a physical disability should be able to tolerate a walk of up to half a mile relatively fine. Older elementary school kids can handle a mile, while most middle schoolers and high schoolers can easily walk up to one and a half miles. This might suggest that more kids would walk and bike to school if home and school were closer together, but a lot depends on what's between here and there.

In 1969, 41 percent of children in the US in kindergarten through eighth grade lived within one mile of their school; 89 percent of those children walked or bicycled there. Forty years later, the percent of children in kindergarten through eighth grade living within one mile of their school had fallen by only 10 percent, but the percent of those children walking or bicycling to school had fallen by a lot more: 54 percent. (In Canada, only 47 percent of students who live within a five-minute walk of their school—which at normal walking speeds comes out to not much more than a quarter mile—bike or walk there.) But why?

Just as a chain is only as strong as its weakest link, a route to school is only as safe as its most dangerous street. Schools in small communities used to be built in central areas near walkable downtowns, but today many new schools are in far-flung areas where land is cheap, roads are wide, and sidewalks are nonexistent. That leads to a lot of young kids, even ones who technically live close to their schools, being driven there.

It also leads to a lot of traffic. According to the US Department of Transportation, 10 to 14 percent of car trips during the morning rush hour are for school travel alone. Add people making dual-purpose trips, such as a parent who drops a kid off at school on their way to the office, and it's estimated that as much as 20 to 30 percent of morning traffic in some metro areas is school related. This creates a vicious cycle: As streets become more dangerous and congested thanks to all the parents driving their kids to school, more parents opt to drive their kids to school to keep them safe, leading to more dangerous and congested streets, especially near schools. The National Poll on Children's Health, published by the C.S. Mott Children's Hospital at the University of Michigan, found that 48 percent of parents said that to get to class, their children must walk through busy areas filled with cars dropping off other children. Thanks to all the traffic—and school buildings located on properties designed to accommodate all the traffic—nearly one third of parents expressed concern about their kids' safety *immediately* outside their own schools.

Their fears are not unfounded. An analysis of nearly one million car crashes in New York City over seven years found that on school days there were 57 percent more crashes and 25 percent more injuries per mile on streets near schools than on other city streets. These elevated statistics disappeared when schools were not in session. A 2016 study in Toronto looked at 104 elementary schools and found dangerous driver behavior at 88 percent of them, with forty-five children sustaining minor injuries requiring an emergency room visit as

the result of being hit by a car. Analyzing twelve years of police reports, the study found that more than four hundred children had
been hit by a car within 200 meters (656 feet) of a school. Schools in
lower-income communities saw higher rates of collisions.

For decades, motor vehicle crashes were the leading cause of death
for children and adolescents in the US, until guns took the top spot
in 2020. Despite this macabre dethroning, an estimated 429 American children were injured *every day* in traffic crashes in 2022. Broad-
ening out, over one hundred thousand adolescents died in traffic
crashes around the world in 2021.

Beyond the immediate threats to the lives of children, there are
plenty of other ways in which a world built for cars harms their physical health. According to the CDC, only 24 percent of children aged
six to seventeen get the recommended sixty minutes of physical activity every day, something a fifteen- or twenty-minute walk or bike
ride to and from school would go a long way toward solving. As we'll
discuss in chapter 5, exposure to air pollution from cars is a major
source of respiratory disease, a big problem for children whose lungs
are still developing.

And those are just the physical effects. Dangerous, car-centric
roads also mean kids have less freedom than they deserve. That
loss, too, can be measured.

A 2024 study by researchers at Polytechnique Montréal showed
that traffic danger reduces children's ability to access destinations
in their communities by at least 75 percent. Looking at kids aged eight
to twelve, the study found that the disproportionate danger imposed
on kids by "adult-exclusive modes"—aka motor vehicles—was so significant it qualified as an "environmental injustice." Whereas most
previous studies measured only children's ability to independently

access schools and parks, this study included dozens of "child-relevant" places such as libraries, shops, supermarkets, fast-food restaurants, sports centers, movie theaters, museums, public transit stops, and more.

The study showed that such places were essentially beyond the reach of kids, due to excessive automobile speed and streets that were not designed with them in mind. "Children are generally neglected in the transportation decision-making process which is primarily based on the needs and capacities of adults," noted the researchers. This exclusion was so widespread and systematic, the study's authors concluded, that children could be considered a marginalized group whose basic human rights are being violated under the United Nations Convention on the Rights of the Child.

This reduced accessibility not only leads to kids having less freedom but also changes the way they experience the world around them. Bruce Appleyard, an urban designer and professor of city planning at San Diego State University, worked with groups of nine- and ten-year-old children from two suburban communities. One community had streets with light traffic where children were generally able to walk and bike safely on their own. The other had heavy traffic, where children traveled almost exclusively in a parent's car. Using a technique called cognitive mapping, Appleyard asked the kids in each community to draw maps of their neighborhoods and include destinations that were important to them, such as their schools and friends' homes, as well as natural markers like trees. He also asked them to mark places in orange or red they disliked or that they felt were dangerous, such as busy streets with a lot of cars.

In the community with heavy traffic, "the children frequently expressed feelings of dislike or danger and were unable to represent any detail of the surrounding environment." For example, children marked a main road in front of their school with lots of orange and red. Even when the street was lined with trees, the children drew very few. Meanwhile, the children in the community with light traffic created far more detailed neighborhood maps, "drawing more of the streets, houses, trees, and other objects, and including fewer signs of danger or dislike and fewer cars." Their maps also noted 43 percent more locations where they played than the maps drawn by children in the neighborhood with heavy traffic.

On top of that, the children in the heavy traffic community who were driven to most places drew far less accurate maps than children who walked or biked. The latter group produced highly detailed maps of their neighborhood street network that practically could have been handed to people asking for directions. Appleyard's conclusion? "In sum, as exposure to auto traffic volumes and speed decreases, a child's sense of threat goes down, and his/her ability to establish a richer connection and appreciation for the community rises."

The good news is that young brains are malleable—and so are streets. After Bruce Appleyard concluded his initial study, the community with heavy traffic improved some of its pedestrian and bike infrastructure. Appleyard followed up with the kids there and asked them once again to draw maps of their neighborhood. This time, they included much greater detail. Plus, "there were . . . fewer expressions of danger and dislike, indicating a greater sense of comfort and well-being."

Appleyard's study and the research out of Polytechnique Montréal speak to the benefits that can come from making children a central part of the planning process. Kids aren't urban planners, but neither are most adults—and plenty of adults still get a lot of say in how people get around, often at the expense of anyone who doesn't use a car to travel. It's not unusual to go to a public meeting about a traffic-calming project and hear someone say, "I've lived in this neighborhood for the past fifty years, I need my car to get to work, and I don't want any bike lanes." It might be strange and even a little scary for children to speak up in front of a room full of angry adults who just want their parking, but it's fun to imagine a kid flipping this script: "I'm going to live in this neighborhood for *the next fifty years*; I need my bike to get to school, the park, the library, and maybe even to work one day; and I want a whole lot of bike lanes."

That's essentially what happened when Doug's daughter Galit was a second grader at Public School 118 in Brooklyn. That year, the school announced that due to limited space, students would no longer be allowed to store their bicycles and scooters inside the schoolyard. With few alternatives for locking up on the surrounding sidewalks other than trees and signposts, a lot of kids stopped biking and scooting to school altogether. When the next school year began, the students started a petition, gathering hundreds of signatures from kids, parents, school staff, and neighborhood residents all in support of installing a "bike corral" at the curb in front of the school that could store at least twelve bicycles and scooters. At the time, the space accommodated just two parked cars.

According to DOT practice in NYC, changing parking spaces into anything other than car storage required the sign-off of a local community board. These volunteer-run groups, which are sometimes pejoratively called "parking boards" due to their obsessive focus on preserving every last parking spot, are not always bastions of progressive change. They also almost never hear from kids. When the Department of Transportation came to present their plan for the bike corral, Galit and her classmates made a special trip. They stood up before the room and, reading from prepared remarks, explained that having a place to park their bikes would allow them to get to school in a way that was fun, healthy, and good for the environment. Even though a few locals showed up to oppose the plan—and even complained that it was part of New York's ongoing "war on cars"— the board voted unanimously in support of the bike corral, with one adult remarking, "Who can resist cute kids?" The bike corral was installed the next year and was so routinely full of bikes that, as of this writing, it's set to be doubled in size.

Not every kid is the daughter of one of the hosts of *The War on Cars*, so your mileage may vary. Still, while we likely won't see hordes of children taking over community board meetings or out marching for safe streets, perhaps we should. That's exactly how some of the safest cities in the world for kids got to be that way.

Stop the Child Death

As we saw in the Copenhagen example in the last chapter, cars had been steadily encroaching on European cities since the 1950s, and by the 1960s and '70s, automobile dominance was increasingly pervasive around the globe. Even in Amsterdam, a place that had a long history with cycling as transportation, neighborhoods were made over for cars. Parking was squeezed into narrow seventeenth-century streets, and even some canals were filled in and paved over to make room for automobiles. The consequences were similar to or even worse than those caused by the rise of cars in US cities in the first few decades of the twentieth century. By 1971, there were about 3,300 annual traffic fatalities in the Netherlands. Five hundred of the deaths were children, making the country one of the most dangerous places in the world for child traffic casualties at the time.

One of those children was six-year-old Simone Langenhoff, who was cycling to school in the village of Helvoirt when she was killed by a driver. Her father was a prominent journalist named Vic Langenhoff, and he decided to use his pen to fight back against the scourge that killed his daughter and so many other children. Langenhoff published a manifesto in *De Tijd*, a Dutch newspaper, arguing that nothing short of a radical rethinking of the nation's priorities and mindset would stop the carnage. He called for the formation of a pressure group that would unite parents "who want to break through the apathy with which Dutch people accept the daily slaughter of children in traffic." The name he suggested for this group was written right into his manifesto's headline: Stop de Kindermoord, or "Stop the Child Murder."

Langenhoff's powerful words attracted the attention of a young mother and experienced organizer in Amsterdam named Maartje van Putten, who became the first national president of the official Stop de Kindermoord organization. According to Van Putten, the perils of traffic had robbed pedestrians in general and children specifically of access to the streets. "We have lost something essential in our societies," she said. "The car has disrupted our way of living." Van Putten and her fellow campaigners soon organized a series of demonstrations, including complete takeovers of neighborhood streets by children, asserting their demands for more space in their communities to walk, bike, and even play. Some kids held signs comparing themselves with small game being hunted by large predators. Eventually, the children would make the case for safer streets directly to the prime minister at the time. It was a junior version of speaking truth to power.

It would take time, a lot more advocacy, and drastic political changes for things to turn around. In 1975, the traffic fatality rate in the Netherlands was 20 percent higher than in the United States. But just three years later, in 1978, cycling policy became a major part of local elections in Amsterdam, helping a new set of elected officials take power and beginning a push for bicycle-friendly streets that continues to this day. Now, the traffic fatality rate in the Netherlands is more than 60 percent lower than in the United States.

When Sean Kenney, an artist, moved from the US to Amsterdam with his wife and two children in 2020, he was aware of this history. The ease of getting around by foot and by bike was part of the appeal. What he was not prepared for was the culture shock that came with moving from a place where kids are uniquely at risk of being harmed by cars to a place that had spent decades making its streets safe for even the youngest pedestrians and cyclists.

After signing a lease on an apartment, Sean received what, to him, seemed like a strange apology from his new landlord. The landlord handed over a few sets of keys: one for Sean, one for his wife, and one for their nine-year-old daughter. The landlord motioned to Sean's six-year-old son and said, "I'm sorry that I only have three sets of keys for the four of you, but you can get another made at the shop around the corner." Sean looked at his young son and then at the landlord. "A key for the six-year-old?" he asked incredulously. She gave him a quizzical stare, as if the two of them were speaking totally different languages. As Sean told us, "I don't think she knew what to say."

Sean and his wife soon learned that most Dutch kids get home from school by themselves from a very young age, especially if both of their parents are working. Hence the need for a set of keys for a six-year-old. The Dutch also recognize that kids make all sorts of trips beyond getting to and from school, such as meeting friends in the neighborhood. In a city that has mostly tamed the car, that means a lot of independence for kids—as well as a lot of freedom for parents. There's freedom from worry, yes, but also the freedom that comes from not having to constantly serve as a child's chaperone or chauffeur.

"My six-year-old would have playdates and many of the kids would just go home by themselves afterwards without a parent picking them up," said Sean. In his trips around Amsterdam, he constantly sees kids playing outside without adult supervision. Sean sees this with his own kids, too, who love hanging out in a small playground that was carved out of about ten parking spaces. Said Sean, "It's a sort of unofficial 'watering hole' for grade school children. They head over there just to see who else is playing."

Sean Kenney's choice of the term "watering hole" is telling. Just as adults need what are called "third spaces"—those places outside of home and work such as bars, cafés, and public spaces that enable them to socialize with other adults—kids need places outside of home and school, especially places like parks, where it's free to hang out and play with other kids.

"The best park for kids is one that they can access easily on their own, that can become their place," said Alexandra Lange, an architecture and design critic whose book *The Design of Childhood* looks at how the built environment influences kids' development and independence. Lange believes that despite the negative stereotypes of overprotective "helicopter parents," Americans who are uncomfortable letting their children wander independently due to the threat of traffic violence have reality on their side. "It's not an irrational fear on parents' part to not want kids to go around on their own if they have to cross a lot of streets. Kids being threatened by cars is backed up by facts. And bigger cars, faster moving traffic . . . all of that has only increased the danger to kids."

Sean Kenney said it took some time for him and his wife to shed their American tendency toward at least a little bit of helicopter parenting. "My kid is responsible, so we got him the keys and were okay with him walking home from school by himself while my wife and I were at work, but I wasn't ready to let him wander the neighborhood at that age." Then Sean learned that his six-year-old was doing it anyway, heading to friends' houses or the playground with his classmates or neighbors' kids. Sean wasn't upset. "I remember saying to him, 'Well, if you'd have asked me for permission to go out on your own, I would've said no, but you obviously did it and were fine, so I guess that means it's OK.'"

It's more than OK. According to UNICEF, the Netherlands ranks first among all high-income nations in the world in terms of child well-being outcomes, which includes things such as mental well-being, physical health, and academic and social skills. The United States ranked just ahead of Bulgaria and Chile at the bottom of the list. New Zealand, Australia, Canada, and the UK weren't that much farther ahead. It isn't all because of the efforts of those early Stop de Kindermoord campaigners—a robust social safety net and a society that puts tight restrictions on guns certainly helps—but safe streets where children can be active and independent are an essential part of the story.

"I Just Walk There"

Many years after she fought for a bike corral in front of her school, Doug's daughter, Galit, spent a couple of weeks in suburban Chicago, getting some quality time with her grandparents and seeing her best friends from summer camp before she started her sophomore year in high school. Her visit was filled with all the things teenagers like to do in the suburbs: trips to the mall and the multiplex, days at the beach or the public pool, and lots of sleepovers at friends' houses—houses three or four times the size of the two-bedroom apartment she lives in back in New York. About halfway into her time there, she called Doug and told him she had something to say. "Papa, I think I figured out why I like living in Brooklyn," she said.

This was a bit surprising to Doug, because after previous trips his daughter would come back home to the bedroom she shared with her little brother and ask when she could get her own room. "Like all of my camp friends," she would say. Doug asked what it was that made her appreciate living in the city. "All my friends here argue with their parents about who can drive them places," she said. "You and I never fight over anything like that. If I ask if I can go to the movies with friends, you usually say yes, and I just walk there." Making a last-minute decision to go anywhere with her friends in the suburbs, she said, required a lot of discussions with various adults, who didn't always have the time to change their schedules. Kids love spontaneity; driving sometimes requires thinking ahead.

Galit was onto something. People live in the suburbs for all kinds of reasons, many of them deeply personal, perfectly legitimate, and beyond the scope of this book. But one of the reasons people tell themselves that suburbs are better for kids than cities is all the space they get, such as big bedrooms, rec rooms, and backyards. For some kids, those things might be great. But most kids don't necessarily need that much space. What they need are other kids. Whether in a suburb or a big city, the way to make that happen is with safer streets where they can wander and play on their own.

What will it take to center the needs of children at all levels of urban planning and design? How can we force a mindset shift that says that kids have as much of a right to their communities as anyone else, and that such a right can be achieved only by radically rethinking the role of cars in their lives? Sam Balto, the physical education teacher and bike bus organizer in Portland, Oregon, believes that in a country as dominated by cars as the United States, efforts like the bike bus could be the spark that ignites the flame. "A bike bus is kind of this gateway drug to the safe streets for children movement," he said. "If bike bus leaders play our cards right and do the right things to build this movement, this could be our generation's Stop de Kindermoord."

4

Cars Ruin Nature

Everybody loved Barry the barred owl. That was what made it all so sad.

For a brief flicker of time during the first year of the COVID-19 pandemic, Barry was the most famous owl in New York (a position later to be claimed by zoo escapee Flaco, a Eurasian eagle owl, but that's another story). Barry was a young female barred owl, common in much of North America but a novelty in Central Park, New York's premier urban oasis. She became a celebrity simply by being her owl self: perching in the trees and soaring over the lawns of the park's 843-acre expanse, attracting legions of birders with cameras and binoculars when she paused to feast on pigeons and rats, or simply to preen her magnificent plumage. Her movements tracked constantly on social media, Barry was a native-born feathery raptor of undeniable star power. The toast of the town.

Until, that is, she was wiped out in a collision with a Central Park Conservancy vehicle on the road that loops around the park, at the tender age of not quite two. The conservancy posted a somber message on Twitter about Barry's death. "Flying low, likely in search of a meal, the barred owl made contact with a Conservancy maintenance vehicle," the post read. "The barred owl's presence in Central Park brought so much joy, reminding all of us that the Park is a vital green-space for all New Yorkers, including the wildlife that call it home."

Rat poison may have contributed to Barry's demise by impairing her overall health and agility, but the most immediate cause of her death, which happened in the middle of the night, was undeniably a motor vehicle—even though the park she lived in doesn't allow regular car traffic, finally banning it in 2018 after decades of advocates' efforts. "Just say your van killed the owl—and then announce that you're going to remove motor vehicles from the park FOR REAL," wrote one commenter on Twitter.

Barry's violent death was an ugly irony: The owl died in a vehicle strike in one of the very few places where she should have been safe from that particular fate.

The whole city seemed to mourn her passing. "Her arrival during the pandemic brought joy to many New Yorkers who had been hunkered down in their apartments, worried about Covid and their jobs and a crucial presidential election," wrote Michiko Kakutani in a lengthy appreciation of Barry for *The New York Times*. "She got people away from their Zoom meetings and TV screens, and out into the light and air of the park."

The unusual thing, of course, is that anyone thought about Barry as an individual worth grieving at all. We don't mourn the vast numbers of nameless owls that are killed on roads every year. How vast are those numbers, exactly? We don't know for sure. But to give you the very roughest idea, according to the Barn Owl Trust, an owl advocacy group in the United Kingdom, as many as five thousand of the twelve thousand owlets born there each year die on British roads.

From those kinds of local figures, scientists have tried for generations to extrapolate the broader toll that motor vehicles take on wildlife in direct strikes. The first people to document roadkill in a methodical manner were Dayton and Lillian Stoner, a husband-and-wife team of scientists who in 1924 started logging the dead birds and other animals they saw on their road trips through Iowa, Illinois, New York, and Florida. (They didn't call it roadkill; that term seems to have been coined in 1943 by an ecologist named Robert McCabe.)

From the flattened garter snakes and ground squirrels and red-headed woodpeckers they saw lying inert on the nation's burgeoning road network, the Stoners drew some alarming conclusions. "The death-dealing qualities of the motor car are making serious inroads on our native mammals, birds and other forms of animal life," Dayton Stoner wrote in the journal *Science* in 1925. "On a summer motor trip of 632 miles over Iowa roads, 29 species of our native and introduced vertebrate animals, representing a total of 225 individuals, were found dead as a result of being crushed by passing automobiles. . . . Assuming that these conditions prevail over the thousands of miles of improved highways in this state and throughout the United States the death toll of the motorcar becomes still more appalling."

Exactly how appalling was and remains a matter of educated guesswork, complicated by several factors that Stoner and other early chroniclers of roadkill realized from the start. Some animals, like frogs, are reduced to little more than a bloody smear on the pavement by the wheels of a car. Other corpses are cleaned away by scavengers. Larger animals might survive initial impact, only to die where they won't be found after making their way off the road.

Despite its inherent fuzziness, the basic methodology pioneered by the Stoners is still pretty much all we have when it comes to figuring out roadkill numbers: Count what you can see, and multiply. While these constraints leave the exact scope of the problem hazy, the sheer volume of death is undeniable. In his 2023 book, *Traffication*, Paul Donald, a researcher with decades of experience in analyzing data about the effect of roads on animals, writes that studies estimate drivers kill some 200 million birds and 30 million mammals every year in Europe alone. Donald notes further that a relatively recent accounting of annual bird fatalities caused by vehicle strikes in the United States ranges "between 89 and 340 million."

The first number is shocking enough. The second veers into incomprehensibility. That would mean just about one bird killed for every human being in the United States.

Avian celebrities like Barry aside, we don't even really think about those birds most of the time, let alone feel any true sadness at their fate. We certainly don't mourn the innumerable snails, or snakes, or toads, or beetles that are flattened every hour of every day of every week of every year. Killed, directly, by people driving motor vehicles. Squished. Squashed. Smashed. Smooshed.

The scale of the carnage quickly becomes incomprehensible, impossible to grieve, as you widen your perspective from the individual victim of road violence—the squirrel that you might spare a thought for as it darts unsuccessfully across six lanes of traffic, or the crow that is crushed as it pecks at the squirrel's carcass, or even the butterfly you find caught in your grille when you park your car.

The thing is, when it comes to the way cars ruin nature, roadkill is only the most visible manifestation of a web of pervasive, insidious, destructive effects. Some of these are global, like climate change; you probably have thought about that before. But a shocking number of them, like the noise cars make and the dust from their tires, are very local and at times practically invisible. All of them begin with roads and the traffic that flows on them with monotonous regularity.

Defining Traffication

You can't talk about how to solve a problem—you can't even say there *is* a problem—if you don't have the words to define it. And the English language has been slow to come up with vocabulary that expresses all the ways that roads and motor vehicles compromise the natural world.

The word *road* itself, in America, is haloed with a romantic sparkle, steeped in positive emotional connotations. We are forever about to *hit the road*. A *road trip* may be our nation's most iconic vacation. We love to let loose *on the open road*, get to the part where the *rubber meets the road*. We long to simply be *on the road*, an existential state of being infused with an almost patriotic significance.

Around the world, roads themselves are viewed—not without reason—as solid, respectable indicators of progress. If industrial capitalism and the gospel of endless growth are the underpinnings of our present-day belief systems, roads are the material expression of that belief, the gospel enacted by the faithful.

The ultimate goal, the unquestioned apotheosis of all this industrious building, is to make the world fully comprehensible to humans. To find the utility in everything. The King James translation of the book of Genesis—a text that would have been intimately familiar to the Anglophone settlers of the North American continent—put it this way: "And God said, Let us make man in our image, after our likeness: and let them have dominion over the fish of the sea, and over the fowl of the air, and over the cattle, and over all the earth, and over every creeping thing that creepeth upon the earth."

Roads are always the first step in our relentless present-day attempt to assert dominion over all the things that grow and creep and fly, our never-ending project to tame, control, exploit, and *own* nature. Without roads, none of the rest of it is possible—not the industrial agriculture, not the suburban sprawl housing, neither the mining nor the clear-cutting nor the fossil fuel extraction.

"Before you can log Alaska's rainforests or convert Bornean jungles into oil-palm monocultures, you need roads to transport the machinery in and the product out," writes Ben Goldfarb in his 2023 book, *Crossings: How Road Ecology Is Shaping the Future of Our Planet*. "Roads are, you might say, the routes of all evil."

So how do we talk about this vast and complex interface between human ambition and the health of our ecosystems? How can we use language to help us better see and communicate the nearly incalculable shadow that a never-ending web of roads casts on our living planet?

In 1993, Goldfarb writes in *Crossings*, a scientist named Richard Forman came up with the phrase and concept of "road ecology" because no one had formulated a term to describe the way roads affected the natural world. Decades after Forman's postulation, that challenge has yet to be met or even fully understood, and *road ecology* is not a term that has entered common parlance. So when Paul Donald set out to write his book about roads and nature, he felt it necessary to come up with another word to describe what he was talking about: *traffication*.

An ever-increasing number of roads where more and more cars

go faster and faster—that's what Donald calls "the unholy trinity of traffication." And traffication is everywhere. "If you look at a country like the UK where I live, that's pretty much the entire country. Pretty much the entire country is within two miles of a road," Donald told us. "So while all these people were working on issues like climate change, agricultural intensification, and habitat loss to try and explain this massive decline in biodiversity that we've had over the last 30 years—nobody's been looking at this other thing, this issue of roads."

It's past time, said Donald, to start looking.

Helping the Mule Deer Cross the Road

The study of road ecology may have begun with roadkill. Yet as disturbing and omnipresent as that phenomenon is, when it comes to all the ways that cars ruin nature, the damage drivers do by directly hitting animals is the easy part—both to understand and to mitigate.

Vehicle strikes, at least of larger animals, are visible and obvious. They can be traumatic to motorists, causing damage to cars, human injury, and even human death. Anyone who has ever hit a deer probably doesn't want to go through that experience again. Aside from the physical effects, there can be psychological ones. Many people love animals and feel sad when they see furry corpses by the highway; they experience shock and dismay when a terrified squirrel goes *thump* under their wheels. A roadkill death is comprehensible and can be emotionally affecting.

Fixing the roadkill problem can be relatively uncomplicated, as well—at least at the local scale. The most popular solutions for vehicle strikes, while they might be expensive, are mechanical and easy to explain to the public. Fences that prevent mule deer from crossing a freeway are a type of technology we can all wrap our minds around. Wildlife bridges that guide animals safely over or under roadways, with their human-designed landscaping, look almost like the world of a video game or a feature at an amusement park, where animals trot along a safe track to go on about their animal ways. These are familiar and cozy solutions that appeal to our aesthetics and our desire for control over the natural world, our sense that we can engineer solutions.

The good news is that, thanks to advocates, road engineers are building many of these safe crossings for animals around the world. In the United Kingdom, for example, where as many as 335,000 hedgehogs a year perish on the nation's roads, community members, nonprofits, and governments have banded together to create secure passages for the spiny mammals and raise driver awareness of how vulnerable to motordom this beloved creature is. In Indonesia, the government has a stated commitment to incorporating wildlife crossings in new infrastructure, providing underpass tunnels big enough for elephants and cable canopy bridges that suit primates.

For *Crossings*, Ben Goldfarb visited some of the most sophisticated wildlife crossing infrastructure in the United States, located in the Snoqualmie Pass, in Washington state. He stood on a bridge that spanned I-90 and admired the effect. "Elk scat lay everywhere," he writes. "Whole herds often bedded on the overpass, cows nursing calves and bulls jousting as trucks hurtled beneath them." Goldfarb details the smaller animals that are using the safe passage as well: jumping mice, shrews, toads, red-backed voles. "The Snoqualmie crossing was less a bridge than an environment, a span both alive and lived upon."

Importantly, wildlife crossings don't require drivers to take any action. Slower speeds are one of the best ways to mitigate roadkill, but with well-designed crossings, motorists don't have to respond to a sign that reads SLOW DOWN, DEER XING. They don't have to risk their safety by swerving to avoid an elk that is desperately trying to make a run for it. They don't have to think about animals at all. The wildlife are living, in Goldfarb's words, "not on the road but over and beyond it."

This type of passive design solution to animal fatalities is ideal, just as passive traffic-calming measures are in preventing human injuries and fatalities. If only we could engineer all roads to have wildlife crossings, you might think. That would solve the problem!

But it wouldn't. Because there are far more insidious and pervasive ways that cars damage nature. Some of them we have known about for decades. Some of them we are just beginning to fathom.

Poison Tires

The coho salmon were dying, and nobody knew why.

This pink-fleshed fish is central to the identity of many Indigenous tribes in the Pacific Northwest, and by the 1980s, its numbers were already decimated by habitat destruction. The traditional spawning runs of the cohos were fragmented and obstructed by dams, their ancestral sources of water diverted by agriculture. But researchers weren't sure why, when the coho salmon did make it into the rivers and streams where they were supposed to lay their eggs, the fish were going belly-up.

"I first started hearing about this acute pre-spawn mortality as a grad student," said Mindy Roberts, Puget Sound project director at the nonprofit group Washington Conservation Action. "When they were cut open, the females had all their eggs." Something was poisoning the salmon, killing them before they ever had a chance to reproduce. But what was it?

Researchers methodically followed the evidence for decades. The cohos, Roberts said, gather where fresh water and salt water meet. One of the triggers for them to begin their final journey upstream for spawning is stormwater coming downstream. Researchers found higher rates of mortality in transportation corridors; high-traffic roads emerged as a potential culprit. "Researchers were exposing captive adult fish to road runoff, and they were dying," said Roberts. So scientists started examining runoff for toxins that might account for the salmon mortality.

Road runoff is a foul stew of chemicals and debris. When a heavy rain washes the asphalt "clean," it sluices away everything that cars shed on the road, along with all the chemicals that are used in maintaining the motorway. Oil, gasoline, road salt, herbicides used to suppress roadside plants, and the dust thrown off by vehicles themselves as they barrel along all go into the mix. It took years of methodical inquiry along with the occasional epiphany, but finally the researchers isolated a chemical compound that they believed was to blame for killing half of the coho salmon that try to make it to spawning grounds each year. It comes from the tires of our cars.

Making tires resilient enough to roll down the road at high rates of speed has always been a challenge. Let's take a little historical—and personal—detour. If you've been wondering whether Sarah's last name has anything to do with the Goodyear tire company, it does, if only in the most tangential way: In 1839, her distant ancestor

Charles Goodyear invented a process for vulcanizing rubber, making it able to withstand extreme heat and cold.

After decades of experimentation, Goodyear figured out, essentially by mistake in the end, that adding sulfur and white lead to rubber would do the trick. He was such a poor businessman, however—and his health was so compromised by all those years of handling toxic chemicals—that he never succeeded in making a significant profit from his discovery. The tire company was named after him in homage in 1898. Charles himself had died in a cheap New York hotel room well before that, in 1860, his financial affairs in disarray and his body in agony at the age of fifty-nine.

Today, as in the earliest days of the rubber business, tire companies are challenged to create compounds that help rubber hold up under incredibly demanding conditions. Tire companies like the one named after Sarah's ancestor guard their chemical concoctions closely, veiling themselves behind a variety of regulations that protect "proprietary" technologies. (Fossil fuel companies do the same with the liquids they use for fracking.)

The tire companies were not going to help figure out the mystery of what exactly was killing the salmon. So researchers at the University of Washington for years doggedly sifted through the dozens of chemicals they found in runoff until they isolated the one they allege is responsible for the salmon deaths. The culprit turned out to be a by-product of a molecule called 6PPD, which for the last sixty years or so has been used as a kind of tire preservative. The ground level ozone that cars give off (a dangerous pollutant that is distinct from the beneficial ozone layer in the atmosphere) can actually harm tires; 6PPD protects them against ozone-induced decay. In so doing, however, it degrades to create a different molecule, 6PPD-quinone, which turns out to be fatal to coho salmon. So the chemical that protects the polluting car's tires from its own pollution creates even more pollution. Animals don't need to die *under* tires, it turns out, to die *from* tires.

The truth about 6PPD-quinone has been clear for several years now. What can be done to stop the ongoing carnage, however, is much less clear. In late 2023, three Indigenous tribes—the Yurok in California and the Puyallup and Port Gamble S'Klallam in Washington—filed a petition asking the Environmental Protection Agency to ban 6PPD, saying that it represents an "unreasonable threat" to the region's fisheries and waters.

Scientists say that 6PPD-quinone, along with the countless other toxic chemicals that run off our roads, could be captured by creating natural buffer zones of plants and wetlands that would filter out the poisons before they could reach the delicate ecosystem of, say, a particular stream that is vital to migrating cohos. Perhaps, like guardrails, this type of solution could be written into road engineering codes, mitigating the damage that roads do to the most sensitive habitats.

No one thinks, though, that a scattering of human-engineered roadside filtration marshes could even begin to address all the harms—many of them yet unknown—that 6PPD-quinone presents to the natural world. A more systemic approach might result from lawsuits, which could pressure tire companies to find a replacement for 6PPD, but what are the chances that the replacement will be completely benign?

In the meantime, the tires keep rolling along, their decay coating the asphalt that spreads across the land, mixing with rain from ever-more-powerful storms caused by climate change, and ultimately washing into bodies of water. There, the poisonous cocktail is metabolized by some of our planet's most delicate and irreplaceable creatures, desperately trying to get upstream.

I Can't Hear You

Sarah was crouching in a muddy field in rural France, a pair of headphones on and her microphone pointed at the sky. If anyone had seen her there, they might well have wondered what the hell she was trying to record in the middle of nowhere—at least in human terms.

She would have told anyone who asked that she was trying to capture the sound of the male zitting cisticola, a tiny warbler whose habit it is to flit high above fields like the one she was in, calling out for a mate. (The little bird's name refers to his song, a high-pitched *zit! zit!*) More to the point, Sarah was trying to record the way passing cars drowned out that exuberant cheeping—along with the lilting songs of the corn bunting, the cirl bunting, the Eurasian skylark, and the goldfinch.

To these songbirds, this soggy, seemingly unremarkable section of farmland was very much *somewhere*—a tangle of bushes, trees, and tall grasses appealing enough that they all were trying to claim a bit of it for themselves at the height of the spring mating season. The only problem was, this choice piece of habitat just happened to be right next to a road.

In *Traffication*, Paul Donald writes extensively about the way noise affects a wide range of animals: "When exposed to prolonged traffic noise, zebra finches become less good at finding food, roosting bats become more susceptible to disease, great tits suffer severe sleep disruption and frogs become unable to produce antimicrobial proteins to fight infection," he writes. "Mice develop problems with motor coordination and their brains shrink." Donald cites research showing that prolonged exposure to the stress hormone cortisol, which is released when animals are exposed to even low levels of traffic noise, is shortening the lives of at least some species by breaking down the telomeres on their chromosomes: "Birds raised in the presence of traffic noise are prematurely aged, and their future lifespans already curtailed, before they have even left the nest."

The effects of road noise are especially concerning because increasingly, in many places, there is nowhere to hide from the cacophony. In Donald's home country of the United Kingdom, he estimates that fully one half of the nation's landmass is within half a kilometer of a road. The animals living on half the landmass of the UK are, inevitably, being harmed to at least some degree by the incessant din of passing vehicles.

The invisible waves of sound emanating from roads, Donald told us, do more than torment individual animals. They can cause entire populations to move in search of peace and quiet. For the most sensitive creatures, even a relatively calm road like the one next to that field in France would be too loud. "The great majority of species— not all species, but the great majority of species—are very adversely impacted by traffic noise to the extent that they will just abandon areas near roads," Donald said. "And this can happen at much lower levels of noise than damages ourselves. . . . This kind of invisible pollutant is stripping wildlife for miles around even fairly minor roads. And I think this is probably not the only, but possibly the single most significant impact—certainly on vertebrates . . . of all of the many environmental problems that cars cause."

Squatting in the mud, Sarah could hear through her headphones how the tiny zitting cisticola's heroic song was obliterated each time a car growled past. And even on this relatively remote rural road, the cars drove by with monotonous regularity. The tiny bird didn't stand a chance of being heard over their din.

How long would he keep trying? How much stress had accumulated in his tiny body? Would a prospective mate ever hear his hopeful song?

Genetic Traffic Islands

The zitting cisticola is lucky, in one respect. Its song may be faint enough to be easily blotted out by road noise. But it can at least fly to the other side of the road to find a mate, if it needs to. Not every creature can.

Roads are cutting our planet into ever-smaller pieces. And because their effects radiate out, in the forms of noise, air pollution, and runoff, their effects are not limited to the actual asphalt. "Pavement itself blankets less than 1 percent of the United States," writes Goldfarb in *Crossings*, "yet its influence—the 'road-effect zone' to use ecological jargon—covers a full 20 percent."

That means, of course, that increasingly fewer animals are out of range of the multitude of literally concrete harms that roads and vehicles cause. The heart rates of bears around the world are elevated. Birds on all continents, except Antarctica, are shouting to be heard. Streams and rivers all over the planet are contaminated with the oil, salt, and tire dust that wash off the asphalt. And of course, creatures from butterflies to salamanders to hedgehogs to moose are ending up flattened and bleeding out on the blacktop.

You might think that simply avoiding roads would be the best thing that animals could do under the circumstances. You would be wrong.

Paul Donald explains that animals can be divided into four different groups: blind crossers, pausers, speeders, and avoiders. The avoiders—animals as various as grizzly bears and beetles—may not end up in the roadkill category. "You might think, 'Well, that makes them kind of safe. If they're not gonna cross the road then they're not gonna get flattened,'" Donald told us. "But in fact, they may be the worst-affected group." The avoiders' evasive instinct serves individual members of the species just fine in the moment. But it turns out that chickens (or any other animal) actually have a very real and important reason to cross the road: to ensure genetic diversity.

"If you can't cross a road, you're kind of locked into an island," said Donald. "You're surrounded on all sides by tarmac. And we know that that has profound implications on the survival probability of the population that's trapped in these little tarmac world islands—I mean, millions and millions of these islands. We've completely cookie-cut our countryside to pieces, to tiny pieces with roads."

This degradation of genetic diversity poses an invisible threat that is easy to ignore. Yet it comes at a time when animals need more than ever to adjust to rapidly changing habitats that are being irrevocably altered by human activity. Genetic diversity makes species more resilient and adaptable, precisely the qualities needed in an environment filled with new challenges in terms of finding food, regulating body temperature, mating, and other crucial functions.

Charles Darwin famously developed his theory of evolution after observing bird populations that had developed distinctive traits by breeding in isolation on the remote archipelago of the Galápagos Islands. Today, with traffication, we are essentially conducting a mass evolutionary experiment, stranding animals on de facto islands amid our raging rivers of asphalt. Some populations are so small, so unable to reach each other safely, that they might not be able to survive.

Ben Goldfarb writes about one such case: the cougars of the Santa Monica Mountains in Southern California, at the northern edge of Los Angeles. Cut off from more numerous and robust populations to the north, the cougars in the Santa Monicas were inbreeding. By the 2010s, scientists knew already the lions' genetic diversity had eroded to the point that they were at risk of disappearing altogether from that part of their traditional range. Then, when examining one young male cougar that they had trapped and tranquilized in 2020, researchers found telltale signs of a catastrophic lack of genetic diversity: an undescended testicle and a kinked tail. Cougars in the Santa Monicas were being "sucked into an 'extinction vortex.'"

The plight of the mountain lions in such a high-profile metro area turned out to be galvanizing, sparking a campaign to create one of the nation's most expensive wildlife crossings. Tens of millions of dollars to build more such crossings around the world have been raised in memory of P-22, a Santa Monica cougar who ultimately had to be euthanized because of trauma he had sustained when a driver hit him.

No one, however, is raising tens of millions of dollars to save the beetles stranded on a traffic island in Europe, or the snails stranded by a new strip mall constructed in Florida. The dollars, millions upon billions of them, are for the most part on the other side of the equation. "Traffication is backed by very powerful political and economic forces," said Donald. "The oil industry, clearly. The motor industry. . . . These are very powerful market forces that are pushing this pollution on us."

Sea Turtle Jesus Wants You to Drive

You may have seen him on your TV in the spring of 2022: a handsome white man with a beard and flowing brown hair, swerving a Kia Sportage SUV over a beach at sunrise at high speed, dragging a clawlike rake behind the rear bumper to collect trash that is strewn across the sand. After the driver loads the garbage he's collected into the back of the vehicle, he sits and watches with benevolent self-satisfaction as baby turtles emerge from the sand and crawl over the beach. Kia called the spot "Beachcomber."

On Reddit, the savior dude came to be known as Sea Turtle Jesus, and he was roundly ridiculed. As one commenter said there, "Nothing says 'save our planet!!!!' like driving a 3-ton, microplastic and CO_x-noxious-emitting urban sprawl tank immediately next to a rapidly acidifying ocean."

While advocacy groups might struggle to break through the cluttered media landscape and communicate the gravity of the climate crisis, carmakers don't have that problem. They are the clutter.

The auto industry, in fact, has made the ability to access nature a core part of its own lavishly funded messaging campaigns. While this may be perhaps the most galling example of a car ad set in nature, Sea Turtle Jesus is hardly alone. Because car manufacturers—perhaps in an increasingly desperate bid to convince consumers that they really *will* use that four-wheel drive—churn out ads showing their products in the wild almost as much, if not more, than they show them in urban or suburban settings.

On our screens, we are constantly served images of huge trucks plunging through limpid streams, ripping across fragile desert surfaces, and crunching into woodlands. In one ad, hikers making their way up a stunning red rock formation get picked up by the driver of an enormous Land Rover Defender so that they don't have to walk to the top. (Because why would *hikers* want to *walk?*)

The American writer, conservationist, and curmudgeon Edward Abbey, who worked in national parks and monuments in the American West for many years, would have been apoplectic if he could have seen that ad. Abbey famously railed against those who thought they could have a drive-by communion with nature. "You can't see *anything* from a car," he wrote in *Desert Solitaire*, published in 1968. "You've got to get out of the goddamned contraption and walk, better yet crawl, on hands and knees, over the sandstone and through the thornbush and cactus. When traces of blood begin to mark your trail, you'll see something, maybe."

Since Abbey wrote those words, though, ads depicting drivers as rugged wilderness explorers have only become an increasingly accepted part of the media ecosystem.

Ben Goldfarb thinks we accept the cognitive dissonance embodied by these ads in part because they simply reflect reality. Even the most well-meaning nature lovers in the United States don't have ready access to green space if they can't or don't want to get there in a personal motor vehicle.

"The paradox of roads that a lot of these ridiculous SUV commercials get at . . . is that they are, in a way, how we access the outdoors," said Goldfarb. "I live in rural Colorado and . . . a big part of the reason that my wife and I moved out here is so that we could go hiking and skiing and fishing and all of the things that we love to do, right? And the way that we access those things is by getting in a car and driving up one of the . . . obscure dirt Forest Service roads that I was railing about. . . . I definitely feel very conflicted about that."

Goldfarb adds that even those places that are supposed to be the most awe-inspiring wild public lands are inherently compromised by the way we prioritize motor vehicle access. "Cars are sort of fundamental to the history of American conservation in a lot of ways," he said. "When the national parks were created in the early 20th century, they were kind of conceived as these fundamentally automotive landscapes that you were meant to visit in a car. And there's a big road running through basically every single one of our iconic national parks."

There may be hope, though, for those of us who are tired of yelling at Kia's Turtle Jesus and his nature-crushing friends at Land Rover, Ford, GM, and many, many others.

In the United Kingdom, at least, there is a glimmer of dawning recognition that these fantasies of crashing through the wilderness in your $75,000 living room (because that is, essentially, what modern cars have become) might have a negative real-world impact. In 2023, activists with a United Kingdom organization called Adfree Cities won a ban on ads for the Toyota Hilux SUV from the Advertising Standards Authority, which regulates ads in the UK. Adfree Cities argued that the ads depicted illegal and dangerous activity by showing the vehicles racing through fragile natural environments, as well as cities. The regulators concurred. "The ads presented and condoned the use of vehicles in a manner that disregarded their impact on nature and the environment," wrote the ASA in its decision on the matter. "As a result, they had not been prepared with a sense of responsibility to society."

It may seem like a small victory. But it opens up the possibility that activists could fight back in a systemic way against the ubiquitous ads that foster the societal norm of impunity for cars moving through natural landscapes and cities alike. Because the idea that cars should be allowed to crunch their way through nature without restraints has to be constructed and promoted. We know this because in some places, it simply isn't acceptable.

Could You Care About a Pigeon?

In December of 2022, a taxi driver was arrested in Japan for running over a pigeon.

Does that sound ridiculous to you? Maybe it does. Maybe it should. But in Japan, they take road safety very seriously. When Sarah toured Tokyo on a bike, she was astonished by the courteous and quiet driver behavior in the city of nearly fourteen million people.

The streets of Japan don't just *seem* safe. In relative terms, they *are* safe. In 2021, Japan recorded a human traffic fatality rate of just 2.7 per one hundred thousand inhabitants; in the United States, by contrast, the number was 14.2 per one hundred thousand inhabitants, more than five times higher.

The Japanese social ecosystem is dramatically different from the one that prevails in North America and Europe. Consideration for others generally takes precedence over individual liberties; the taxi driver's alleged action—accelerating deliberately into a flock of the birds, crushing one—was seen as antisocial, according to an article about the incident in *The New York Times*: "Atsushi Hosokawa, an animal rights lawyer, said the police appeared to see someone who would run over any animal at 35 m.p.h. as a danger to society at large."

The idea of respecting all forms of life when driving a car may seem radical. But maybe our attitude toward the way driving damages nature can help us cope, philosophically and practically, with the damage driving does to human society as well.

Maybe it's easier for us to see the brutality of our current systems when we look at the effect on animals rather than humans. Losing a beloved pet under the wheels of a careless driver is often a person's first real lesson in the destructive power of motordom, a devastating introduction for many children into the grim reality of auto carnage. As we grow up, we are often warmhearted enough to support wildlife crossings, even if we are sometimes irritated by crosswalks that let humans get from one side of the road to the other. We are charmed by a line of ducklings scurrying across the asphalt behind their mother, although we might roll our eyes impatiently at a human mom holding a toddler's hand and pushing a stroller as she tries to get her kids to day care. We allow ourselves to gaze sadly at the furry corpse of a groundhog on the shoulder, feeling emotions that are perhaps too terrifying to explore when the body crushed on the pavement is the same shape as our own.

Maybe allowing ourselves to care about individual owls, or bears, or cougars, or other "charismatic fauna," could help us care about the smaller animals, the butterflies and snakes and midges that are obliterated in a vast *whoosh* that is drowning out the sound of the natural world—the *whoosh* of the motor vehicle.

Maybe we can build an ethics of care around roads precisely by seeing the value of an individual pigeon, and what it means to disregard that value. "The practice of road ecology," writes Ben Goldfarb, "is not merely a set of engineering principles but a moral mandate."

Perhaps by learning to understand and care about the way tire particulate runoff affects a vulnerable, culturally important species such as salmon, we can also care about how these toxins affect another species we ostensibly care about—human beings.

We cared about Barry the barred owl. Can we muster the same concern for our human neighbors? Or even for ourselves? As we'll see in the next chapter, when it comes to death and illness caused by cars, we may be more hardened to the fate of millions of our fellow human beings than we think—especially compared with the mourning we witnessed for one well-liked owl on Central Park Drive.

5

Cars Are Killing Us

For over half a century the automobile has brought death, injury, and the most inestimable sorrow and deprivation to millions of people."

So wrote Ralph Nader in his 1965 bombshell book, *Unsafe at Any Speed: The Designed-In Dangers of the American Automobile.* It would only get worse, he predicted: "A 1959 Department of Commerce report projected that 51,000 persons would be killed by automobiles in 1975. That figure will probably be reached in 1965, a decade ahead of schedule."

Nader was desperate to convey his message: Despite the grandiose claims that boosters made about automobiles' unmitigated positive effect on the human condition, cars were killing us in hideous numbers—most obviously by collisions between their chrome and steel bodies and our own bodies of soft and vulnerable flesh, but also through the pollutants they spewed into our air.

Nader was basically right in his predicted automotive death toll, if his estimate was a year early. By 1966, the number of Americans killed directly by traffic violence hit 53,041. That figure stayed above 50,000 for most of the next fifteen years, peaking at 56,278 in 1972 and then slowly abating to 40,982 in 1992, when the numbers started heading up again. Fatalities remained above 40,000 annually until 2008, when they started falling, attaining a modern-era low of 35,303 in 2011.

The steady, gradual decline and stabilization of traffic deaths was due in great part to regulations and safety measures spurred by Nader's own exposure, in his book and in congressional testimony, of the automobile industry's reckless disregard of human suffering in pursuit of profit. Thanks to his activism and the reforms it inspired over the next two decades, personal motor vehicles now come equipped with seat belts, collapsible steering columns that won't impale us if we crash, doors that don't fly open on impact, airbags, and dozens of other features that mitigate the inherent dangers of traveling at high speed in a metal box. Nader sparked one of the most effective safety campaigns in modern history, saving countless lives and preventing exponentially more injuries. For a short time, it seemed like we might have a chance of keeping the US fatality number below 40,000 for good.

But car crashes are still killing people today. And in recent years, the United States has started moving in the wrong direction once more. Bucking the continuing trend of declining traffic fatalities in most of the wealthy world, American motoring deaths have been steadily creeping up. In 2022, 46,027 people died in vehicle crashes in the US—and 9,188 of those were pedestrians, a worrying development that researchers believe may be due to the ballooning size of American cars and SUVs, as well as the proliferation of screens and other distractions.

These raw fatality numbers don't account for the growth of the country's population, it's true. Nor do they take into consideration the exponential boom in vehicle miles traveled, or VMT (itself a profoundly depressing statistic). Factoring in how many people there are in America and how many miles they drive, fatality figures are slightly more reassuring. When Nader was writing, we were looking at 5.3 deaths per 100 million VMT; in 2022, that had dropped to 1.35. And the traffic death rate per one hundred thousand population went down by almost half over the same period, from 25.4 to 13.8 since 1965—although both of those more hopeful figures also represent a worrying upward trend from the lows of the 2010s and compare unfavorably with other wealthy nations.

The thing about fatalities, though (the thing about *people dying*, we should say), is that the per capita or per VMT death rate is meaningless if the person who died on their way to work or coming home from a basketball game is *your* person—*your* wife or brother or father or best friend. Or, god forbid, your child.

Each time a person is killed in a crash, a ripple of trauma spreads through that individual's community. Even if you've never lost one of your nearest and dearest on the road, you've almost certainly experienced the news that someone you are separated from by just one or two degrees has died as the result of traffic violence. You've almost certainly seen and felt some measure of the pain that just one of these sudden, preventable deaths causes.

When children are involved, the pain is almost unbearable. Sarah will never forget how in 2010, the mother of one of her son's classmates, a woman she used to chat with every day at pickup, was killed on her Vespa scooter by a driver speeding through a light that had just changed from yellow to red. At the memorial service, Sarah watched the dead woman's pale, quiet six-year-old son crawl onto her flower-bedecked coffin and lay his head down on the polished wood.

Just three years later, the nine-year-old boy who had the locker next to Sarah's son at the same school was killed by a driver who ran him over on a sidewalk as he walked with his brother and mother. The dead boy's best friend dealt with the trauma by fantasizing about a pair of sneakers that could stop cars.

You almost certainly have been close to a traffic violence death yourself. And you know that, to the human beings picking up the pieces after a crash, information about skyrocketing VMT is irrelevant. No amount of statistical rationalization wipes away the reality that in 2022, driving inflicted unfathomable pain and damage on the families, loved ones, friends, colleagues, and acquaintances of 42,514 unique and irreplaceable human beings in the United States.

Forty-two thousand. Five hundred. And fourteen.

Another 5.2 *million* people, or about 1.6 percent of the US population, were injured in an automobile crash seriously enough to seek medical attention. A significant percentage of those injuries were "life-altering"—a phrase that includes paralyzing spinal cord injuries, traumatic brain injuries, and loss of limbs.

These deaths and injuries are only more heartbreaking because so many of them—almost all of them—are preventable. In the twenty-first century, wealthy nations outside of North America have concentrated on reducing death and injury through a combination of design, enforcement, and incentivizing non-car travel, and it has worked. In Germany, for instance, the per capita fatality rate is 3.7 per one hundred thousand inhabitants, nearly four times safer than the US, down from 9.6 in 2000. In France, the number of traffic deaths in the same period has plunged from 13.4 to 4.8. And in the Netherlands, from 7.5 to 3.0.

So why aren't we following their lead?

Cognitive Dissonance and Rugged Individualism

Cognitive dissonance is defined as "psychological conflict resulting from incongruous beliefs and attitudes held simultaneously." Cars and car infrastructure demand a lot of it from all of us. Drivers, in order to keep firing up their vehicles every day and going to work or the grocery store, must block out the knowledge that every day, about 110 people in the United States don't come home from exactly this kind of mundane trip.

Those of us who have the luxury of not driving every day, mostly in big cities, still must perform a similar sort of mental gymnastics. We must convince ourselves that being relentlessly assailed by the roar and honk of cars is essentially harmless, just the ironic price to be paid for living in one of our nation's few walkable communities. We must pretend that our soft human bodies are somehow tough enough to resist the forces that we know can't be resisted by other animals. We must ignore the soot on the windowsill, or else we would have to admit it is also inside our lungs.

The details and the scale of suffering represented by the cold, hard statistics of automobile-induced injury and fatality are difficult to comprehend. So we mostly don't try.

Toward the beginning of *Unsafe at Any Speed*, Ralph Nader quoted a transportation specialist named Wilfred Owen, who wrote way back in 1946, "There is little question that the public will not tolerate for long an annual traffic toll of forty to fifty thousand fatalities."

"Time," wrote Nader in his 1965 attack on the negligent auto industry, "has shown Owen to be wrong."

More time has shown more of the same. Nearly eighty years since

Owen's optimistic prediction about our unwillingness to accept mass death on the road, the 40,000 to 50,000 motor vehicle fatalities each year have become what you might call the standard American unit of mortality—let's abbreviate it to the SAUM. We use the SAUM as the benchmark against which all other scourges are measured, like gun deaths ("In 2017, there were 1.44 million years of potential life lost due to firearm deaths, edging out that of motor vehicle crashes [1.37 million years]") or drug overdoses. When the fatal force of cars was surpassed by opioids in 2019, the milestone was duly noted on the National Safety Council website: "For the first time in U.S. history, a person is more likely to die from an accidental opioid overdose than from a motor vehicle crash. . . . The odds of dying accidentally from an opioid overdose have risen to 1 in 96, eclipsing the odds of dying in a motor vehicle crash (1 in 103)."

The difference between cars and guns, or cars and opioids, is that nearly every single person in the United States is forced, by our infrastructure—by deliberate and well-financed government plan—to accept that 1 in 103 chance as part of their daily routine, often multiple times every day. The most responsible and risk-averse parents, who would never let their kids get near a Glock or a Percocet, are compelled by the structure of our transportation system to expose their children to one of the leading causes of child death every single day, simply to get them to school, or a doctor's appointment, or a friend's house.

Even if you don't drive, your kids are vulnerable to potential vehicular violence when they are crossing in the crosswalk or waiting at a bus stop or just playing in front of your home. In 2022, 1,129 children aged fourteen and younger were killed in motor vehicle crashes in the US, and tens of thousands more were injured. Yet loading the kids into the car is an unquestioned action—indeed, an unquestionable one.

The SAUM is a number that society accepts as the price of doing business with cars. It's a price we've been paying so long that we can't imagine not paying it. And it's worth asking what our ability to accept this bloody structural foundation for our society is doing to us.

"Does the fact that our whole lifestyle is sort of predicated on a lot of people dying in car wrecks desensitize us to other forms of violence or mass death?" asked Angie Schmitt, author of *Right of Way: Race, Class, and the Silent Epidemic of Pedestrian Deaths in America*. "Or is there something about the United States that's just a little bit callous about that, culturally?"

We've been practicing losing our loved ones to preventable causes, with cars. We've been getting used to the idea that we have to accept the risk of violent death and injury as part of quotidian life, thanks to cars.

America is famous for its "rugged individualism," a cowboy-tough attitude that puts responsibility on each of us to take care of ourselves, rather than acknowledging that people need help from each other to live happy, safe, and productive lives. Instead of creating a robust public health system, we expect people to cobble together their own medical care. Instead of building a comprehensive network of childcare providers, we tell parents that "maybe Grandma or Grandpa wants to help out a little bit more." (Yes, then–Republican vice presidential candidate JD Vance actually said that in 2024.) Instead of building supportive housing for people with mental health issues, we let them struggle to survive on the streets, maybe getting an occasional hot meal from a local soup kitchen.

Car dependence manifests that same philosophy. "It's a dangerous world out there" is the message we get from our perilous transportation system. Suck it up. Get out of the way. Drive defensively. Keep your wits about you, if you don't want to end up a statistic. It's on *you* to stay safe, and if you end up dead, well, you probably were doing something stupid.

But no matter how self-reliant and cautious you are, no matter how big and tough your SUV is, there are some deadly effects of cars that you won't be able to protect yourself against. You still are in a human body on a planet with 1.47 billion cars. You still have to breathe.

It's All Around You

Air pollution is estimated to cause between 100,000 and 200,000 "excess deaths" annually in the United States. Globally, that number is 6.7 million each year. According to the World Health Organization, 99 percent of the world's population lives in places where the air quality does not meet WHO guidelines for human health.

Even when it doesn't kill you, air pollution can make you sick. Very sick. Air pollution created by cars has been definitively linked by researchers to asthma, premature births, cognitive delays in children, and cardiovascular disease. It contributes to dementia. It may even negatively affect male fertility and sexual function. (Hmm, maybe emphasizing the risk of ED could make a certain population take notice of the issue?)

Everyone suffers from air pollution, including people inside of cars. (Yes, the fumes from the car in front of you get sucked into your bubble, and that "new car smell" is pretty toxic as well.) Health outcomes associated with pollution are dramatically worse in poorer countries, as well as in low-income and marginalized communities in even the wealthiest nations. The very people least likely to own cars are the ones who suffer the greatest medical burdens caused by their use—although because of the high cost of health care in developed nations, it's actually the wealthiest countries that take the biggest financial hit from car-induced disease.

This is not news to the people in power. Doctors, politicians, and carmakers have all known about the disastrous effects of automobile pollution for generations. When Nader wrote *Unsafe at Any Speed*, air pollution was so extreme that it was literally causing crashes: "Emissions have frequently curtailed highway visibility to the point where freeways have been temporarily cleared of traffic to avoid chain accidents," he wrote. Even so, it was already widely recognized that "the health hazard posed by various combustive by-products is of a far more serious nature than the problem of reduced visibility."

The automakers knew they were spewing deadly gases, even then. In fact, in 1965, the same year that Nader published his book, *The New York Times* reported that physicians were picketing the New York Auto Show demanding a reduction in tailpipe emissions, among other measures to protect human health from the scourge of the automobile.

Eventually, policymakers did insist. Amendments to the Clean Air Act, passed with bipartisan support in 1970 and signed by then-President Richard Nixon, created enforceable standards for air pollution and resulted in a dramatic improvement in the air we all must breathe. Yet pollution generated by motor vehicles still is a major contributor to dirty air, and it is still killing and disabling us in numbers that would be unacceptable if they were the fallout of any other consumer product.

It's worth noting, too, that eliminating tailpipes altogether, as electric cars do, doesn't get rid of pollution that harms human health, because electric cars don't eliminate the spread of microplastics and other toxic chemicals. Scientists in California looking at plastic particles in ocean water believe that tire dust and fragments probably are the largest source of this pollution. Particles from brake wear contribute to high levels of magnetite in the environment that have been linked to the development of Alzheimer's disease, one of the leading causes of death among older people globally.

Cars also contribute mightily to the industrial-grade sonic wallpaper of our modern lives. And while most people may be even less conscious of the negative health effects of traffic noise than they are of how bad air pollution is for us, that doesn't mean the noise doesn't hurt us, as we learned in the last chapter.

"It's a massively serious health problem," said *Traffication* author Paul Donald. "Road traffic noise probably kills hundreds of thousands of people around the world each year, and it's nothing to do with the damage it does to your ears, it's the fact that your body . . . detects traffic noise as a threat, and what it does is it squirts stress hormones into your bloodstream."

Those hormones, such as cortisol, trigger a fight-or-flight response that was extremely useful in the environment we lived in for most of human history, one in which quick reaction to sudden and intermittent threats was imperative for survival. But when stress hormones are dumped over and over again into our nervous systems— when the perceived threats are ambient and continuous—they have a host of corrosive effects. Exposure to road noise, more and more studies are showing, can contribute to cardiac disease, dementia, and even some forms of cancer.

Get Moving

Despite the feeling of security that many people seek in their oversized automobiles, sitting in a big protective car bubble whenever you need to get somewhere is not too healthy for drivers or passengers, even if you're never involved in a collision.

The World Health Organization has called physical inactivity a global crisis that is poised to crush our already overwhelmed health care systems, projecting that if we don't start moving more, hundreds of millions of people around the world will get sick with noncommunicable illnesses such as cardiac disease, at a cost of some US$27 billion annually. Reducing systemic car dependence would go a long way toward shaping a world in which we would move more just going about our daily lives, instead of having to drive the car through traffic to get to the gym.

That's not the way things are going in a lot of the world, though. We talked with Texas-based journalist Megan Kimble about her book *City Limits: Infrastructure, Inequality, and the Future of America's Highways*, which documents how policymakers there, in America's second-most-populous state, are doubling down on widening freeways and expanding road networks, spending billions on locking in car dependency while continuing to leave transit, pedestrian facilities, and bike infrastructure underfunded or unfunded. For Texans forced to look for housing ever farther from urban boomtowns such as San Antonio and Houston, where housing costs are soaring, these pricey freeways—one of them already twenty-six lanes wide—have become the place where they spend significant portions of their days. And that isn't good for them.

Kimble interviewed one young woman who with her husband

had bought a house twenty-five miles out from the Austin city center because they couldn't afford anything closer. The wife hated the lengthy car commute for all the reasons you'd expect—if the traffic was bad, it could be as long as two hours one way—but Kimble said she has been haunted by one very specific detail of the woman's story.

"She had . . . an Achilles' heel . . . injury because she was just, like, hovering her foot above the gas-brake-gas-brake, because I-35 is stop and go," Kimble told us. "This is . . . a small injury compared to the violence that happens on our roads, but I think about it a lot as . . . commuting sucks. And she really experienced . . . on her mood, on her well-being and happiness, how that commute impacted her life. . . . Her perspective is like, 'Why don't we have a train? Why can't I get on a train to go up I-35 and get to my job?'"

That train that young woman would love to ride doesn't exist, because generations of planners and politicians, right up to those who hold the power today, have made sure that she has no alternative to driving. And her sore Achilles' heel is a red flag for all the different ways that sitting in a car for hours every day takes its toll on your body. A recent study in Australia, for instance, found that the risk of cardiometabolic disease increased in tandem with distance from the city center: "Residents of peri-urban areas were at higher cardiometabolic risk than those of inner urban areas, partly due to the former's car-dependent lifestyles."

On the flip side, giving people transit as an option can substantively improve their health. Japanese researchers took the opportunity to look at the data from a natural experiment that occurred when planners added a transit station to a line that passed through a rural area. Annual health care costs for people in the area affected by the change went down by more than US$600 per year in just four years. "This study's results are consistent with previous studies suggesting that increased access to transit may increase physical activity among transit users and may lead to decreased healthcare expenditures," the researchers wrote.

The World Health Organization emphasizes that the deleterious effects of car dependence on our health can be addressed by policy measures that are well-known and have been proven effective. Prioritizing cycling and pedestrian infrastructure so that people feel safe, providing high-quality public transit so they can leave the car at home sometimes, even if they sometimes have to drive—these are not any more difficult to understand than the concept of widening a freeway. And yet, according to the WHO, while three quarters of the world's nations have policies to increase transit use, fewer than half encourage walking and cycling with a comprehensive infrastructure-based approach. "Safety concerns are the leading reason why people choose not to walk or cycle, meaning road design that provides safe environments for all users is essential."

So why do we have so much trouble treating cars like the manageable public health problem they are? Maybe because they're so relentless and omnipresent that we simply haven't been able to imagine the landscape without them.

Until, for a strange and terrible reason, we suddenly saw what that might look like.

The Anthropause

In the spring of 2020, when the world shut down because of the COVID-19 pandemic, we entered a brief period that some dubbed the Anthropause. During that strange time, as we huddled in our homes wondering if things would return to "normal"—if we would ever go back to work, if we would someday be able to hug each other again—the skies of the world began to clear. In Wuhan, China, air pollution went down by as much as 30 percent; in Turin, Italy, some intersections saw reductions of up to 65 percent in nitrogen dioxide levels. Looking across New York Harbor, the shoreline of New Jersey, usually covered by a thin brown veil on the best of days, was instead crisp and clear.

Stuck behind our keyboards in spring 2020, many of us found a shred of hope in the satellite imagery that showed major metropolitan areas emerging from the haze of pollution that is caused, in great part, by motor vehicles. Ironically, the greatest global respiratory virus crisis in one hundred years temporarily made it easier for humanity at large to draw a breath, even as some researchers posited that air pollution may have exacerbated the spread of COVID and led to worse outcomes for those who were infected. No one wanted the lockdowns, but the recovery of natural systems that we witnessed—immortalized in the "nature is healing" meme—gave some people hope that positive change was imminent.

People were hungry, it turned out, for the chance to reconnect with nature, even in an urban setting. They liked seeing blue skies instead of muddy brown ones. They liked looking at clean water in the harbors of their cities. They found in the natural world one of the few reliable respites from the anxiety and distress engendered by the pandemic and resulting shutdowns. It was a huge and terrible natural experiment in which the variable of cars suddenly was clearly isolated for the first time in generations.

In those early weeks of lockdown, we put out a call for voice memos from our listeners to see whether we could get a sense of what people were seeing on their streets. What came through, from countries around the world, was the enormous difference that removing huge numbers of cars from the transportation mix had on people's perception of safety when walking or riding bikes.

We heard from Becky, who lives in London, Ontario, Canada. "I've noticed from my bedroom window that there are a lot more kids on bikes biking around my neighborhood," she said. Sebastian told a similar story from his vantage point in Los Angeles. "During this pandemic as people are staying home and not driving to work, the number of cyclists on our streets has greatly increased, including what seems to be a lot of families and new cyclists," Sebastian said. "In one sense, it's kind of sad because it shows how dangerous our streets are, but I hope that more and more people will continue to bike even after this pandemic ends." In Paris, Cécile reported: "If I still need to go to my office, I bike, and it has never been as freeing because I don't have to worry about cars anymore. Paris's streets are eerily quiet. You see people on the sidewalks, a few joggers, but cars have virtually disappeared."

As the pandemic dragged on and it became clear that gathering outdoors was relatively safe, many cities embraced outdoor dining and open streets to give people more access to social opportunities in fresh air and to help businesses stay alive. Parks were jammed with picnickers. Everything about public space, it seemed, was suddenly up for reconsideration. On the podcast, we talked about the potential these changes represented for the movement to reduce car use in cities. "Is the world witnessing the wrenching, difficult birth of the car-free city?" we asked. "Or are we merely living in the brief moment before cities snap back into even deeper automobile dependence?"

Mike Lydon, an urban planner, was cautiously hopeful when we put the question to him. "More and more cities are taking on multiple measures," he said. "I think some cities will revert back to status quo at some point, but more and more, I'm starting to be convinced that citizens and political leaders will not want that. That there's going to be a lot of positive change that is the result in terms of the spatial reallocation on our streets. . . . But for any of that to happen, it's going to require much stronger political leadership in cities to carry this forward."

So, did that leadership materialize?

Four years later, at the writing of this book, the verdict is mixed. Some cities, like Paris, have moved decisively to extend the decarring of their streets (more on that in chapter 9). Others have been backsliding a bit, rolling back open streets programs and reversing initiatives that allowed for more open-air dining.

While such reversals can be discouraging, it's important to remember that progress is rarely linear or continuous. Two steps forward, one step back may be a frustrating way to get ahead—but it still results in forward motion. And even before the pandemic, even in car-dependent North America, many cities were moving to create streets that put people first. Many COVID-era initiatives were in fact simply amplifying progress that had been building for years, thanks to pressure from advocates on elected officials, some of whom showed the courage to change what seemed immutable for generations.

I Can Hear Clearly Now

Stand on the southern edge of Union Square, one of the most well-traveled spots in New York City, and you'll experience something almost freakishly unusual on the chaotic streets of downtown Manhattan: You can hear.

From the other side of Fourteenth Street, which at a hundred feet wide has always been one of the city's busiest crosstown thoroughfares, you can hear a woman laughing with her friends. You can hear the rise and fall of conversations among the chess players at the tables outside the subway entrance. You can hear the whir of a derailleur as someone rolls by on a bike. You can even hear the jingle of a collar as a dog gets taken on its lunchtime walk.

What's going on here? It's actually pretty simple: They took away the cars.

For decades, the M14 crosstown bus had been a joke, moving so slowly along the auto-choked two-mile length of Fourteenth Street that walking was often a faster option. In 2019, the M14 won the dubious distinction of being the slowest high-ridership bus route in the city, receiving the Pokey Award from the Straphangers Campaign, a local transit advocacy organization. It moved, the group reported, at an average speed of 4.3 miles an hour.

Then, in fall of 2019, the city made Fourteenth Street a dedicated busway. From 6:00 a.m. to 10:00 p.m., no private vehicles would be allowed from Third to Ninth Avenues, with exceptions for some local traffic. A few neighbors filed lawsuits to block the plan, but the city administration, under the leadership of then-Mayor Bill de Blasio, held firm, and ultimately the community backlash failed.

The bus got faster and more reliable, and that was great. Side streets remained relatively peaceful, which was terrific. And the ancillary benefits were stunning to anyone familiar with the old Fourteenth Street. Now, any day of the week, you can cross the street without encountering the bumper-to-bumper traffic that used to take over crosswalks, leading pedestrians to scurry like rats through a maze of potentially lethal vehicles. Emergency vehicles heading to the many hospitals nearby can swiftly get where they are going. And once again, you can hear. The angry honks and revving engines that used to be a reliable feature of the landscape have disappeared. And people's health benefits materially from all that, even if they never think about it.

Dedicated busways are just one example of how quickly and easily we can make healthier environments for people. In Bogotá, since 1974, the tradition known as Ciclovía opens seventy-five miles of the city's streets to bicyclists and pedestrians every Sunday, offering citizens car-free public space. In Oslo, incentives for driving electric vehicles have reduced air pollution in the city center by 35 percent. In Seoul, a highway removal in 2003 allowed for the rehabilitation of a stream that flows through the city and the creation of a park that has become a beloved haven for wildlife and people alike. In Hoboken, New Jersey, a commitment to the Vision Zero approach to traffic engineering, which originated in Sweden and aims to reduce traffic deaths and severe injuries to zero through a data-driven approach to policy and infrastructure reform, resulted in seven consecutive years of zero traffic deaths recorded.

All these initiatives have encountered virulent opposition, some of which has dragged on for years. In London, since 2019 drivers have been charged £12.50 to bring emissions-producing vehicles into an Ultra Low Emission Zone (ULEZ) that now encompasses all of the city's boroughs, reducing deadly nitrogen dioxide pollution in the zone by 21 percent in Outer London and 53 percent in Central London. When proposing the expansion of the zone in 2022, Mayor Sadiq Khan knew he was facing opposition from much of the Conservative political establishment controlling the United Kingdom's central government. The ULEZ was denounced as "Mr. Khan's much-hated road charge" by right-wing media. But he stood firm, saying it was necessary to think of his constituents' health: "We have too often seen measures to tackle air pollution and the climate emergency delayed around the world because it's viewed as being too hard or politically inconvenient," he said. "It's clear the cost of inaction—to our economy, to livelihoods, to the environment and to the health of Londoners—would be far greater than the cost of transitioning to net-zero and reducing toxic air pollution."

In May 2024, after the expanded ULEZ was implemented, Sadiq Khan was reelected by a decisive margin, thumping the Conservative candidate whose platform called for the ULEZ to be "scrapped on day one" of her administration.

Politics remains a stubborn sticking point when it comes to treating cars as the public health disaster that they are. A lot of elected officials don't have what it takes to stay the course. But increasingly, buoyed by grassroots support, many are showing the courage required.

In 2024, the Biden administration's Department of Transportation introduced regulations that would, for the first time, require car manufacturers to make their vehicles safer—for people *outside* the car. The new rules would require automakers to conduct tests that would assess the likelihood of pedestrians sustaining head injuries when struck by ever taller and heavier cars, SUVs, and light trucks. "This is a huge step in the right direction—and long overdue," wrote journalist David Zipper. "If this proposal comes into effect, carmakers will finally have to address how car bloat endangers pedestrians." In 2024, the California legislature passed a law that would require intelligent speed assistance technology on new vehicles, a relatively simple feature that would alert drivers when they're going more than ten miles over the posted speed limit. If implemented, the California law would almost certainly lead to a wider adoption of such regulations in other states, and ultimately at the federal level.

Rules like these would provide an important foundation for future safety technology aimed at protecting pedestrians, bicyclists, and drivers alike. It's a promising trend that could end up being as important as the introduction of seat belt requirements back in 1968, because it not only acknowledges the problem—it puts the onus on car manufacturers to solve it.

These are the types of actions that give us hope. Many people in power know what we need to do to make our societies healthier, just the way those auto executives back in Ralph Nader's day knew what they had to do—and now we need to force them into action. All the evidence points to reducing car dependence as a vital public health measure. All the evidence tells us that reducing the number of cars, and the number of trips we take in cars, would significantly lengthen our lives and improve the quality of those lives. And we don't need a global pandemic and a complete shutdown of our society to do it.

It won't be easy, and it won't happen overnight. But we are making progress, two steps forward, one step back, two steps forward.

Cars Ruin Society

We become the people we are, and act the way we do, because of a complex interaction of nature and nurture. But what if our environments play a larger role in our ability to form social networks than we realize or would like to admit? What if our ability to relate to the people around us is determined, to a significant degree, by the number of cars that roar past our homes each day, or the amount of time we spend looking at the world through a windshield? What if cars make us bad neighbors? What if cars bring out the worst in us? What if cars are literally driving us apart?

In 1969, San Francisco embarked on the development of an urban plan that would define that city for generations to come. As part of its research, the city decided to look at how people living on streets with differing levels of traffic rated their quality of life. The results, written up by participating UC Berkeley professor Donald Appleyard, provided a startling insight into just how destructive cars are to the patterns of urban human socialization that had endured for millennia before the age of the automobile.

Appleyard (whose son Bruce we cited in chapter 3) and his fellow researchers chose three different streets in the same part of town to study, with automotive traffic that they characterized as heavy, medium, and light, with the specific goal of figuring out whether and how traffic intensity affected people's lives. The team compiled data about the frequency and type of vehicles passing through while also documenting neighborhood demographics and interviewing residents about conditions. What they observed was that car traffic appeared to erode, and in some cases destroy, the delicate human social environment of the streets they were looking at. The more cars, the worse the damage.

Perhaps most startling was the way residents described social life on their respective streets. On the heavy-traffic street, people reported an almost total absence of interaction with their neighbors. "It's not a friendly street—no one offers help," one respondent told the planners. "People are afraid to go out into the street because of the traffic." The atmosphere on the less-trafficked street was dramatically different. "LIGHT street respondents had three times as many local friends and twice as many acquaintances as those on HEAVY street," reported Appleyard in his 1981 book building on the research, *Livable Streets*. And on the medium street? Rising traffic was endangering the increasingly fragile alliances that still existed there. "There was a feeling that the old community was on the point of extinction," Appleyard wrote, quoting a respondent who said: "'It used to be friendly; what was outside has now withdrawn into the buildings.'"

The highly trafficked street was also repelling the healthy multigenerational mix that could be found on the calmest street. "LIGHT street was predominantly a family street with many children," Appleyard wrote. "Grown-up children were even returning to bring up their own children there." The heavy-traffic street, in contrast, had few children; many aging residents, mostly older women, had become "trapped" there by circumstance, and young families were not moving in.

In effect, it appeared that the cars were killing the human social life on heavy- and medium-traffic streets. This at a time when Americans were being told that urban decline was an inevitable scourge that could be solved only by "slum clearance" to replace dwellings and business districts, often belonging to Black and brown people, and that "crime" was driving people away from urban life. (Appleyard and his team found that in fact more people cited concerns about traffic degrading their neighborhoods than about crime.) What replaced those dense and complex urban neighborhoods, of course, were freeways and surface parking lots catering to suburban motorists. Many of them used the city simply as a place to drive through on their way to earn their paychecks, before returning to the quiet cul-de-sacs of a mostly white suburbia. Planners widened the remaining surface streets in many cities, shrank or removed the sidewalks, and raised the speed limits, ensuring that more and more urban American streets could be classified as "heavy"—and that the cycle of social degradation and hollowing out of relationships could begin there, too.

Appleyard well understood that the decline of "street life" in the nation's cities posed a deep threat not just to individuals, but also to the collective enterprise of neighborhood vitality. The community's most affected members included San Francisco's best hope for the future—its children. "The protection and creation of livable streets is not simply a matter of increasing the safety or comfort of urban living," he wrote in *Livable Streets*. "The street has other functions. As the place where most children grow up, it is a crucial mediator between the home and the outside world, where the child learns to confront strangers and environments on his own. It should be a receptive and reasonably safe environment that the child can explore, manipulate, and use as a setting for all kinds of activities. . . . The social relations that take place on the street, its potential for neighborliness and street life, are values of urban life to be treasured."

In a senseless irony, a speeding drunk driver in Athens, Greece, killed Appleyard in 1982, just after the publication of *Livable Streets*. His work, however, has been hugely influential on generations of planners since, and his findings have been replicated several times, including in a 2011 study in Bristol, United Kingdom. Appleyard's genius was that he was able to quantify and document intuitive common-sense truths about how traffic affects us on the community level. Among those who study urban design, his research is well known; it underpins the intuitive understanding that in general, car traffic degrades urban quality of life and community.

And yet streets are being built all the time that disregard this widely and well-documented truth. As Mimi Sheller writes in her 2018 book, *Mobility Justice*, traffic engineers and elected officials persist in seeing streets as conduits for a flow of vehicles that can and must be measured solely by their productivity—by the same capitalist "cost-benefit analysis" metrics that are destroying our planet on so many levels.

"When transport is isolated as a matter of efficient movement, it becomes disconnected from the wider meanings of streets, neighborhoods, and communities and thereby ignores the valuation of diverse peoples' livelihoods, well-being, and health," writes Sheller. "[Cost-benefit analysis] also presumes that space is an empty background that transportation infrastructure simply moves through."

The tragedy is that so many of our modern streets are exactly that—an empty background filled only by a sizzling, snorting, roaring parade of ever-more-bloated vehicles. Most American cities and suburbs are filled with street-road hybrids, or "stroads," as engineer and planner Charles Marohn likes to call them. A stroad is a place that repels human life, its four or six or eight lanes of traffic baking under a sky that grows ever hotter, lined with mostly empty asphalt parking lots that reflect yet more heat upward on whatever person might choose, or more likely be forced, to walk through the bleak landscape. And yet by traffic engineering standards, this type of thoroughfare is a "success."

Streets used to be for people. They were incubators for style, slang, politics, love, and simple neighborly affinity. They were places where we could do things together, make things together, simply *be* together. Cars roll over all of that human activity and crush it. Cars send us scurrying to our respective dwellings like mice who fear the hawk in the sky above. In the words of one of Appleyard's respondents, "This street is murder."

Cars make us scared and suspicious of one another. Cars make us lonely.

Driving Alone

The picture-postcard version of the American dream has long been a detached home surrounded by greenery and, of course, that legendary white picket fence. Plenty of room to be yourself, without any interference from the neighbors. Plenty of space to be alone. But every dream can turn into a nightmare if it's twisted right. And the flip side of blissful solitude is loneliness.

We've all heard about the "loneliness epidemic" in American

society and how it's contributing to a host of ills—depression, anxiety, self-harm, apathy, paranoia, political division. The book *Bowling Alone*, by Robert Putnam, came out in 2000 and caused a wave of self-examination about the increasing isolation of the average American, especially in the suburban context, and how this isolation was leading to the slow death of "community" in much of the country. Putnam names autocentric sprawl development as one of the major factors in what he identified as a dwindling supply of "social capital" in the nation. "One inevitable consequence of how we have come to organize our lives spatially is that we spend measurably more of every day shuttling alone in metal boxes among the vertices of our private triangles," writes Putnam, referring to the home/work/shopping trajectory of the average suburbanite. "Metropolitan sprawl appears to have been a significant contributor to civic disengagement over the last three or four decades."

And yet when we talk about the American loneliness epidemic today, cars and car infrastructure are rarely, if ever, part of the conversation. The living memory of a time when things were different is now almost completely paved over. As a result, we almost never ask ourselves whether the way we build our communities, and the way we are forced to get around as a result, might be contributing to the problem.

That's not for lack of hand-wringing at the highest levels. The loneliness crisis in the United States is severe enough that the surgeon general under the Biden administration, Vivek Murthy, issued a whole report about strategies for combating life-threatening isolation. Yet you will search in vain for the words *traffic* and *cars* in the report. While there are a few nods to the importance of public spaces such as libraries and parks, streets and transportation are never discussed. You could read the whole report and never once encounter the idea that the increasingly loud, dangerous, bleak, and polluted conditions of our streets might be affecting our ability or desire to gather in community. Nor does the report consider whether the death of "the street" as social space could be part of the reason that we are now conducting so much of our social lives online.

You would never know, from this report, that over the past few generations, most Americans have been forced into dependence on a transportation system that inherently isolates them, each in their own metallic bubble—atomized individuals piloting death-dealing machines and condemned to compete every day for space and speed in a featureless roadscape that isn't even halfway as interesting as a 1990s-era video game.

Maybe it's not that surprising that we don't think about what we have lost in the fabric of our communities. The number of people who know what it is like to go about the business of daily life outside of a motor vehicle is dwindling. As we saw in chapter 3, in 1969, 89 percent of kids in kindergarten through eighth grade who lived within a mile of school walked or biked to get there; by 2011, that number was down to 35 percent. No wonder the kids are hanging out on the social media platforms adults so often decry—there are barely any physical platforms left where they can stand safely.

In *Livable Streets*, Appleyard wrote about how people's relative experience over a lifetime affects their perspective: "A longtime resident of Army Street in San Francisco, for example, would remember the time before Army Street became one of the major exits and entrances of the Bayshore Freeway. . . . A new resident would not even think of the street as having less traffic than it does today."

Traffication author Paul Donald agrees that the incremental nature of the change that has happened over a very long timeline is at least partly responsible for our obliviousness to the threat posed by an autocentric lifestyle. "It has crept up on us so slowly," Donald told us. "If you look at the rate of change in the number of vehicles on our roads, the billions of vehicle miles that they drive each year, it's kind of been about one percent per year. . . . One to two percent per year. And I think that we simply haven't noticed it." He continued, "If we could wave a magic wand and go back 50 years, I think we'd be astonished by how few vehicles we saw on the roads."

If you do make the effort to shake off this generational blindness to the proliferation of cars, what you see is shocking. In the US, per capita vehicle miles traveled have soared over the last forty years, from 6,767 per year in 1981 to near 10,000 today (an overwhelmingly upward trajectory that has been slowed or reversed here and there by financial crises, spikes in gas prices, and, of course, the pandemic). The average length of commute has also been steadily rising, in part because many people are being forced by price to live farther and farther from their jobs.

In the wake of the COVID-19 pandemic, the commutes that were happening got even lonelier. More people bought cars, even in cities with robust public transportation systems like New York City, where car ownership rose by 12.1 percent between 2012 and 2021. As Sarah said on the podcast back in 2020, people started using their SUVs as personal protective equipment. And while the virus may have receded, it doesn't seem as if our inclination to isolate from others has done the same.

In so many communities there is no street life, no corner store, no local bar to meet friends for a drink, no diner where you can grab a coffee and hang out with your neighbors. Human contact might consist of seeing the Amazon delivery driver through your house's Ring camera. Building our cities and towns to accommodate cars first and people as an afterthought, if at all, has created a world in which many of us never have to think about what anyone else needs or wants. A world in which we can entirely detach from the whole enterprise of "building community" or even "being polite." A world in which the street is our trash can, not our common ground.

A world, in other words, in which we are encouraged to act like jerks.

Motor Mania

It's no secret that cars make us act like jerks a lot of the time. So much so that researchers, advocates, and the general public have for years been coming up with words and phrases to describe the altered emotional state that cars put us in: *Windshield perspective. Car brain. Road rage.* Or maybe . . . *motor mania?*

Motor Mania was the title of a 1950 Disney animated short starring Goofy. In it, the friendly cartoon dog first appears as a mild-mannered suburban fellow named Mr. Walker, who "wouldn't step on an ant . . . courteous, punctual, and honest." Getting behind the wheel of a car, however, quickly transforms him from someone who "believes in live and let live" into a nightmarish figure named Mr. Wheeler, who "is charged with an overwhelming sense of power," and becomes all at once "an uncontrollable monster, a demon driver . . . a murderer." The short, which has long been a staple of drivers' ed, shows how once Goofy parks, he becomes the kindly Mr. Walker again, endangered by the rageful, reckless drivers around him—only to revert to the psychopathic Mr. Wheeler as soon as he gets back in his car.

More than seventy years after Disney animators created this spot-on spoof, a British scientist named Ian Walker and some colleagues got the idea to explore just how completely driving can transform our personal ethical code. The result is a paper, published in 2023, called "Motonormativity: How Social Norms Hide a Major Public Health Hazard." The basic question the study is trying to answer is this: Do we have different standards for moral behavior when cars are involved than when they are not? Is there a type of deeply ingrained thinking—Walker and company call it "motonormativity," a coinage that riffs on the concept of heteronormativity— that makes it impossible to act according to our usual codes once motor vehicles enter the equation?

"We've all seen this, we've all noticed that people do things in cars or do things for cars that they wouldn't do in other circumstances," Walker told us. "Like for example, you know, if you were in a shop, you would never just scream at somebody in front of you saying, 'Get out of the way! I want to be in front of you because I'm more important!' And yet people actually did that all the time on the road."

To explore how people change their ethical stance once cars are involved, Walker and his fellow researchers asked two thousand respondents one of a nearly identical set of questions, in which the only variable that changes is the presence of a car. Most telling was a question about air pollution. Respondents were asked if they agreed with one of two statements. The first was "people shouldn't drive in highly populated areas where other people have to breathe in car fumes." And then that was changed to "people shouldn't smoke in highly populated areas where other people have to breathe in cigarette fumes."

Changing *car* to *cigarette* made a stunning difference. "This was the biggest one," Walker told us. "We went from 17 percent agree that you shouldn't make people breathe car fumes to 75 percent agree you shouldn't make people breathe in cigarette fumes."

What explains our flexible morality when it comes to driving? Walker said part of the problem can be attributed to what is known in sociology as "special pleading." "Special pleading is where certain cases or certain situations just get a free ride in your discussion or even at a social level within our society," Walker said. "We just give something a free ride uncritically without actually justifying it."

But how have cars attained that "special pleading" status? Well, as a rule, we humans imitate those around us, starting with our parents, and we develop a belief system based on the way we see things functioning. That's called the social-ecological model, and Walker took us deep into the annals of philosophy to explain how it works.

"You can actually take this all the way back to the work of David Hume back in the 18th century," said Walker. "He talks about something called the Is-Ought fallacy. . . . He suggested that what we do as humans is . . . we see that something is a certain way, and from observing how something is, we say, 'Well, it is that way, therefore it ought to be that way.' . . . That's what I would argue is happening in the streets. . . . We observe a world where cars come first, we observe a world where fast, antisocial motoring is condoned or even encouraged, where the externalities of motoring are picked up by the state even amongst the most rugged individuals." Feeling perfectly fine about belching exhaust fumes into someone else's face is the least of it, Walker suggests. "It's a world where there are basically no consequences for killing another person as long as you do it the right way."

In the motonormative world, changing the way people think about what *is* and what *ought to be* is further complicated by the fact that cars are perceived and used as status symbols and markers of social standing. Other research has revealed, perhaps unsurprisingly, that people who drive expensive cars are far less likely to yield to pedestrians in the crosswalk or to wait their turn at a four-way stop sign. Mr. Wheeler is even more of a jerk, it seems, if he is driving a BMW.

As the Disney animators behind *Motor Mania* intuited, it's easy to become a monster when you get behind the wheel. It's also easy, as they illustrated, to become a decent human again—simply by getting out of the car. A group of German researchers recently conducted a study to look at "how mobility behavior relates to the orientation towards the common good." Using data from Germany, where more than 50 percent of trips are taken by car, they concluded that "cycling rather than driving was positively associated with orientation towards the common good in all models. . . . These findings are significant for policy and planning because the benefits of cycling over driving are more profound and sustainable than previously thought."

In other words, cyclists make better neighbors. Why, then, do we make it so hard to choose biking and walking?

Power Likes Horsepower

The politics of cars are incredibly complex, and it would be foolish to make simplistic statements about how they work. At this point in history, the automotive industry has enormous de facto power by virtue of its sheer size. In the United States alone, it provides millions of jobs and constitutes 3 percent of US GDP. More than 90 percent of American households own at least one car. So it's only natural that elected officials would be particularly responsive to motoring interests. That's why it wasn't much of a shock when the Obama administration pumped $80 billion into saving the US industry in the 2008 recession.

But in recent years, a darker kind of pro-automobile rhetoric has been escalating, and increasingly, it mirrors the most disturbing aspects of our ongoing civic breakdown.

In May of 2020, at the height of the first surge of COVID in the United States, President Donald J. Trump made an appearance at a Ford auto plant in Ypsilanti, Michigan. The factory had been contributing to the pandemic response by manufacturing much-needed ventilators, and Trump praised the workers and their employer for their efforts. Things got a little weird, though, when he referenced the company's founder, "a man named Henry Ford—good bloodlines, good bloodlines, if you believe in that stuff. You got good blood."

It was, at best, an unfortunate choice of words. Henry Ford was, of course, the man most responsible for inaugurating mass production of the automobile—the man who refined the car as the ultimate expression of American consumer culture. He was also a man who had some exceptionally repellent ideas about "bloodlines." As Jonathan Greenblatt of the Anti-Defamation League said on Twitter at the time of Trump's remarks, "Henry Ford was an antisemite and one of America's staunchest proponents of eugenics. The President should apologize." (Spoiler alert: the president did not apologize.)

Cars have been politicized ever since they started rolling down the road for the first time. And during the period when Henry Ford was developing and refining the automobile assembly line, he and others were also developing some of the auto-related political tropes that have flourished and persisted over the last century, such as making the personal motor vehicle affordable to the masses—a goal he achieved by being staunchly anti-union in an effort to keep labor costs down.

Ford was also busy documenting and promoting his own eugenicist, and specifically antisemitic, beliefs, at great personal expense. In 1918, he gained control of a newspaper, *The Dearborn Independent*, and made it into the premier press outlet for antisemitic hate propaganda in the United States. Ford published eighty-one articles between 1920 and 1922 on "the Jewish question," under his own name (although they were ghostwritten by another man). The vile antisemitism that was the paper's raison d'être was an on-ramp for Ford's doggedly pro-Hitler stance as National Socialism took hold in Germany over the years that followed. (Ford received the Grand Cross of the German Eagle, the highest commendation available to non-Germans, from the Third Reich in 1938.)

Exposure to Ford's hate speech was baked into the Ford Motor consumer experience. *The Dearborn Independent* was distributed through Ford dealerships around the country, given as a bonus to anyone who drove a Ford off the lot. Its circulation reached seven hundred thousand readers at one point. And its influence was undeniable.

"Because *The Dearborn Independent* was published by Ford . . . it got much greater currency than if it had just been a small-town newspaper in some equivalent-sized town in Wisconsin or Montana," scholar Hasia Diner told PBS's *American Experience* in 2012.

"Henry Ford's ability to gain a national audience with his words made him a very dangerous person," Diner added. "And Hitler was very much inspired by Ford's writing. And the idea that this could happen in the United States, I think, was very important to Hitler as well, because as people in the United States were speaking out against Nazism and were using a kind of rhetoric, 'Well, it could never happen here,' and 'We are the bastions of democracy,' I think Hitler would have derived a degree of satisfaction to be able to point to Ford as, in a way, just as good an anti-Semite as he was." (In 1933, Hitler commissioned his own "people's car," the "Volkswagen," which was supposed to embody "strength through pleasure.")

It would be easy to dismiss the resonance between Trump's aside about "bloodlines" and Ford's obsession with the same. But the historical echo has only gotten creepier over time as debates over cars and car infrastructure have steadily become more prominent in the culture wars and the electoral battle for the future of the United States and Europe as well. In early 2024, Trump used inflammatory rhetoric about the need to put tariffs on Chinese-manufactured cars. His prediction of what would happen if he wasn't allowed to do that? "If I don't get elected, it's going to be a bloodbath for the whole— that's gonna be the least of it. It's going to be a bloodbath for the country." Funny how often blood and cars seemed to go together in his mind.

When we took *The War on Cars* as the name of our podcast, we were doing so in a spirit of trying to expose the absurdity of that phrase and to appropriate it for our own (ironic) use (see the introduction). Claiming that there was a "war on cars" was an easy way for virulently pro-car, mostly suburban forces to sanitize the anti-urban and frankly racist arguments that undergirded their opposition to transit, bike, and pedestrian improvements in the urban core. The political rhetoric around cars, and the insistence on making any challenge to automotive dominance into a culture war issue, sows fear and division in society and festers into something truly ugly.

Case in point: The advent of electric cars has caused a fresh wave of anxiety in motordom. Suddenly, after generations of complaining about gas prices, the pro-motoring lobby decided to cling to gas-powered vehicles as a last bastion of freedom. Before he became Trump's 2024 running mate, JD Vance proved his pro-gasoline bona fides by introducing legislation eliminating tax credits for electric vehicles and replacing them with credits for gas-powered vehicles (it didn't pass). Senator Ted Cruz reacted to Kamala Harris's candidacy by saying, "Kamala can't have my guns. She can't have my gasoline engine. And she sure as hell can't have my steaks and cheeseburgers." Indeed, the scare tactics used by the fossil fuel lobby eerily mirror the gun lobby's framing of supposed threats to Second Amendment rights.

"Are you ready for the government to take away your car?" asked the right-wing think tank Heritage Foundation on its website in 2023, basing that question on exactly nothing real. "Under Uncle Sam's Grand Theft Auto plan, Americans would be sacrificing their cars, paying more for transportation, and giving up their personal mobility without benefits for the environment. It's time to stop the theft." Perhaps unsurprisingly, the Heritage Foundation also came up with Project 2025—the plan floated during the 2024 election season that called for increased fossil fuel extraction and reduced research into climate change, among other things.

The performative panic over the concept of fifteen-minute cities is another example of how the rising global Right has effectively sown political strife over any policies that decenter the automobile. In this fevered narrative, the relatively anodyne concept of being able to access services and amenities within a fifteen-minute walk or bike ride in your own neighborhood was painted as the work of a totalitarian state that wanted, in the words of British right-wing media personality Katie Hopkins, to create a world in which "you will have only 15 minutes of freedom."

These addled conspiracy theories and juvenile displays of machismo might seem merely absurd. But they have real-world consequences. Some of them are political, like New York Governor Kathy Hochul's last-minute decision to pause congestion pricing in New York City in what was apparently an effort to placate wealthy suburban voters and persuade them to vote for Democratic candidates in the 2024 election. (Autocentrism is one of the few remaining bastions of bipartisanship.)

And sometimes, the consequences are fatal.

In August of 2017, a young woman named Heather Heyer was killed in Charlottesville, Virginia, by the driver of a Dodge Challenger who used his vehicle to plow into a crowd of protesters who had assembled to counter the infamous "Unite the Right" rally. The driver was later convicted of first-degree murder, his claims of self-defense rejected by the jury. But the practice of using vehicles to menace, injure, and kill protesters reemerged during the Black Lives Matter protests in 2020. In fact, legislators in several states have moved, with varying levels of success, to protect drivers who strike protesters with their vehicles, on the grounds that they are engaging in some kind of self-defense.

Ari Weil, a PhD candidate at the University of Chicago who researches political violence, shared some of his findings with us back in 2020. Weil tracked seventy-two incidents of vehicular violence against protesters between May 27 and July 7 of that year, only twenty-eight of which resulted in charges against the driver. Seven of the incidents were perpetrated by law enforcement officers. Weil also found cops sharing memes about using cars to hurt and kill protesters on several forums. "I worry that that then tacitly encourages future behavior," Weil told us. "We heard on an NYPD scanner, an officer saying they were dealing with some group of protesters, and you can hear over the chatter someone says, 'Well just run them over.' And it worries me if they too begin to see this as legitimate or a tool in their arsenal."

Walk and Learn

So how can we fight back against the isolation and bad feeling created by cars?

Maybe we can start by simply getting out of them and seeing what it's like to rub up against the real world for a change.

That's what Jonathon Stalls tries to do. Stalls calls himself a "walking artist." He has lived almost his entire life without a car, now in Colorado. In 2010, faced with a daunting set of life challenges, he decided to "reset the defaults" by walking across the country. His experiences connecting with other people as he trekked through America's sometimes unforgiving streetscape convinced him of the essential value to be found in simply being physically present with others who were walking and rolling down the same streets.

"One of the things that was really loud from the beginning was just what happened when I was moving with other people," Stalls told us. "I walked with . . . and moved with so many people of different backgrounds, people that wanted to join for an hour or half a day or a day, people that I just ran into and stumbled upon along the route at a bus stop or underneath an overpass bridge while we shared a shade break from the sun," he said. "The things that we were able to connect on because we were moving in an unhurried way. . . . It was simple and basic, but profound in comparison to kind of car-centric frameworks of just bypassing each other and everything around us all the time, all day."

Stalls went on to write *Walk: Slow Down, Wake Up, and Connect at 1-3 Miles Per Hour*, a combination of self-help book and advocacy manual that suggests that simply walking (or rolling in a wheelchair) can be a radical impetus for social change. In the years since his cross-country walk, he has led workshops and group walks that help people explore their communities outside of the car bubble. Some of the people he walks with are planners and elected officials—who bear at least some responsibility for the unhealthy built environment in their communities. Many of them, Stalls told us, have never truly experienced what it's like to get around the places they live without the protective shell of a personal motor vehicle.

His goal, he said, is to help these transportation professionals to move away from thinking about streets in an abstract way and to awaken their "body brain" so that they can understand the reality that pedestrians, wheelchair users, and bicyclists feel on the street—the whoosh of a semitruck passing fast and close, the struggle to get a stroller to a bus stop when there isn't a sidewalk, the long slog to reach a marked crosswalk. The practice can have a profound effect. "I see over and over and over every single time, every time there is a kind of a vibrational shift," said Stalls. "You just feel it with everyone involved, especially those working within the systems, working within cities and states and transit agencies. . . . You feel the empathy expanding."

Stalls's book contains many exercises that readers can try at home, like drawing a one-mile radius around their homes and committing to only walking or rolling within that line for a day, a week, a month, or longer. "For those who grew up in cars and have only seen the world through cars, that lived experience is informing all the defaults—feeding it, sustaining it, maintaining it," he said. "Just experience another way. Replace your trips for a week or a day, or part of your trips. Drive and park the damn car half the way to work, 15 minutes outside of the grocery store. Don't park the damn thing right up in the grocery store. . . . What would it be like to approach this grocery store on foot or in a wheelchair?"

The reality is that in many places, the environments are so hostile that it's hard for people to imagine walking through them for even half a mile. Maybe that's why so many Americans like vacationing in Europe (or in the Disney bubble of simulated Euro-style walkable streets).

Pretty much anywhere you go in Europe these days, you will find cities that have limited cars and increased space for human beings. Oslo, Madrid, Paris, London—these are the cities that make international headlines with their congestion pricing initiatives, bike lane networks, and freeway removals. But in dozens of smaller cities, from Bilbao to Malmö to Toulouse to Ljubljana, city officials are pedestrianizing downtowns, limiting automobile access in residential districts by using simple infrastructure like retractable bollards—simple cylindrical traffic barriers that go up and down to admit permit holders, delivery drivers, and emergency vehicles—and creating new parks in industrial areas or where roads used to be. On street after street, people walk without fear of cars and relax in plazas where the sound of humans laughing and chatting and clinking glasses at outdoor restaurants doesn't compete with the roar of personal motor vehicles.

North America isn't Europe, they'll tell you, as we learned in chapter 2. That's true—and there are plenty of places in Europe where cars still dominate, as well. Does that mean we humans who live in autocentric societies are condemned to isolation and increasing alienation from others? Is motonormativity inevitable?

Ian Walker said that his research into the phenomenon has led him to believe that we must raise awareness of what cars do to our humanity. "I think one of the things we have to be exploring is showing people this," he said. "Look, I'm sure in every other context of your life, you are a lovely person. You would never dream of committing violence in any other setting. You would never dream of demanding that other people get out of your way in a shop or a supermarket. You would never murder a person because you've taken a slight dislike to them in half a second. And yet in this context, you are doing that. And we need to be calling this out, I think. And I think that's got to be one of the most powerful tools available to us."

If you can only recognize what cars are doing to you, in other words, you might be moved to demand a better system.

The problem is that many people in our society are too pressed by the requirements of daily life—by the struggle to make the rent, pay for health insurance, figure out how to get the kids to the dentist—to be looking for a paradigm shift. A lot of people *aren't* in Europe on vacation, marveling at car-free streets, because a lot of people can't afford to even think about taking a vacation at all.

And in many parts of the world, including the United States, a comfortable walkable lifestyle has become a luxury good. The few cities—and neighborhoods within those cities—where you can get around reliably on public transportation or by biking and walking have become mind-bogglingly expensive (New York, we're looking at you). In most other places, if you're walking or riding the bus, it's only because you can't afford to go by car. Many of your community's amenities and advantages will be out of reach for you because the bus doesn't go there, or it runs just a couple of times a day, or it takes so long that it doesn't make sense to try using it. As for walking or rolling? To be avoided, unless you have a death wish.

The automotive industry told us that cars would bring us together; instead, it turns out, cars keep us apart from one another, each in our own bubble of metal, glass, and plastic, blasting through communities, trailing a cloud of exhaust and dust, engines roaring to drown out the sound of the human voice on the street.

Cars Are Unjust

At the heart of car culture is a series of paradoxes. Cars open new vistas of social mobility; cars also erect barriers that keep populations in their place. Cars are liberating; cars are also burdensome and confining. Cars enable freedom, but only on their own terms—terms that include a steep financial cost and the assumption of a variety of risks, some of them life-threatening.

These paradoxes are never more evident than when we discuss cars and people who are traditionally disenfranchised and excluded in our society—Black and brown people, people with disabilities, children, older people, and women, to name a few groups. Together, they represent the majority of the population. But our transportation system is stacked against them. Too often, our autocentric way of life exacerbates and magnifies the inequalities that already exist. If you can't afford to drive, or you can't drive because of your age or disability, you're condemned to using a public transit system that, in North America, is almost certainly going to be underfunded—and as a result, infrequent, erratic, inconvenient, and sometimes so neglected that it doesn't feel safe. If you're driving and you're a member of a racialized minority, you might find yourself the target of police violence.

We talked with historian and author Gretchen Sorin about her groundbreaking 2020 book, *Driving While Black: African American Travel and the Road to Civil Rights.* The phrase *driving while Black* is usually employed to highlight the dangers Black people face on the road, particularly when it comes to inequitable law enforcement. Those dangers are real and ongoing. Sorin's book, however, is also interested in exploring another side of driving while Black—the way that access to personal motor vehicles opened up the world for Black people in the twentieth century and gave them unprecedented independence and agency.

"For African-Americans who were living during the period of Jim Crow, the alternative methods of travel—the bus or the train—required that you depend on the decency of someone else," Sorin told us. "You depend on the bus driver. You depend on the . . . train staff. And very often those people would be extremely rude. . . . They would insist that you get on the rear of the bus or they would insist that you move to the Negro car on the train. So, when you had your own automobile, you got to control how you were treated. You got to control where you went. . . . You were able to maintain dignity when you traveled. And that was particularly important for people with families, because they wanted to make sure that their children did not have to face the same kind of humiliation that they faced when they were growing up."

Not that getting behind the wheel magically erased the barriers of segregation or the threat of anti-Black violence. Sorin documents in heartbreaking detail the lengths to which Black drivers had to go to stay safe, making plans for extreme situations that would never occur to a white motorist. "Generally, African-Americans favored the Buick . . . because it was a good, sturdy, sensible car that had a great reputation," Sorin said. "It was a car that wouldn't strand you when you were going out on the road. And it was also heavy, and a heavy car would be harder for a mob to turn over if you encountered an angry mob on the road."

An essential tool in a Black road tripper's kit was *The Negro Motorist Green Book*, a guide to the United States that was tailored to help Black drivers find secure accommodation and supplies as they traversed an often hostile country. Updated annually from 1936 to 1966, it aimed, in the words of its creator, "to give the Negro traveler information that will keep him from running into difficulties, embarrassments and to make his trip more enjoyable." On the cover, which featured a picture of dozens of cars traveling closely together down a scenic road, was an idealistic quote from Mark Twain: "Travel is fatal to prejudice."

Unfortunately, that aspirational maxim did not always hold true. Driving a personal motor vehicle may have meant that Black people could travel without risking the humiliation of outright segregation— riding on the back of the bus or on Jim Crow–era train cars that were custom-built with inferior facilities for Black people. The road, however, had a different set of perils. Prejudice was anything but dead in midcentury America, and it was often accompanied by violence. Black drivers were forced to take extreme measures to keep their families safe on the road, carrying all the supplies they might need with them in case they couldn't find a place where they knew they could stop without fear of harassment—or worse.

And then there were the cops.

"It was a double-edged sword because when you go out on the road, you are exposing yourself to the police," said Sorin. "One of the cardinal rules for most African-Americans who were traveling was to stay on the interstates . . . because you'd rather encounter a state policeman than you would a . . . local policeman. But no matter what, you wanted to encounter the police as little . . . as possible. . . . In many states, . . . they tended to stop proportionately more Black drivers, even though African-American drivers were not speeding or committing crimes at any higher rate than any other drivers. . . . And there was an assumption that if you were a Black driver and you were driving a nice car, that you were a drug dealer or that you were driving a stolen car."

This stark reality—that merely driving a car down the road can make you a target for racist police—is not just history. It is a living reality in the United States of America today. In 2024, the US Justice Department brought charges against local law enforcement officials in the town of Lexington, Mississippi, arguing that starting in 2021 they had conducted a systematic campaign to arrest and ticket local residents, raking in $1.7 million in fines and debts and ultimately arresting about a quarter of the town's population. Black residents were the prime target of these escalating police actions in Lexington, according to the report, which showed that by 2023, "Black people were 17.6 times more likely to be arrested by LPD than white people were."

A huge number of these arrests and tickets had to do with driving, which essentially exposed Black people in Lexington to police who were waiting for any chance to move in and make a cash grab. Every arrest, no matter how minor the infraction, netted a fifty-dollar processing fee. "Officers arrested anyone they caught driving without a license," read the DOJ report. "They arrested people for crimes like playing loud music and improper parking. LPD arrested and jailed one man for four days because he bought coffee at a gas station, then refilled his coffee without paying for a second cup."

While the actions of Lexington's police department were so egregious that they attracted federal civil rights action, they are part of a pattern that is all too familiar to Black drivers. And one of the reasons corrupt cops think they can get away with this kind of thing is that back in the twentieth century, the Supreme Court created a loophole that made anyone driving a car vulnerable to the police.

Searching and Seizing

As more and more people took to the roads over the first half of the twentieth century, legislators were passing ordinances to control the way those people drove—a perfectly reasonable response to the wave of death and injury caused by the introduction of the automobile. The consequences of these new laws, however, would reverberate for generations, long after the reasons for their adoption were lost in the mists of history.

With more people driving, more people were breaking the law and getting caught doing it. Legal scholar Sarah Seo, in her book, *Policing the Open Road: How Cars Transformed American Freedom*, examines the way that an explosion of traffic regulations—covering everything from turning to speeding to taillights—led to a parallel explosion in the numbers of cops empowered to enforce the new rules. "The traffic code became bigger and bigger and bigger," Seo told us. "All of a sudden everybody became a misdemeanor offender. Everybody broke traffic laws and it was a huge problem. . . . They realized they needed the police to enforce them."

This new army of cops was simultaneously enforcing another new set of laws caused by Prohibition. Like driving, the constitutional ban on liquor, which lasted from 1920 to 1933, turned legions of "ordinary" folks into criminals. Some people used cars to transport that illicit booze, and that's where things got legally complicated.

The case of one specific Michigan bootlegger named George Carroll, who was caught with boxes of liquor stuffed into the upholstery of his snazzy Oldsmobile Roadster, went all the way to the Supreme Court. The cops who stopped and searched the vehicle did so without a warrant, based on their suspicions that the vehicle might contain contraband. Carroll's lawyers argued that the search violated the Fourth Amendment, which protects citizens against "unreasonable" searches and seizures by the government.

The Supreme Court, however, didn't see it the way that Carroll's attorney did. Chief Justice William Howard Taft wrote the court's decision against Carroll. In it, he articulated a distinction between the legal protections that people could expect in their homes and in their cars. Normally, a cop must go before a judge and demonstrate probable cause for a search warrant. But the mobility of cars posed a special problem. How could the police deal with the moving threat posed by the driver of a personal motor vehicle who might be using that vehicle as a base for criminal activity?

"Basically, what [Taft] said is, 'When it involves cars, if the police have probable cause to believe that there's evidence of a crime in the car, then they don't need a warrant,'" Seo told us. "What the Carroll case did was transfer that decision making from the judge . . . to the police on the road. . . . That gives the police great discretionary power."

That discretionary power has led to millions of traffic stops in the hundred or so years since the cops ripped open George Carroll's back seat and found a few crates of booze. In fact, Seo writes, "The law's accommodation of discretionary policing profoundly altered what it meant to live free from state intrusion in the Automotive Age. . . . Unforeseen by midcentury jurists, their solution . . . led directly to the problem of discriminatory policing against minorities."

In her book, Seo highlights the way traffic stops have played a role in some of the most shocking instances of police killing Black and brown people in the twenty-first century. She cites the infamous 2015 case of Sandra Bland, a Black woman who was pulled over by a policeman in Texas for failing to use her turn signal. The encounter, captured on body cam and on Bland's own phone, quickly escalated as the officer ordered her to put out her cigarette and Bland insisted on her right to smoke in her own car. Then he told her to get out of the vehicle and threatened to tase her. "For a failure to signal, you're doing all this . . ." Bland said, before the cop pulled her out onto the side of the road and arrested her as she lay writhing in pain on the ground. Just three days later, Bland was found hanging lifeless in her jail cell. Her death was ruled a suicide.

Bland had a history of traffic stops, which is why Seo used her story to illustrate the pervasive effect that "routine" traffic enforcement can have on a person's life. "Even though she doesn't die during the traffic stop . . . when you look at her entire life and look at the reasons for why she's unemployed, the reason why she's self-medicating with marijuana and arrested for marijuana possession, the reason why she has traffic fines that she can't pay for and goes into debt—all of those setbacks in her life happen in the context of traffic stops,"

Seo said. "And that's because our society is a car society. And the number one place where most Americans encounter the police is in their cars."

Evidence has shown time and again that members of racialized minorities are disproportionately targeted by the police for the kinds of traffic stops that ended so catastrophically for Bland. A 2020 analysis of one hundred million traffic stops conducted by the Stanford Open Policing Project showed that Black drivers were 20 percent more likely than white ones to be stopped, and that after a traffic stop, they were 1.5 to 2 times more likely to undergo a search for contraband and weapons—even though "[B]lack and Hispanic drivers were searched on the basis of less evidence than white drivers." This is why we, and many other advocates, call for automated camera enforcement of moving violations like speed limits and red-light running (as well as passive controls on reckless driving, such as speed governors). Cameras don't discriminate. Too often, cops do.

"That's where the police get the minority citizens," Seo told us. "They get them for minor traffic violations and rack up their fines. And so the problems with . . . unequal justice, and poor people not being able to pay their fines, and late fees and fees for not appearing in court—all of that begins with traffic violations."

Each one of those traffic stops also comes with tremendous risk. The year Sandra Bland died, according to a survey cited by Seo, 27 percent of police killings of unarmed people resulted from the same type of inciting incident—a traffic stop. As Seo writes of the story that emerged about Bland's life and death, "the automobile stood in the background . . . but it played a prominent role as a site of violence, poverty, and discrimination."

For too many Black and brown people, the promise of autonomy and independence offered by the car has turned into a deadly trap. But when your transportation system is systematically rigged for cars, as ours is in the United States, it's not just the drivers from marginalized communities who suffer. It's everyone who moves.

Nowhere to Turn

For many Black and brown people, the streets of their communities, the places where they should feel safest, too often represent instead a site of unpredictable peril. We're not talking here about gun violence or gang activity, although those can be factors in some neighborhoods. We're talking about scenarios that are purposely created by the people in charge, the ones who are supposed to be keeping us all safe. We're talking about autocentric design and policy decisions that make going about your daily business a threat—streets without sidewalks, multilane suburban arterials that are impossible to cross safely, unreliable public transportation, bus stops without benches or shade, and an all-encompassing law enforcement infrastructure that seems more invested in controlling marginalized populations by intimidation than in creating true and lasting safety—much less a vibrant and accessible public realm.

The Black Lives Matter movement, for a time, forced the nation to confront the consequences of maintaining a status quo that systematically patrols and limits the movement of Black people no matter what transportation mode they choose. As a result, we now know the names of some of the countless people who have been killed by law enforcement officers while trying to move about the communities where they live. Michael Brown was walking down the middle of a street in Ferguson, Missouri, when he was shot by cops who told him to move onto the sidewalk and then blocked him with their SUV before killing him. In Minneapolis, George Floyd was pinned to the asphalt and killed in the street next to a police vehicle after being pulled from a car he had borrowed from a friend. Elijah McClain was injected with a fatal dose of ketamine after police confronted him for waving his arms while walking down a sidewalk in Colorado. Walter Scott was shot three times in the back when he tried to flee from a policeman who stopped him for a broken brake light in South Carolina.

Unfortunately, we could go on and on.

Historian Rod Clare notes that the Black Lives Matter movement highlighted an issue that has long poisoned American society: what he calls "the long-standing issue of [B]lack mobility. That is, *where* [B]lack people can go and *when* can they go there." Clare emphasizes the way that the "movements and associations" of Black Americans have been monitored and regulated since the first enslaved people were forcibly brought to this continent centuries ago. "This remained the case in the South and indeed in other parts of the country well into the twentieth century through the implementation of Black Codes, Ku Klux Klan terrorism, sharecropping contracts, city zoning laws, segregation, and various other means."

These days, the work of limiting Black mobility is in great part performed by a hostile built environment and systematic disinvestment from public transportation, bike, and pedestrian infrastructure in American cities and suburbs. And on one spring evening in 2011, a Black woman named Raquel Nelson found herself in the middle of a four-lane arterial road in suburban Atlanta, caught in a terrible confluence of all those malign forces.

Who's the Guilty One?

Nelson, then twenty-nine, was coming home by bus from a long day out with her three young children. They had missed a bus on their way back to their suburban Atlanta apartment complex after having a pizza dinner to celebrate Nelson's birthday, which was the following day; they had to wait another hour for the next one, because service was so infrequent. The bus stop where they got off was directly across the street from their home, but the nearest crosswalk was a third of a mile away. That meant the family, laden with grocery bags, would have had to walk an additional two thirds of a mile in the dark along the busy four-lane roadway to cross in the one place where they were "allowed" to and then back to where they were trying to go. Like others on the bus who lived at the apartment complex, Nelson made the decision to cross the road at the bus stop.

She and the kids got halfway across without a problem. But then four-year-old A. J. went out ahead of his mom to cross the second set of lanes. He was hit by a car and killed right in front of her.

Nelson's nightmare didn't end with A. J.'s death. The car's driver, who was partially blind and by his own admission had been drinking and taking painkillers, was charged with a hit-and-run (he eventually served six months for the offense). But *she* was the one charged with vehicular homicide in her son's death—on the grounds that she endangered A. J.'s life by crossing where there wasn't a crosswalk. Nelson was quickly found guilty by an all-white jury and sentenced to a year's probation.

The case was so egregious that it attracted national attention. Nelson—supported by the NAACP and a petition drive that garnered

135,000 signatures—fought the charges. Two years later, she won. "This is for everyone," Nelson said on the *Today* show after she was cleared. "This is for—on a more personal level, myself, my children, single mothers, anybody who has to take public transportation. This is for anyone who has ever had to be in a scary situation like that."

The reality is that countless families every day find themselves in this exact type of scary situation. Studies have found that single parents like Nelson are more likely to use public transit than other people. They are also more likely to face financial challenges. And in much of the United States, living in a neighborhood with safe, walkable streets and frequent, reliable transit service is an unattainable luxury.

As we've shown in this chapter, the laws are too often written and enforced in a way that targets Black people and majority-minority communities. Our society routinely and systematically disinvests from these same communities, leaving their residents to endure neglected infrastructure and cuts to all kinds of services, including transit—although there always seems to be money for hiring more cops.

First, huge swaths of urban neighborhoods were demolished for highway construction that enabled white flight, with millions of Black and brown people displaced and hundreds of majority-minority business districts gutted. Then those cities were systematically starved of the funds they needed to maintain services. When white people decided to come back, part of the much-touted twenty-first-century trend of the "creative class" revitalizing long-disinvested neighborhoods, Black communities were the last to see improvements in the public realm—and Black residents were often priced out when basic services and amenities did show up. Which meant that suburbs like the one where Raquel Nelson endured the horrifying loss of her child became a refuge for those fleeing gentrification—a refuge that was never designed for anything other than cars passing through in huge numbers at high speeds.

Raquel Nelson's intersectional identity as a Black woman meant she was doubly marginalized. For generations, planners and engineers have ignored the transportation needs of women—women like Nelson who just need a safe way to cross the street with their kids; women coming home late from shift work and forced to wait for sporadic transit service in vulnerable locations without proper lighting or shelter; women who need to get their kids to school and sports, take an older relative to the doctor, go to the grocery store, and get themselves to work, none of that happening on the "regular" nine-to-five workday schedule that dictates transit timetables.

For women, as for so many other marginalized groups, the promised freedom of an autocentric society can start looking more and more like false advertising. Especially if, like Raquel Nelson, they are depending on a public transportation system that is routinely starved of funding, while roads get all the money they need.

Not Driving? Take Your Chances

Safety when riding and waiting for public transportation is one of the most obvious areas where women's concerns and needs are different from men's—and where their movement is limited by the threat of sexual assault, something that men rarely consider when they travel through public space. In some countries, such as India and Mexico, all-women cars have been introduced to metro systems to account for the inherent vulnerability of women. When Sarah rode the metro in Delhi in 2012, she had the chance to ride on one of these; it was a pleasant enough experience, except for the few men who stood on the adjacent car and stared persistently through the open gangway at the women they were prevented from getting close to.

If you're a woman, you know the calculus of safety all too well. The list of variables goes on and on: What time is sunset, what is the bus schedule, will there be other travelers on the subway platform, what are the sight lines like in the parking garage, is that sidewalk properly lit, what should I wear, could I run in these shoes, should I take out my AirPods? Is that man looking at me? Is there someone behind me? Could I stick my keys in his eye if he grabbed me? Who would hear me if I started screaming?

Add to that incessant internal litany the things that people say to you on the street, no matter what form of transportation you're using. The London Cycling Campaign recently surveyed one thousand women about their experiences riding bicycles on the streets of the city. Nine out of ten said they had experienced verbal abuse and aggression while biking. Ninety-three percent said drivers had used vehicles to intimidate them. One in five said they had given up riding permanently or temporarily after they had been harassed. And when women reported incidents of aggression to the police, the cops almost never followed up.

Harassment from drivers has a chilling effect on women's mobility. "It causes people to travel less, to become potentially more socially isolated, just miss out on a lot of what's out there in the world," said Kate Bartlett of the London Cycling Campaign. "It just chips away at . . . your confidence, your self-esteem. . . . Those things happen, and we probably all try not to, but you carry them with you the rest of the day, the rest of the week. Some people carry them forever."

Women travel differently from men, too. They are more likely to do errand-based trips along with their own commute to work, a phenomenon called "trip-chaining" that has been studied for decades. Women's unpaid roles as caregivers and their likelihood to do more of the household labor both contribute to the phenomenon, which has changed relatively little over the last thirty years, despite women's changing role in society.

Women's perspectives remain dramatically underrepresented in transportation planning. In the United States, according to a 2019 survey, less than 15 percent of the transportation workforce is women, and only about one fifth of leadership positions in the field are held by women. Our cities are, for the most part, designed for men's bodies, men's habits, and men's tastes.

It might not be surprising, then, that many women feel safer inside the metal bubble of a car. Yet as automobile infrastructure has steadily and exponentially increased over the last century, the freedom that the automobile promised to women has turned too often into a different type of servitude. Now, car sprawl enables and enforces social isolation. Cars themselves keep us neatly separated from the people around us, and sprawling car-dependent development means that traditional support systems for families—the proverbial village it takes to raise a child—has been smashed to bits. Women today, still bearing the lion's share of domestic labor and childcare, not only have to deal with punishing car commutes but also must figure out a web of other destinations connected by often-congested urban and suburban arterials—the kids' school, the doctor's office, the shopping center, the soccer practice field, and on and on. When a woman walks out her front door, she will see a street that is designed and maintained for maximum motor vehicle access.

Women, as we saw so clearly in Raquel Nelson's story, are continually navigating a transportation system that was not designed with them in mind.

Toxic Petro-Masculinity

The boy driving the Ford F-250 was just sixteen years old, from a well-known, affluent family in his community outside Houston. He was the recipient of dozens of "excellent report cards," according to his attorney, and he had never been in trouble with the law.

That changed one day in the fall of 2021, when he decided to use his parents' three-ton vehicle to harass a group of people out for a weekend ride on their road bikes in Waller, Texas. The teenager was "rolling coal" onto the bikers—blasting them with black diesel smoke from his tailpipe. It's a not-so-fun trend that has gained popularity among some motorists in the twenty-first century, often targeting pedestrians, bicyclists, and non-gasoline cars; some aficionados call it "Prius repellent." In 2020, the EPA estimated that more than half a million diesel trucks in the United States had been modified to burn fuel and spew smoke, just for laughs.

According to a police report, the young driver in this case "failed to control speed as he accelerated to intentionally blow black diesel smoke in the path of several bicyclists." He hit six of them, leaving their bodies and bikes strewn across the roadway. All six miraculously survived, although several sustained life-altering injuries. The local district attorney closed the case without charging the kid, who graduated from high school a couple of years after the crash. Funny, who faces consequences and who doesn't.

Scholar Cara Daggett wrote about rolling coal in her seminal

2018 article, "Petro-masculinity: Fossil Fuels and Authoritarian Desire," in which she unleashes a detailed analysis of the way the oil and automobile industries have fostered a toxic masculinity that is expressed, in part, through vehicular domination. "Spectators and coal rollers express pleasure in the noise, the smell, and the beauty of the smoke, all of which give them a sensation of power that, not coincidentally I suggest, is directly related to the smoke's violent effects," writes Daggett. In her framing, rolling coal is a relatively minor manifestation of the petro-masculinity phenomenon, an indicator of some of the dark forces beneath the normalized facade of car culture.

Daggett's thesis explains a lot about our current moment, one in which "muscle cars" roar through our streets unchecked and bicycles still serve as cultural shorthand for male failure to be forceful and dominant. She suggests that in an unstable, rapidly changing world, men can seek solace in the roaring power of car culture. "Petro-masculinity is helpful to understanding how the anxieties aroused by the Anthropocene can augment desires for authoritarianism," Daggett writes. "The concept of petro-masculinity suggests that fossil fuels mean more than profit; fossil fuels also contribute to making identities." Daggett makes a compelling case that by gendering energy—fossil fuels male, alternative energy female—the oil industry and its political allies have cemented their hold on the psyches of consumers.

When it comes to designing transportation systems, most policymakers in the United States seem more interested in the masculinized might of the car than in creating a network of transit, bike, and pedestrian infrastructure that would provide safe, reliable, pleasant, and affordable passage for people like Raquel Nelson and her children. When our transportation system and our justice system intersect, as they did in the case of Nelson and Sandra Bland and so many others, the inequity that is so deeply baked into our society is only heightened.

Cars promise freedom and agency for everyone. But too often, they have proven a more reliable vehicle for reinforcing the power of those who are already powerful. They impoverish those who are already poor, disproportionately endanger the most vulnerable among us, and widen the already yawning gulf that separates the haves and have-nots in our society.

Part III

How We Get Free

8

Designing a Better World

First, we shape the cities," wrote architect Jan Gehl. "Then they shape us."

What shape do we choose as we go forward? Will we move toward a renewed norm of streets at a human scale, where people can move freely and safely outside of the metal carapace of a car? Or will we perpetuate the status quo—the bleak hardscape of the multilane suburban arterial, the incessant roar of multiton vehicles, the alienation from the world beyond our windshields?

That choice is still being made every day by people who dole out money for transportation infrastructure. It will determine the way the rest of us live our lives. And despite a lot of terrible infrastructure out there, we *are* capable of making good choices about how our streets are configured. Bringing our cities and suburbs back to a human scale is something we can do by design, if we decenter the car. It's already happening in some communities around North America and the world.

We shape our streets. Then they shape us. We can choose a human shape.

The Curb-Cut Effect

Not long after Sarah started classes at UC Berkeley way back in 1981, she noticed that more than a few of her fellow students used wheelchairs to get around. Where Sarah came from—New York City—she almost never saw people with wheelchairs on the street. It was a moment of revelation. What caused this difference? Inspired by a paraplegic student she got to know, Sarah began to do some research—and discovered that Berkeley was a hub for the disability-rights movement.

In the 1960s, a group of quadriplegic students at the school had come together and started fighting for their rights to live as fully as anyone else. They became known as the Rolling Quads, and they advocated for the full inclusion of people with disabilities in the community. That inclusion depended fundamentally on their ability to simply move about with the same access to classrooms and public amenities as others.

When it came to the inaccessibility of sidewalks, the Rolling Quads turned to direct action. As the 1970s dawned, the city of Berkeley had created a few curb ramps near campus to help wheelchair users navigate more easily. But then the improvements stalled, and the activists decided to take charge of the streets themselves. "We had a Wednesday-night poker game in those days, and a lot of good ideas came up over those games," Michael Pachovas, one of the activists, told a reporter decades later. "One night, we decided to put in some curb ramps on our own after the game. A couple of our attendants did construction work, so they had access to cement, and I had a wheelbarrow," said Pachovas. "We didn't cut curbs; we just added skirts to existing curbs." While local police threatened to arrest the group, they never made good on those threats.

The actions of these and many other disability-rights activists, with their radical vision of self-advocacy and inclusion, led directly to the Americans with Disabilities Act of 1990, which required curb cuts in new construction. It may seem hard to believe for those who came of age after the ADA became law, but there was a time in the United States when the curb cut was almost entirely absent from street design. The exception was driveways, which people in wheelchairs were often forced to use to get on and off the sidewalk. This simple fact explained why Sarah so rarely saw people navigating the streets of New York by wheelchair.

In the vastly improved streetscape we all move through today, curb cuts are increasingly common. Stand on any street corner with an active flow of pedestrians, and you will see how frequently and instinctively people use this low-tech feature: caregivers pushing strollers, delivery workers rolling dollies loaded with packages, older people using walkers, tourists pulling wheelie suitcases. For all of them, the simple slope in the sidewalk as it meets the roadway enables seamless mobility. For all of them, walking instead of driving becomes a viable choice.

Make infrastructure to provide access for people with disabilities, and you'll get better infrastructure. Civil rights leader Angela Glover Blackwell calls it the "curb-cut effect." It's easy to see when you start looking. (Closed captions on video, developed for deaf viewers and now used by everyone, are another great example.)

Now, widen your perspective. Look at the larger transportation infrastructure picture through that same lens of disability—the cars moving through cities at high speeds, the bus stops where riders wait in all weather for buses that come infrequently or not at all, the sidewalks and crosswalks that disappear at the end of a multilane road.

You'll quickly see how inaccessible much of our autocentric environment is for people with disabilities, whether permanent or temporary.

If we are going to move our society away from car dependence, we will have to change the way we build our communities. And the humble curb cut can show us the way. Imagine what we could achieve if we tried to broaden the curb-cut effect.

Designing for Nondrivers Helps Everyone

Regardless of physical ability or wealth, absolutely everyone benefits, in the long run, when we design for people and not cars. As it is, our communities are built in a way that excludes almost one third of Americans. Because that's how many residents of the United States can't drive. Nearly one in three.

Despite this stunning statistic, the vast majority of people in the United States live in places where independent access to a full life and basic services is almost exclusively available if—and only if—you can slide into the driver's seat of a personal motor vehicle, start the engine, and press the accelerator yourself. More than 30 percent of people living in this country just don't qualify for that vantage point in the pursuit of happiness, because they don't have driver's licenses.

Some are too young. Some have disabilities, visible and invisible, that prevent them from driving. Many have age-related physical and cognitive impairments. Some can't afford a car. Some are prevented from getting licenses by their immigration status.

What is the message for these members of our society?

You're second-rate. Second-class. You can't expect as much from life as people who can drive. Suck it up.

When President Biden was under pressure to leave the presidential race in 2024, we heard a lot of jokes about taking the car keys away from Grandpa. It was a popular analogy because almost everyone knows the scenario: An elder in the family just doesn't have the visual, motor, or cognitive skills to drive safely anymore, but they cling to that car because they know that the alternative to driving is, in most parts of the country, a life of total dependence on others and—paradoxically—growing isolation.

"I think there's this real fear to give up that mobility access and to talk about life without driving," said Anna Zivarts, an organizer and videographer who wrote a book called *When Driving Is Not an Option: Steering Away from Car Dependency* and came on the podcast to talk about it in 2023. "In my own family, I know my grandma who lived in southern Indiana refused to give up driving. She was having heart problems. She kept on passing out, driving off the side of the road and the cops would find her and she was fine. And she'd get back in her car and keep driving. . . . [She] definitely shouldn't have been driving, but didn't want to give up that access. . . . That is something . . . we need as a country to reckon with."

Zivarts, who herself can't drive because of a vision disability, wrote her book in part to help raise awareness of the sheer size of the nondriving public—and by so doing, help to create a more clearly defined group of stakeholders in the fight against autocentric development. "All together we're a really large constituency, but we don't think of ourselves as a constituency because there's so much shame and stigma around both disability and not being able to . . . afford to drive," Zivarts said. "Let's figure out ways to build our cities and our towns and even our rural communities in ways that don't require car dependency."

Yes, for some people with disabilities, cars are the best or the only option for mobility, and those people are the ones whose access to motor vehicles and motor vehicle infrastructure should be prioritized. But as it is, we have built a world that favors what scholar Mimi Sheller has called the "kinetic elite," those who have the physical ability and financial resources to access our autocentric transportation system.

The curb-cut effect is widely recognized in contemporary urban design circles. We know just how much better our communities can be for everyone if we build cities to accommodate people with disabilities. We know, too, that nearly all of us are going to be disabled at some point in our lives, temporarily or permanently. Why is it so hard, then, to implement other design changes on our streets that would improve access for people who can't drive? Why aren't we allowing denser development in urban areas where nondrivers could live with greater access to services? Why are we allowing the "kinetic elite" of drivers to dictate how the rest of us live?

In many cases, it all comes down to a one-word answer: parking.

Free Parking Isn't Free

"I think that parking is one of the deepest problems that we have in the United States, and in the rest of the world," Donald Shoup told us.

Shoup, an engineer and urban planning professor who died in 2025, is best known as the author of a 2005 book, *The High Cost of Free Parking*, that has become a seven-hundred-page touchstone for people fighting back against car culture in the twenty-first century. Shoup, born in 1938, brought a generational perspective to our collective obsession with free parking, arguing that it lies at the foundation of our dysfunctional streets. His work has a lot of fans who are decades younger than he was, some of whom are proud to be known as "Shoupistas," and his detailed analysis of the flawed nature of the way we price parking—or, let's call it what it is, "car storage"—has catalyzed an international movement to reform building codes that call for parking minimums in new residential, retail, and office developments.

After a century of building more and more spots in the hopes of finding a place to put our cars wherever we stop driving them, we are left with anywhere from a billion to two billion parking spaces in the United States. No one is really sure how many; at the same time, everyone also seems to be sure that there could never be enough. Because while we've been striping all those parking spaces, we have also been building up an enormous sense of entitlement among drivers, who expect to be able to bring their vehicles up to the front door of whatever their destination might be.

At the core of Shoup's argument is a recognition of curb space as a classic "commons"—a resource that is freely available for public use and that is routinely abused as a result. He writes, "Free curb parking is an asphalt commons: just as cattle compete in their search for scarce grass, drivers compete in their search for scarce curb parking spaces. Drivers waste time and fuel, congest traffic, and pollute the air while cruising for curb parking, and after finding a space they have no incentive to economize on how long they park."

The larger problem, according to Shoup, is that the people who run our cities have "misdiagnosed" the problem that the curb commons represents. Instead of disincentivizing driving by charging a fair price for curbside parking, he writes, "[p]lanners have identified the source of the problem . . . as the market's failure to supply enough off-street parking. . . . In effect, urban planners treat free parking as an entitlement, and they consider the resulting demand for free parking as a 'need' that must be met."

And here is where the cascade of negative effects comes crashing down on our cities, towns, and suburbs. Those consequences include things you might expect—like difficulty in building bike lanes or traffic-calming infrastructure that makes direct use of curb space. But the ramifications are far more pervasive than that.

Most cities have so-called parking minimums, codes requiring new developments of any kind to provide off-street parking for a given number of vehicles per residential unit or per expected shopper. These minimums, which vary wildly from place to place, are based on "market requirements" that consist of little more than guesswork, according to Shoup. "Market requirements are more like astrology than like astronomy," he told us. "I mean, you might as well look at the signs of the zodiac to say how many parking spaces are required. But you have to do it. . . . Everyone wants to park free, including you and me."

The fake science of parking minimums, over the decades, has led to acres of surface parking lots, downtowns where parking garages dominate the streets, and higher costs for developers. It's all based on flawed assumptions, according to Shoup and his disciples. "Cities require off-street parking because the market supposedly fails to provide enough of it," Shoup writes. "But the market fails to provide many things at a price everyone can afford. For instance, it fails to provide affordable housing for many families. Advocates for affordable housing usually find themselves in an uphill battle, but without a second thought cities have imposed requirements to ensure affordable parking. Rather than charge fair-market prices for on-street parking, cities insist on ample off-street parking for every land use. As a result, most of us drive almost everywhere we go."

Shoup called out our priorities with devastating clarity: We are so eager to accommodate the hunger of drivers for free or cheap car storage that we will do anything to feed their bottomless appetite. Downtowns become vast parking lots while people go unhoused.

In 2023, journalist Henry Grabar published a book, *Paved Paradise: How Parking Explains the World*, that details just how destructive our parking fixation is, and how we cling to it at any cost. He writes about how people will literally kill each other over a parking space—it happens dozens of times a year in the United States. Those physical confrontations, however, are merely a surface manifestation of a much deeper struggle over what we prioritize when we plan our cities and towns, and how those priorities affect the way we build.

Grabar details a particularly bitter fight over the construction of an affordable housing project in Solana Beach, California, that illustrates Shoup's point about prioritizing cars precisely. The city had committed to helping create housing for people who had been displaced from a motel that was condemned back in the 1990s. After decades of delay, the local council was considering a proposal from a developer to build ten affordable housing units on—wait for it—a parking lot, which was located near the site of the old motel. The parking spaces that would have been lost by building on the lot would have been replaced in the underground garage the developer was required to build.

Initially, the plan was to allow the developer to help finance the project by charging for parking in the garage. But the community fought hard against the proposal, forcing further and further concessions that included making the parking free. They hung their fight on the idea that the parking lot as it existed was a vital community resource.

"You will not be surprised to know they spent 10 years fighting over whether this housing should be permitted on the parking lot," Grabar told us. "It's tragic. . . . This is not like an affordable housing lottery, these are real people who've been promised homes who now do not have homes because the neighbors put up such a fight about the parking lot."

Not for nothing, the parking lot in question was situated on a bluff overlooking the Pacific Ocean. Grabar makes the point that the residents of Solana Beach, a community where the median household income is more than $100,000, were able to use parking to create cover for their desire to keep less affluent residents out of the community.

"One of the questions that comes up with this Solana Beach case is: are the neighbors really concerned about parking, or are they concerned about having low-income people living in their neighborhood?" Grabar said. "You can't file a lawsuit saying these poor people are gonna mess up the neighborhood, but you can file a lawsuit over parking. And so that's what they did."

Parking, in other words, is a way to block anything you want to block.

But that is beginning to change.

Parking Reform Is Contagious

Founded in 2019, the Parking Reform Network is a national organization that aims to educate the public about the impact of parking policy on "climate change, equity, housing, and traffic," as well as to support and push for the adoption of parking reforms. This fight against parking minimums might have seemed like a quixotic quest when the organization was founded, in 2019, by Tony Jordan, who calls himself a "full-time parking reformer and rabble-rouser." But the Parking Reform Network now can point to ninety-one (and counting) examples of cities around the world eliminating their parking minimums.

The movement has been spreading across the country, and the cities and towns in question represent a true cross section of America—red counties and blue, big cities and small. Austin, Texas. Branson, Missouri. Longmont, Colorado. Minneapolis and St. Paul in Minnesota. Anchorage, Alaska. Buffalo, New York. Birmingham, Alabama. All of these, and many more, have moved to allow developers to build housing without requiring them to construct a set number of parking spaces for each unit. And don't leave out Canada, where Toronto is just the largest of several cities to jettison its minimums, allowing developers to save money and build more spaces for people to live rather than for cars to park.

Somehow, despite what opponents of parking reform might want you to believe, the world has kept turning. And as municipalities see the examples of successes multiply rapidly across North America, the movement for sane parking policy is gaining strength.

The push for adoption of such reform, according to sustainability professional Sarah Stuetz, is a great example of the "contagion" phase in political diffusion theory, which explains how policy innovations spread exponentially: When a policy succeeds and proves popular and effective, legislatures that are initially reluctant to embrace change grow bolder and begin to adopt measures that once seemed out of the question, "until only a few lagging or hesitant legislatures are left," wrote Stuetz in a post on the *Parking Reform Network* blog. "If this holds true, we can expect this number to continue to rise rapidly over the next few years."

Stuetz also suggests that this period of exponential growth in adoption is a great time for advocates to push for change in their own jurisdictions. *"There is likely a vast untapped political viability for parking reform across the US,"* she writes. *"Supporters of reform are well-positioned to successfully advocate for change no matter the community they are fighting for."* The italics are hers, and the point deserves the emphasis.

If the rejection of parking minimums continues to spread at its current pace, it will mean that in all kinds of communities all over, a fundamental shift in thinking will have taken hold. The stranglehold that ubiquitous free parking has had on the design of our cities is loosening. The curb is freeing up. And that makes a whole lot of great things possible.

No Free Parking

What do cities look like if you don't just let people park there for free?

Sarah found out on a trip to Japan, where parking policy is pretty much the exact opposite of what it is in the United States—despite the enormous influence Americans had on popularizing cars there during the postwar occupation.

In suburban and rural areas of Japan, where land is more available, you can park for free outside malls and grocery stores and the like. But in the densely populated cities where most of the archipelago's people live, on-street parking is essentially prohibited. People who drive in town must pay to park in lots (some of which are very ingeniously designed with elaborate elevator systems to make the most of tight spaces). To even buy a car in Japan, you must prove you have a dedicated car-storage (aka parking) spot where it can live long term. Parking on the street overnight is completely forbidden (as it was in New York City until 1950).

Japan's supertight parking regulations, coupled with excellent and ubiquitous regional and local transit, create a streetscape that is almost shockingly relaxed by North American and even European standards. No one is cruising around the block looking for a space, impatient and angry and distracted. It just isn't enticing to drive if you have to think very much about where you are going to put the damn car when it isn't moving.

In the Asakusa neighborhood of Tokyo, people of all ages can ride bikes (and trikes) safely.
Sarah Goodyear

As a result, in Tokyo, while there is ample car traffic on main thoroughfares, narrow neighborhood streets are peaceful and inviting for pedestrians, to the point where even first graders can safely walk to school. Indeed, they are expected to.

"Parents we met on our trip said walking to school is a basic principle of Japanese life, and that their roads cannot accommodate the traffic that would result from driving to school," wrote Margo Pedroso of the Safe Routes Partnership after visiting Japan. "They value their children learning how to navigate their neighborhoods and be independent. Parents also noted that when everyone walks, it is the safest because there is no mixing of cars, bicycles and pedestrians in small spaces."

As for bicycles, there are plenty of those, including the famous "mamacharis," or mom chariots, which often come with two or three seats for small children, enabling parents (usually women) to ride around safely with their kids, their groceries, and whatever else they can stuff in their panniers and baskets. This relaxed and safe environment isn't just good for kids and parents—it's great for older people, too, and you'll see plenty of gray-headed folks riding around central Tokyo and other Japanese cities.

Even if it's hard to imagine Japan's hard-line approach to car storage taking hold in less dense North American cities, parking reform could lead quickly to more livable, safer, and healthier cities. Donald Shoup proposed that cities start by fairly pricing the curb and putting the money they collect toward improvements like street trees, trash pickup, and plantings.

And that's just the beginning.

Because if curbside parking were eliminated or dramatically limited, the most important thing that freeing the curb from parking does is open a whole toolbox of design improvements that make the street work better for human beings. Some of these require removing all car parking spaces on a given street, but many of them can be achieved by taking just a few at strategic locations.

You may already be familiar with a lot of the infrastructure that freeing up the curb could make possible. Things like protected bike lanes. Bike parking. Dedicated bus lanes. Curbside dining structures. Parklets. School play streets. Loading zones for deliveries.

There are also lesser-known tools that are familiar to human-friendly urban planners, but aren't exactly household words. Things like curb extensions. Also known as bulbouts or neckdowns, these are extensions of the sidewalk at crosswalks; they make the crossing shorter for pedestrians, naturally slow turning traffic, improve emergency vehicle access, and provide a place for landscaping. Chicanes

Sidewalk extensions, known as bulbouts, are one of the design elements that can make streets calmer and safer for all users. From *Urban Street Design Guide*, by NACTO. Copyright © 2013 National Association of City Transportation Officials. Reproduced by permission of Island Press, Washington, D.C.

are a similar treatment used mid-block on a street to slow traffic. Daylighting is the practice of removing parking spaces near intersections, with or without curb extensions, to improve visibility for drivers and pedestrians.

All these techniques are being used around the world to make streets safer and more pleasant. But in North America, such treatments are often controversial and difficult to implement because of community opposition, whether real or perceived. A lot of politicians and planners reflexively resist this type of street improvement even when there is local support, often because small-business owners insist that their patrons need that on-street parking and that taking it away would destroy their ability to attract customers.

This autocentric mindset, even in cities like New York and San Francisco, is hard to overcome, despite numerous studies that show bike lanes, for instance, often have a positive rather than a negative effect on small business, drawing in more people rather than deterring them.

Why is it so hard to combat the idea that we need to roll out the parking welcome mat for drivers everywhere and all the time? Probably because in the 1950s, in the United States, we started building out a transportation scheme that sucks cars from surrounding communities by the millions and deposits them like so much debris into our nation's cities.

It's called the Interstate Highway System.

Highways to Hell

If you live in a North American city, chances are there is an interstate highway near you. Maybe, like Sarah, you live close enough to one to hear its miserable whine from your bedroom window late at night when the surface street traffic has gone quiet, punctuated by the occasional distant shriek of a muscle car drag racing through the dark (looking at you, I-278).

Maybe you live in a neighborhood or a city that has been cut in half for generations by a freeway, like Seattle, where I-5 plows straight through the heart of downtown. That freeway, like so many others, gutted several thriving neighborhoods, including a historic Chinese American enclave that has survived in a butchered form. This massive conduit for personal motor vehicles, like all American freeways, has enabled suburban commuters nominally seamless access to the city—from which they extract wealth in the form of wages without having to worry about giving anything back to the community in taxes or any other way.

The I-5 story is a familiar one. To build the road, some 4,500 plots of land in central Seattle were cleared, wiping away businesses, razing homes, and reducing historic buildings to rubble. The places where people once walked and played and lived their lives were utterly erased, as if they had never existed. Seattle architect Paul Thiry had this to say about the before-and-after effects of the massive road project: "It was with the Freeway, cutting through the very heart of the city, that Seattle began taking one of its wrong turns and started to lose its identity as a city."

Residents of the First Hill neighborhood fought for years against the planned road, which severed the connections between many residents of that blue-collar area and their jobs downtown, previously within comfortable walking distance. A group called Lid I-5, which is now fighting to have the highway covered, or "lidded," to reconnect the riven city, highlights the history of the nearly forgotten anti-freeway movement on its website, along with a picture of people marching against the road in 1961, right before the wrecking balls turned blocks upon blocks of human-scale community to dust.

In the city's heart now is a thirteen-lane-wide sewer of concrete, asphalt, and steel in which the people of the now-sprawling Seattle metropolitan area, population four million, shuttle back and forth from their destinations in metal boxes. A lot of the time, they are staring at the taillights of the vehicle in front of them and breathing in its fumes, because the road is one of the most congested in the country. During peak travel hours, I-5 is congested nearly 80 percent of the time, causing about fifty-five hours of delays each year for the people condemned to use it.

Urban highways are the most aggressive, obnoxious, destructive infrastructure that car culture has to offer. A freeway going through a densely populated neighborhood is as brutal as a punch in the face and as pervasively poisonous as an oil slick. In the short term, its construction erases communities and displaces people; in the long term, it radiates toxic pollutants and unhealthy noise levels into the homes, schools, businesses, and surface streets that remain in place along its ruthless trajectory. Once a freeway exists, it assumes an air of inevitability, like a natural feature of the landscape, determining the fate of hundreds of square miles around it.

If what we build shapes us, freeways distort and deform the human social world as surely as they do the natural world. You might postulate a corollary to the curb-cut effect, which improves the quality of life for everyone in a community: The freeway effect brings everybody down.

When the Interstate Highway System was inaugurated, in 1956, President Dwight D. Eisenhower sold it to a booming nation with the promise that it represented modernity, security, wealth, and strength. At the time, the minority and working-class communities that bore the greatest brunt of the destruction were treated by planners as at best an inconvenience, and more often as a blight that needed to be cleared.

The last twenty-five years have seen a radical rethinking of the interstates and what they have done to American cities. A lot of people, including many who now work in government and have at least some say over the way we build, have been influenced by reading (or reading about) *The Power Broker*, Robert Caro's classic biography of New York's midcentury builder king, Robert Moses. (In fact, having finished all 1,344 pages of Caro's magisterial history is something of a badge of honor among urban-studies nerds.) Janno Lieber, the chair and CEO of New York's Metropolitan Transportation Authority, was quoted by *The New York Times* on the occasion of the book's fiftieth anniversary as saying that "anybody who shares Moses's view that mass transit is the past and not the future will be proven wrong."

One of the things that was apparent even in Moses's time was something called "induced demand"—a remarkably consistent phenomenon in which building more lanes on a road attracts more users, so that congestion never really goes away. It's a pattern that was crystal clear in 1936, after the completion of the Grand Central, Interborough, and Laurelton Parkways on Long Island. When the roads opened, writes Caro, "one editorial opined that the new parkways would, by relieving the traffic load . . . solve the problem of access to Moses' Long Island parks 'for generations.'" As it was, "the new parkways solved the problem for about three weeks."

You might think that current-day planners, engineers, and elected officials would have digested the lessons of the twentieth-century freeway spree and by now would be making different decisions. Some of them have, and in many places you can see the results. Freeways are being taken down across the country, from San Francisco to Rochester, New York. The Inflation Reduction Act of 2022 included $3 billion for tearing down highways and rebuilding the ravaged urban landscapes that scar so many of our cities.

But learning the lessons of history is never easy. Texas journalist Megan Kimble details several modern-day highway widenings and expansions, including one in Austin that will bloat I-35 from twelve lanes to twenty and one in Houston that will destroy 1,100 homes and 300 businesses, almost entirely affecting "minority and low-income populations," by the admission of the Texas Department of Transportation itself.

"Seventy years of evidence shows when you add lanes to a highway, cars fill it up. Why are we still doing this?" Kimble told us. "I have spent, like, four years reporting that and . . . don't know that I have a good answer beyond people still persistently believe that driving creates prosperity."

Not only do today's ongoing road megaprojects in places like Houston, Austin, Phoenix, and New Jersey destroy people's homes and businesses. Not only do they require enormous amounts of spending. Not only do they incentivize sprawl and lock future generations into the same exhausting drive-till-you-qualify nightmare that nobody wants to live. The toxic legacy of "urban renewal" road projects, Kimble's book shows us, has so damaged community trust in the whole concept of urban planning that local residents are sometimes very skeptical of teardown projects, seeing them as another possible engine of displacement, with rising property values and potential gentrification the threat this time, rather than wrecking balls and bulldozers. That leads many to reject participation and resist change.

"See, this community has been hurt so much," a Rochester woman named Nancy told Kimble about a neighbor's skepticism of that city's plan to repair a highway-damaged area. "When they stripped this neighborhood away from us, they just knocked all these homes down and relocated all these families. . . . But if we don't stand and if we don't make our voices heard, then we're never going to be heard."

We have built a world in which our voices can rarely be heard over the roar of traffic. Our transportation infrastructure is a complicated web of cause and effect that is, for the most part, determined by the insatiable need of the motorcar for space. Space to park, space to drive, space to idle while waiting to park or drive. Every human aspiration and desire is pushed aside in favor of the car.

Those of us who want a human-scale world where we can live in health and safety must push back against the automotive imperative at every level, from the parking space to the interstate. We must raise our voices above the malevolent hiss of the freeway traffic and make them heard. Like Nancy in Rochester, we must demand that planners design for the people in a community, not for the cars.

Political Will

What does it take to reclaim a city from cars? Well, to implement reforms on any significant scale, you're going to need allies in power. That means elected officials who are willing to take some heat in order to do what they know is right, and who empower their administrations to implement changes that are sometimes initially unpopular. Politicians with principle, in other words.

You may have noticed that this type of person isn't necessarily easy to find.

Many who talk a good game before they get the keys to city hall become suddenly wishy-washy when they actually get a taste of power. Others, however, show some backbone and push through reforms that benefit all the people who live in and visit their cities—even the ones who were loudest in opposition at the outset.

We talked with officials who showed political will to the benefit of three very different cities—one a small European gem, one a top-tier world capital, and one an overlooked sliver of a sprawling American megalopolis.

Here's what they told us.

Ghent: "Monday Morning, Everything Was Different"

In 2017, Filip Watteeuw, deputy mayor for mobility, public space, and urban planning for the city of Ghent, was on the verge of implementing one of the most ambitious car reduction initiatives anywhere in the world. Even though he and his colleagues had every confidence their plan would work—and had run through various war room–like scenarios in case it didn't—Watteeuw understood some things might not go so smoothly. After all, the last time this small Belgian city tried something similar, its mayor had received a bullet in the mail.

For much of the twentieth century, Ghent did what most other cities around the world were doing—it conducted a grand experiment that centered cars in its urban design and policymaking. As a result, many of its most significant and beautiful sites were overrun with automobiles. The plaza in front of the Ghent Belfry, a stunning medieval tower, had been converted to a parking lot. The Gravensteen, a castle dating from 1180, often had bumper-to-bumper traffic outside its imposing stone walls. In the 1960s, the city drained and paved over the Reep, a historic canal, to provide—you guessed it—more parking for the ever-growing number of cars.

By the late 1990s, city officials wanted to try reclaiming some of Ghent's ancient streets, and in 1997, they launched a plan to pedestrianize the innermost part of Ghent's historic city center. The initiative sparked protests from shopkeepers who feared customers would no longer be able to patronize their businesses and residents who worried visitors wouldn't be able to access their homes. Tempers were running high.

Then, one morning in the middle of the conflict, Ghent's mayor at the time opened his mail to find a bullet. He was under police protection for three weeks and even wore a bulletproof vest until the man who sent the bullet to the mayor was identified and arrested. The culprit turned out to be the owner of a shoe store who believed that restricting cars in the city center would hurt his bottom line. Thankfully, the situation cooled down, and the initial pedestrianization of the inner part of the Ghent city center was a resounding success—so much so that as years passed, many younger residents never knew things had ever been different.

Cars still held a lot of territory in Ghent, though, and when Filip Watteeuw began working in city government in 2013, he believed that more needed to be done. Nearly twenty years of growth had created all kinds of traffic problems, from danger to noise to poor air quality. Watteeuw, a regular bike commuter, also understood that all those cars were keeping a lot of people from seeing biking as a viable transportation option. So, with the full backing of the administration, Watteeuw and his team began brainstorming ideas for how to expand the existing pedestrian zone, increase cycling, and take bigger steps to significantly reduce the number of cars in the rest of the city center.

For inspiration, Watteeuw visited several other European cities famous for their cycling cultures, focusing not just on how cities promote cycling as transportation but also on how they use it as a tool for improving quality of life in general—even for people who never get on a bike. "I wanted Ghent to become a cycling city," he said, "a city that is livable, healthy, safe, and civil." His travels took him to the Netherlands and the city of Utrecht, a place known for its wide bike lanes, dedicated traffic signals for cyclists, and other sophisticated bike infrastructure. He also visited Copenhagen, another place with world-renowned bike infrastructure such as raised bike lanes running along the curb of many busy streets to separate people on bikes from cars.

Watteeuw was indeed inspired, but he was also intimidated. Utrecht and Copenhagen had spent forty years evolving into the cycling cities they were by that point. He and his colleagues in Ghent had to face the political reality of the next election cycle, which wasn't that far away in relative terms. "The infrastructure they have there has such a high-quality level that it was amazing," Watteeuw said. "But at the same time, it was also paralyzing because I thought, I have six years, I have no huge budget. How can I come to that same level? That's impossible."

Ghent had another challenge, and that was a lack of space. Some of Copenhagen's bike lanes had been carved from wide boulevards that could easily afford to lose a lane of car traffic or parking, and even parts of Utrecht outside its medieval center had streets with room to spare. Cédéric De Clercq, a mobility adviser for Ghent, told us the planners realized what worked in those places wouldn't translate. "We have a lot of narrow streets," he said. "So that means that it's not even technically possible to put in bicycle lanes and keep the cars."

Keep the cars. It might seem surprising to focus on how to maintain an appropriate place for automobiles when planning a people-based urban nirvana. And it's true that in some contexts, the total elimination of cars makes sense—cars would not make Vatican City or Disneyland more pleasant places to visit. But some motor vehicles still serve necessary functions in cities. Think of the children's book *Cars and Trucks and Things That Go* by Richard Scarry, and you'll get the full picture: There are ambulances, fire trucks, police cars, sanitation vehicles, delivery trucks, heavy construction vehicles, taxis, and more. As we've noted in earlier chapters, many people with disabilities depend on cars for basic mobility. Even residents who prefer cycling, walking, and transit for their daily needs like to have occasional access to a car for the times when other modes won't do.

"The most important part of an effective walking and cycling plan is the car plan," say our friends Chris and Melissa Bruntlett, two urban mobility advocates living in the Dutch city of Delft. Figuring out a way to restrict the cars that aren't essential—the ones that are just cutting through on the way to somewhere else and creating nothing more than noise, traffic, and headaches for everyone else—is difficult, but it can be done. The trick is to change the way cars fit into cities rather than changing cities to accommodate cars.

Eventually, Filip Watteeuw found a model that made sense for Ghent. That was the lesser-known Dutch city of Groningen, which does a great job of *keeping the cars*—and keeping them in their proper place. Since 1977, Groningen has had a highly successful "traffic circulation plan" that makes it impossible to drive directly through the city center. Under Groningen's plan, the center of the city is divided into four sections. Motorists cannot go directly from one section to another; instead, they must head out to the city's ring road, drive a little bit, and then come back in. As a result, it's almost always faster and more convenient for people of nearly all ages and abilities to bike or walk when traveling *within* the center. It's pleasant and safe, too. While Groningen has no shortage of excellent bicycle infrastructure outside the ring road, there are so few cars within it that bike lanes are hardly necessary in the center. The streets themselves become, in effect, bike lanes.

"The great irony of this is . . . it sounds like . . . it's making things super inconvenient for people that are driving cars," said Melissa Bruntlett. But, she emphasized, the opposite is true. Because people aren't forced by design to drive for every trip, the ones who do have to drive find it relatively easy to get where they need to, because the roads are less congested and chaotic. "Everyone's kind of winning in this situation, as opposed to pitting [people] against each other," she said.

Groningen had figured out a way to reduce nonessential motor vehicle traffic and grow cycling to the point where 60 percent of all trips were now made by bike. It also had the cleanest air quality in the Netherlands. All of this in a place that, much like Ghent, didn't have a lot of room or money to build bike lanes. Best of all from the perspective of officials looking at a tight political time horizon, Groningen's transformation back in the 1970s happened literally overnight, when the city erected hundreds of signs and changed the traffic configuration of dozens of street directions over the course of mere hours. Groningen was proof that the results Ghent wanted could be achieved, and quickly.

By 2014, Watteeuw and his team began sketching out their own version of a traffic circulation plan for Ghent. Instead of four zones, Ghent would have six. The existing pedestrianized zone would double in size. Most car traffic would have to stick to the R4, the ring road that encircles the city. Other traffic would be managed by reversing the direction of streets or with strategically placed bollards, cement blocks, and planters that would divert vehicles elsewhere while still allowing people on bikes or on foot to filter through. A network of cameras and license plate readers, paired with a residential permit system, would enforce who could access certain neighborhoods by car, with fines for violators and exemptions for medical personnel or other essential service providers. Taxis would still be allowed to drop off and pick up passengers, while commercial deliveries would be limited in some areas to early mornings or late evenings to avoid hours when pedestrian and cyclist traffic was at its highest. Visitors arriving by car would largely be directed to parking garages in places that minimized their need to drive through neighborhood streets. Public parking would not be allowed at all in the expanded pedestrianized zone in the very center of the city.

In the fall of 2014, Ghent launched a long community consultation and education process that continued right up through the plan's implementation, which was scheduled for about three years later. This gave people ample time and opportunity to weigh in with suggestions and point out potential issues that planners, working from their perch in city hall, might not be able to see. The process—which also featured public service announcements, flyers, posters, and direct outreach across the city—was designed to prepare citizens for a change that would require huge behavioral shifts from everyone.

Watteeuw expected some pushback, but he felt good about the plan; the beauty of his team's approach was that it was nimble and cheap. Instead of building permanent infrastructure that would be time-consuming and expensive to undo, it made use of materials such as bollards, signs, and paint—things that could be changed quickly in response to real-time feedback. If new traffic patterns didn't work out the way that the models predicted, or if citizens identified problems the planners hadn't foreseen, finding a solution would be easy. Watteeuw and his team had thought of everything. Or so they believed.

As the public engagement period kicked off, the intensity of the opposition took Watteeuw by surprise. Just as in 1997, business owners complained that making it difficult for drivers to reach their stores would force them to close. More conservative members of the region's political establishment whipped up a small culture war, with some saying the plans would deny people living outside the ring road access to the center city. "There was a loud minority," said Watteeuw. "The only problem was that I didn't know at that moment that it was a minority. And that group was very loud. Immediately it became rough."

Over the next two and a half years, things got ugly. Opponents of the plan shouted and hurled insults at public meetings. While there were plenty of positive comments from residents as well, they often got drowned out by the most vociferous critics. The opposition party attempted to force a citywide referendum on the plan; even though they failed to garner enough signatures, it kept negative stories in the media for months.

Watteeuw never got a bullet in the mail, but he was on the receiving end of some frightening and violent intimidation tactics. "It was a very difficult period for me," he said. "I got death threats, and not only for me, for myself, but also for my family. And so, that was really frightening." Things got so scary that Watteeuw needed round-the-clock police protection for six weeks.

Watteeuw was undeterred. He knew his colleagues supported him. Advocates from the Fietsersbond, the local cycling advocacy organization, organized group bicycle rides and other campaigns to generate even more support. "I had also the support of my family, so that took me through this difficult period," Watteeuw said. "And it's not in my personality to back down."

He never did. After years of preparation and community engagement, Ghent's traffic circulation plan was implemented over the course of just one weekend. One Friday night in April 2017, city crews waited for rush hour to end. Then, with all the coordination and precision of a major military operation, they got to work. Workers removed or erected two thousand five hundred signs, changed the traffic flow on about eighty streets, and completely blocked cars from fourteen locations. Bollards, blocks, and planters were placed in strategic spots on canal bridges and other pinch points around the city. Traffic cameras were adjusted and turned on in time for the start of a new week—or, as Watteeuw thinks of it, a new era. "Friday evening everything was like it was," he said. "And Monday morning, everything was different."

At eleven o'clock on Monday morning, April 3, 2017, Watteeuw set out on a bike tour with a journalist through the freshly transformed streets of Ghent. He knew agreeing to be accompanied by a reporter on the very first day the traffic circulation plan was in effect was a huge gamble. If angry citizens confronted him, the headlines would be unforgiving. "This could end [up on] the front page, people yelling at the deputy mayor," he worried.

As Watteeuw and the reporter cycled through the city, the opposite happened. Everywhere he went, people stopped Watteeuw to say how much they already liked the changes, with some wondering why it hadn't been done ages ago. "From the first minute I got out to the last minute of the tour, I got thumbs-up, I got congratulations, people who said, 'We are so glad you succeeded.'" Having only recently shed his police detail, it was hard for Watteeuw to process. "This was very strange for me because after two and a half years, a rough period, I came out and I said, 'My God, where were you all that time?'"

That was the moment when Filip Watteeuw realized that the people who had complained the loudest about the traffic circulation plan had only ever been a small contingent. Most people lead busy lives and don't have the time to attend a public meeting, even if they otherwise support progress. "The people who are in favor, that's the trustful majority," Watteeuw calls them. He likes to remind his counterparts elsewhere that this untapped support for better cities is out there. "That's very important to know," he said.

On Ghent's *fietsstraten*, or "bicycle streets," cyclists have priority. Doug Gordon

The impacts of Ghent's traffic circulation plan were immediate and dramatic. The number of cars in the city center dropped by 20 percent. This led to a drastic improvement in air quality; nitrous oxide levels and other pollutants fell by 18 to 20 percent. Traffic crashes fell by about 40 percent in less than a year.

Before the implementation of the traffic circulation plan, 22 percent of all trips in Ghent were by bike. The goal had been to increase that figure to 35 percent by 2030, the kind of bold-yet-distant target date that's set—and often quietly abandoned—by many city leaders around the world. Ghent met its goal by the fall of 2018. Today, people make about 200,000 bike trips in Ghent per day, an impressive figure for a city with a population of just 264,000 permanent residents and 75,000 students. All this for a plan that cost only €5 million, or less than most cities spend to repave a short stretch of highway.

In many ways, drivers have been the hidden beneficiaries of Ghent's traffic circulation plan. "The decrease in the traffic meant that the congestion also declined," said Cédéric De Clercq. "So for certain car users who need their car to get into the city center, like homeowners, it's less difficult." The data bear this out: Even though drivers must travel longer distances to reach their destinations, the time it takes to get from the R4 to the center of Ghent has decreased by 35 percent.

Since 2017, Ghent has cashed in on the spatial dividend left by the absence of cars. Much of the area that was once devoted to personal motor vehicles has now been repurposed for public seating, plazas, greenery, and more. About 450 on-street parking spaces for cars were transformed into parking for 8,500 bicycles. Streets outside dozens of Ghent schools prohibit car traffic for about thirty minutes at the beginning and end of each day so that kids and families feel safer walking and biking.

And while the city has built a lot of impressive new cycling infrastructure, such as the Louisa d'Havé cycling bridge over the Scheldt river, some of Ghent's best cycling routes are often its simplest. The city has a network of *fietsstraten*, or "bicycle streets," that, other than a bit of red pavement and special signs, look the same as regular streets. By law, drivers must travel no faster than 30 kilometers per hour (18.6 miles per hour) on these thoroughfares and are forbidden from overtaking even the slowest cyclist. Riding on a *fietsstraat*, especially when school gets out or at rush hour and the city fills with people on bikes riding in every direction, is glorious.

Ghent is calm yet lively, tranquil yet filled with pleasant sound. One resident went so far as to tell Filip Watteeuw he was "the best orchestral composer the city has ever had," because the noise created by excessive automobile traffic had been replaced by an urban symphony of people talking, bicycle gears cranking, and birds singing. While we were in Ghent, we stood at the intersection of two major bike routes. There we heard the joyful sound of children laughing and playing, presumably from a schoolyard or playground just out of sight. It was a beautiful reminder that cities aren't loud, *cars* are loud.

Ghent's traffic circulation plan represents a complete inversion of the typical transportation hierarchy that puts cars at its apex, regardless of the consequences. "The dominant paradigm of our streets as places for car traffic really undermines the quality of life that our cities can afford to us," said Meredith Glaser, a professor of cycling studies at Ghent University. "Whether that's enjoying a sunny day outside or talking with your neighbors or getting to essential services like health care and education and employment, if we shift that paradigm to thinking about our streets as places for access and well-being, then what comes naturally is walking and cycling and lingering."

As Ghent demonstrates, no city can achieve this paradigm shift and become a cycling city—or a walking city, or a lingering city, or a "hear children laughing and birds singing" city—without coming up with a car plan or, more specifically, a car-reduction plan. "There's this carrot and stick approach that I think other cities are very scared to implement," said Chris Bruntlett. "The carrot's easy, the carrot is just building some bike lanes and patting yourself on the back. The stick gets harder when we talk about congestion pricing or traffic circulation or car-free or low-car city centers, but they're necessary to really achieve the things that we want to achieve in terms of building great places for us and our children to live."

"The fundamental discussion is the space in the city. To whom does that space belong?" said Filip Watteeuw. "Does it belong to the people? Does it belong to the pedestrian and cyclist, or does it belong to the cars? That's the real discussion. The democratic redistribution of the streets." Leaders who are elected on promises of making life better for their constituents have a duty to question the status quo and fulfill such promises, even if it makes some people upset—or leads to death threats. As Filip Watteeuw told us, "If you are in politics, you are in politics to change things, to have results. And at that moment, you can't hesitate."

Paris: "It Is Worth It to Have a Better Life"

It was one of the iconic non-sports moments of the 2024 Paris Olympics: Phoenix Suns superstar guard Devin Booker, wearing the gold medal he had just scored as a member of the United States men's basketball team, leaving the Paris restaurant where he'd been celebrating—on a Lime bike.

"If you're an international star who gets mobbed by paparazzi and fans regularly, how you get to places matters. You need to be able to be whisked away from all that commotion in privacy and style," *Velo* magazine reported. "That's why . . . NBA player Devin Booker chose to leave a restaurant on a bicycle—wait, seriously?"

Yes, seriously. Booker was just one of thousands upon thousands of people in town for the Olympics who took advantage of the city's abundant bike-share offerings, which had been beefed up in advance of the games. And like those other visitors to the City of Light, Booker got to experience firsthand what has become one of the easiest and most convenient ways to get around Paris: on two wheels.

Under the leadership of Mayor Anne Hidalgo, a member of the Socialist Party who took office in 2014, this city of 2.16 million has created hundreds of kilometers of new bike lanes and huge new car-free green spaces along the River Seine, with a strong emphasis on improving public health and quality of life. A recent study found that in central Paris, where the changes have focused, 11.2 percent of trips are now made by bike, up from just 3 percent in 2010, and the proportion of people using cars and using bikes has flipped. The change is visible everywhere you go, as Parisians and visitors alike cycle along bike lanes that now are omnipresent on the major boulevards, including the fabled Rue de Rivoli, which now has more space for bikes than for cars. Bike parking is everywhere, often taking space at the curb that used to be devoted to automobiles; more space has been taken away from car parking to serve delivery vehicles.

These changes, which built on initiatives inaugurated by Bertrand Delanoë, who held the mayor's office in the early 2000s, have made Hidalgo a wildly popular figure in international urbanist circles. At home, however, it has not always been an easy political ride for the mayor.

In late 2020 we talked with Christophe Najdovski, who at the time was Paris's deputy mayor in charge of initiatives to increase green space and biodiversity under Hidalgo. He talked about how, like officials in Ghent, Hidalgo and her administration have faced backlash—in the Parisian case, from a well-organized motoring lobby, among other forces. A drivers' advocacy organization mounted bitter opposition to the mayor's plan to pedestrianize the roadway along the Seine that was built in the 1960s and that brought forty thousand cars into the city center every day. "We went to the court," Najdovski told us, with Gallic cool. "We lost the first time. Then we won the second time, and definitely."

Many Parisians, however, have continued to vilify Hidalgo. "Everybody hates her," said Sarah's stepsister, who lives in Paris, with a shrug—although she herself has loved seeing the streets become calmer and greener. It's true that the mayor's approval ratings have been less than stellar, and when she made a run for president in 2022, she got only 1.75 percent of the vote in a multicandidate first round before dropping out. At one point, anti-Hidalgo forces mounted a social media campaign with the hashtag #SaccageParis, or, roughly, "#vandalizedparis." "They are philistines," one protester told *Politico Europe* in 2021.

Despite the backlash, Hidalgo ran for reelection in the summer of 2020, at the height of the pandemic, winning a plurality in a tight race, in part on a platform of ensuring that Paris would be a "fifteen-minute city" with easy access to services and amenities for all its residents. In our talk with him a few months after the vote, Hidalgo's deputy Najdovski emphasized the administration's commitment to following through on promises about planned improvements despite resistance. "During all the three or four years of resistances and fight to have this pedestrianization [on the Seine], we still had the support of the majority of the people," he said. "So it shows that there is a strong social demand of the citizens to have more spaces for life, more spaces to breathe, to have more livable cities. . . . The streets are not just channels to bring just cars and motorized traffic from a point A to a point B, they are also places to live. . . . And no one would propose today to come back to the former situation."

Now the people of Paris have a twelve-acre riverside park where all those cars used to be. And despite the vocal disapproval from some disaffected Parisians, Hidalgo and her administration have continued to push to decrease not just the number of cars in the city, but also the size of those vehicles. In an early 2024 referendum, voters approved a measure to triple parking fees for large SUVs in the city's core.

During the Olympics, the whole city took enormous pride in showing off the "new" Paris—a city that is still in recovery from car-centric planning decisions that obliterated many historic buildings to create auto infrastructure in the 1950s and '60s. Those twentieth-century urban-renewal schemes echoed similar initiatives across North America and Europe, building highways like the Périphérique ring road that encircles central Paris. That road itself became a target in late 2024, when Hidalgo's administration moved to mitigate the noise and pollution affecting the surrounding neighborhoods by lowering the speed limit from seventy to fifty kilometers per hour (roughly forty-five to thirty miles per hour).

As is customary in France, there has been plenty of grumbling and skepticism about the change. But Hidalgo and her administration have shown they can take the heat, forging ahead by creating a new low-traffic zone in central Paris in the fall of 2024. "It is worth it to have a better life," Najdovski said back in 2020. "If we want also to keep the people in the big cities, we have also to improve their quality of life. And you can't have a better quality with more traffic. . . . If you have the political will, then the changes are possible."

Emeryville, California: "People Will Change Their Minds"

The day Sarah showed up at Emeryville City Hall to meet with John Bauters—known on social media as "America's Bike Mayor"—he was standing out front next to a cargo bike with his fluffy white dog, Miss Reyna, in the box. She was wearing a pair of goggles. It was all almost too adorable.

Sarah was there to see what Bauters and his allies in Emeryville have been working to create as part of the city's Active Transportation Plan, adopted in 2023—a well-connected bike infrastructure network that links the entire small city, expands and improves green space, and improves pedestrian and bike access to public transit. She unlocked a bike from the Bay Wheels bike-share dock on the sidewalk and gave Miss Reyna a pet on the head. "You ready to go?" Bauters asked. And then they were off to ride Emeryville's bike network, with the mayor proudly narrating every turn, bridge, and park along the way.

Bauters became mayor of Emeryville in 2021. The city of thir-

As mayor of Emeryville, California, John Bauters rode around town with his rescue dog, Miss Reyna, and became known as "America's Bike Mayor."
Sarah Goodyear

teen thousand, wedged between Berkeley and Oakland in California's Bay Area, has long been a regional afterthought, a kind of infrastructural trash can for the wealthier communities that surround it. A freeway blasts through the heart of Emeryville, cutting off the San Francisco Bay waterfront from the neighborhoods where most residents live. Freight and passenger trains rumble through all day and all night on one of California's busiest rail corridors. The entire thing is built atop some of North America's biggest Indigenous shell mounds, vast and priceless archeological heritage sites that were destroyed for the construction of a municipality that has long been unloved and denigrated.

Emeryville, in other words, might not seem like the most obvious place to go all in on active transportation. It's pretty much the opposite of a sophisticated capital like Paris or a historic city like Ghent. Yet the three places share a lot—namely, the need to repair the damage done by the automobile, and the nerve to get the job done.

Bauters and his allies on the city council and city staff were committed to pushing through better bike and pedestrian facilities. The city had been changing and growing for the past couple of decades, with Pixar and major biotech employers setting up shop since the early aughts, new condo developments, and big-box stores. And while Bauters and his colleagues did encounter opposition to their plans to create a comprehensive bike lane network around the city, they also gathered strong and robust support for the changes. Now, elected officials from around the country come to Emeryville to ask him how he got it done.

"There is a desire for this," Bauters told us. "It is the future of urban living and sustainable living. And I think when other mayors call me, it's because they see the excitement and the palpable support we receive."

That support doesn't just come out of nowhere, Bauters emphasizes. It comes from long-term, consistent, and research-based policy decisions that make true positive change in the community, and it comes from treating the community members as partners in that change.

"Time and again I have found that one of the most important jobs I have . . . is engaging and educating the public," said Bauters. "I simply share my values and articulate the reasons behind why we do things, so that people have time to sit with that for themselves and evaluate it. People often say, you know, 'You're trying to get me to give up my car.' No, I'm not. I'm trying to give other people who are curious about and want to experience the joy of cycling the opportunity to do that on their own time. People will change their minds if you give them the spaces to do that [cycling], and I really believe that."

In 2024, Bauters gave up his seat on Emeryville's city council, and the mayor's office, in order to run for Alameda County supervisor and to bring his agenda of improving housing, transportation, and mental health services to the wider community. People told him not to take the risk, saying, "You won't even get 3 percent of the vote. You represent the smallest city and nobody knows who you are," Bauters told us. Ultimately, Bauters lost the race by just a couple of hundred votes, getting more than 49 percent of the tally against a much better-known opponent. He said he has "zero regrets. . . . I had the courage and will to run a campaign where I talked openly about the issues and my priorities and values."

Bauters is clear-eyed about the political risks he takes anytime he makes decisions based on his convictions about safer streets and active transportation. For him, it's all part of a political ebb and flow. While the fight for safe streets has been steadily advancing over the past two decades, elected officials have to be willing to withstand occasional defeats and keep pressing the cause.

"I think political will is probably the biggest barrier," said Bauters. "When mayors reach out to me, I ask them what degree of political will do they have. They say, 'Well, I really want to do it.' And I say, 'Are you willing to lose re-election over it?' And that gives them a lot of pause. And I say, 'When you've decided the answer to that question is yes, you will be able to do whatever you want.'"

Do It Yourself

On a pleasant October evening in 2019, people in the Prospect Heights neighborhood of Brooklyn were greeted by a curious sight: a large electronic message board, the kind cars might speed by on a highway, curbside on Vanderbilt Avenue. Instead of alerting drivers to construction or a temporary road closure, the twelve-foot-by-six-foot sign was displaying a provocative and very uncharacteristic statement:

CARS

RUIN

CITIES

That same night, barely half a mile away on Union Street in the nearby neighborhood of Park Slope, a producer for New York's public radio station happened to be passing by another large electronic message board. It, too, had apparently been hacked:

BAN CARS

STOP

DRIVING

The producer snapped a photo and posted it to social media, tagging the New York City Department of Transportation with a sarcastic comment: "Wow! @NYC_DOT is really getting radical!"

News of the hacked signs spread like wildfire, transfixing the city and the internet. Who was the mysterious force out there hacking these electronic message boards? Why the heck was it so easy to reprogram what appeared to be official New York City Department of Transportation signs? And where would the hacker strike next?

Others raised bigger and more fundamental questions. Sure, the sign hacks were amusing, but why was the city deploying massive expressway-style equipment in two of the most pedestrian-friendly neighborhoods in New York City, if not the entire country? What these enormous highway signs did was send a signal that transportation officials didn't look at a map of the city and see places where people lived, but traffic sewers.

The DOT deflected the criticism, saying only that the message boards did not belong to the department but to independent contractors, who were immediately dispatched to reprogram the signs to their original traffic-related messages. Nevertheless, the mysterious hacker—who, in homage to the anonymous British guerrilla graffiti artist Banksy, came to be known as Bikesy—was not deterred.

One week later, a different sign was hacked, this time with a rotating series of messages appearing at three-second intervals:

CARS ARE

DEATH

MACHINES

CARS
KILL
KIDS

CARS
MELT
GLACIERS

HONKING
WON'T
HELP

Local community members, long sick of drivers clogging up their neighborhood with space-hogging, noise-making, exhaust-spewing, danger-creating automobiles, hailed Bikesy as a hero. Drivers cursed Bikesy as a car-hating villain. The law was on the drivers' side: City and state ordinances against tampering with official roadway communication signs meant that Bikesy could be arrested and charged with a felony. That is, if anyone could ever figure out who Bikesy was.

As for figuring out how the signs had been hacked, that was easy. Each message board was programmed via a small computer located inside a control box mounted on the sign's base. These control boxes had been left unlocked. Not only that, inside the control boxes was a blue binder containing the instruction manual for the Three-Line Message Sign System from Wanco Inc., which boasted "the easiest programming game in the industry." Inside this manual, under a section subtitled "Normal User Password," was the factory default password for the computer: "ABCD." According to Wanco's instructions, this password was supposed to be changed immediately upon deploying the message board for the first time. The contractors obviously skipped that part. Bikesy had gotten lucky.

Days passed. Then another sign on Union Street was hacked, this time with some advice for frustrated motorists:

**USE BUS
SUBWAY
OR BIKE!**

Just as before, city contractors immediately reprogrammed the hacked sign. This time, they also thought to lock the control boxes, and presumably changed the passwords to something more cryptic than the first four letters of the alphabet. These oversize variable message boards, which were probably trucked in from a New Jersey warehouse to be plunked down next to nineteenth-century brownstones and tree-lined sidewalks teeming with pedestrians, were restored to their original purpose of recommending alternate routes to drivers—even if those alternate routes were neighborhood streets. The car-based order was restored. The news cycle moved on. Meanwhile, the identity of Bikesy remained a mystery, as it does to this day.

Acting with Speed

Whoever Bikesy was, the anonymous message board hacker did more than directly confront motorists with the consequences of their transportation choices. By baiting the city into fixing the hacked signs immediately, this person also showed that governments can act fast when they want to. And when it comes to doing things for drivers, they *really* want to.

On June 11, 2023, a tanker truck headed from a terminal in Wilmington, Delaware, to deliver gasoline to a convenience store in Pennsylvania overturned beneath a bridge in Philadelphia, spilling nearly 2,500 gallons (9,460 liters) of fuel, which then ignited. The ensuing blaze killed the tanker's driver and caused the bridge, which carried the northbound lanes of Interstate 95, to collapse. The southbound lanes were also severely damaged. In a flash, a nine-mile (fourteen-kilometer) section of one of the most important highways in the United States was completely shut down. (Had 2,500 gallons of fuel spilled in the ocean, it would have been seen as an environmental disaster, but 2,500 gallons of fuel spilling in a major American city, lighting on fire, and choking the air with poisonous smoke was seen primarily as a major headache for drivers.)

Experts predicted it would take months to repair the highway. Instead, Pennsylvania Governor Josh Shapiro immediately declared a state of emergency, launching a massive and well-coordinated effort of federal, state, and local forces to fix the damaged roadway. Crews worked around the clock, using innovative materials such as crushed glass aggregate from local recycling facilities rather than asphalt trucked in from much farther away. As a result, a temporary six-lane roadway was up and running in just twelve days. A permanent replacement, which restored the highway to its full eight lanes, opened less than a year later.

What a difference a transportation mode makes.

Bike lanes are frequently subject to months or even years of politicking, community forums, and expert studies, especially if they might delay drivers by even a few seconds. Proposals to improve bus service in low-income communities are often blocked by wealthy suburban motorists—the very people creating the traffic that slows buses in the first place. Even widening sidewalks to accommodate pedestrians can be delayed by angry homeowners who want to preserve "their" parking.

Earlier, we mentioned Doug's daughter's effort to get a bike corral installed at her elementary school. The entire process, from idea to installation, took more than a year and a half, an absurdly long timeline for something involving little more than swapping out two cars for a handful of bike racks.

The contrast says a lot about our society's priorities. Granted, the short section of highway through Philadelphia carries 160,000 vehicles per day and is part of a crucial corridor for interstate commerce, so fixing it quickly was imperative. But you don't need to look very far for other examples of elected officials doing everything they can for what sometimes feels like their most important constituency: cars.

We believe that the twin crises of traffic violence and climate change—not to mention the many other problems caused by cars explained elsewhere in this book—should give governments all the permission they need to move as fast on transit, bike, and pedestrian infrastructure as they do after a highway collapses. Given that the solutions to our traffic safety and environmental woes can be implemented far faster than even the impressively fast work seen on I-95 in Philly, is it any wonder advocates like us—or anyone who's tried to get so much as a crosswalk painted or a stop sign installed on their corner—are frustrated with the pace of change?

Tactical Urbanism

Thankfully, there is an effective, inexpensive, and ingenious technique even ordinary citizens can use to demonstrate that change not only is possible but also can be achieved faster than a highway replacement in Philadelphia. It's called tactical urbanism. According to Mike Lydon and Anthony Garcia, two expert practitioners in the field who defined the term, tactical urbanism is a creative, do-it-yourself approach that "employs short-term actions for long-term change" using "low-cost . . . interventions and policies." It takes the planning out of hostile public meetings or stuffy government offices and brings it directly to the street, almost like an urbanist version of

A pop-up protected bike lane made of traffic cones and flowers, installed covertly by the "New York City Department of Transformation." Doug Gordon

show-and-tell, only with much more emphasis on "show." It turns abstract concepts or renderings of how streets should look, feel, and function into real-world demonstrations of exactly those things. These temporary actions can even involve stealing—or shall we say repurposing—a bunch of traffic cones.

On the morning of Friday, August 7, 2015, in Boston, a thirty-eight-year-old surgeon and researcher named Anita Kurmann was killed by the driver of a flatbed tractor-trailer while bicycling in a painted bike lane on Massachusetts Avenue. Advocates had warned the city for years about the inadequacy and danger of the painted bicycle lane, arguing that it was only a matter of time before a cyclist would be run over. The city kept dragging its feet, even after Kurmann's death. Weeks after the tragedy, nothing about Mass. Ave. had changed at all.

That's what motivated an architect and regular bike commuter named Jonathan Fertig to take matters into his own hands. On Sunday, September 6, one month after Kurmann had been killed, Fertig went to Mass. Ave. near the intersection of Beacon Street where the crash had occurred. He swiped some orange traffic cones from a construction site and placed them along the edge of the bike lane, creating a much more visible separation between cyclists and drivers. To make sure everyone understood his action was very much intentional and not related to some street repair or utility project, Fertig lined the bike lane with six pots of flowers he picked up at Home Depot. In all, he spent about forty dollars.

Thanks to Fertig's simple design intervention on Mass. Ave., bike commuters felt safer and more comfortable immediately. The flowers also made them smile, adding a level of playful subversiveness to an action that had been motivated by tragedy. If this was all it took to make the street feel that much better, maybe saving lives was a lot easier than most people had been led to believe.

Fertig's improvised bike lane attracted a lot of attention, and the activist knew he had to keep it going—both to continue protecting his fellow cyclists and to maintain pressure on the city. He also knew he couldn't keep stealing traffic cones, nor could he keep dipping into his own pocket to pay for potted flowers, so he launched a Go-FundMe campaign. In his appeal to donors, he cited Boston city government's "complete lack of will to do what is required to protect the safety of vulnerable road users" and promised he would use the money to "execute more interventions along the Mass. Ave. corridor, the most dangerous stretch of road in the city." Fertig raised $1,100 in just two days.

By Wednesday, *The Boston Globe* ran a story on Fertig's "flower lane." By Thursday, five weeks after Anita Kurmann had been killed but just five days after Fertig's improvised intervention, the city began installing green paint, plastic delineator posts, and other features to better protect cyclists on Mass. Ave. Fertig's impromptu pressure campaign had worked.

Fertig eventually raised more than $6,000, which he used to purchase enough supplies to "drop cones," as he put it, anywhere he saw a street where people needed protection from cars. In a traffic-choked city like Boston, that's a lot of streets. Still, Fertig's small interventions sent a clear message: Safety can't wait, and it doesn't have to. After all, if he could improve a few streets here and there by himself using only the most basic off-the-shelf materials, imagine what a city could do if it brought the full force of its resources to bear on the problem. Like it might, say, with an emergency highway repair.

Jonathan Fertig's actions inspired a wave of tactical urbanism demonstrations across the country, many of which resulted in permanent improvements. In New York City, an anonymous group of advocates calling themselves the Department of Transformation (or DOTr) dropped traffic cones also topped with flowers in an unprotected bike lane near the Manhattan Bridge to demonstrate that the vital bike route had plenty of room to be fully separated from cars. The city's real Department of Transportation installed a protected bike lane a year later. A group calling itself the San Francisco Municipal Transformation Agency—a similar play on the name of that city's official transportation department—installed plastic flex posts on streets to slow down drivers and keep them out of bike lanes, often staging its interventions immediately after a fatality involving a pedestrian or a cyclist. In at least one case, their posts stayed up until the city replaced them with an official set.

A group of activists in Wichita, Kansas, spiced up their tactical urbanism efforts with a bit of humor. They lined an unprotected bike lane on both sides with toilet plungers, the handles wrapped with reflective tape, to simulate flex posts and keep cars at bay. Inspired by their actions, New York City's DOTr did the same on Fifth Avenue in Manhattan, installing seven plungers at a busy corner to protect cyclists from turning drivers. In Providence, Rhode Island, a bike commuter named Jeffrey Leary must have cleared out a Home Depot's entire stock of toilet plungers, installing seventy-two of them along the outer edge of a curbside bike lane to deter cars from parking in it. The city seemed to take Leary's demonstration in the intended spirit, and said it wouldn't remove the plungers unless they created a problem.

In California, a group called Crosswalk Collective LA painted rogue crosswalks at locations where the Los Angeles Department of

Transportation had rejected or not responded to community requests. Many of the collective's crosswalks would be removed by LADOT crews within days or even hours, proving in a somewhat ironic way—just as Bikesy did in New York—that cities can in fact change streets quickly when they want to. The Crosswalk Collective takes its own requests from concerned Angelenos and has successfully shamed LADOT into making some of its crosswalks permanent. As its website says, "The city of Los Angeles doesn't keep us safe so we keep us safe."

Making the Water Visible to the Fish

Tactical urbanism has the power to pierce the automotive bubble that so frequently surrounds politicians—sometimes in an almost literal sense, because so many elected officials are driven everywhere. It can force them to see that they can become catalysts for rapid change if they really want to. But the value of these tactics goes well beyond the safety (and frequent smiles) that these interventions provide for cyclists or pedestrians who pass by while they're in place—or even the permanent infrastructure changes they might inspire.

A key benefit of tactical urbanism is that it helps, or even forces, the average person to see our car-based reality for the social construct that it is. As the philosopher and noted media theorist Marshall McLuhan wrote in 1968, "One thing about which fish know exactly nothing is water, since they have no anti-environment which would enable them to perceive the element they live in." Just as water is invisible to the fish, hardly any of us can perceive the swirling sea of cars and car-centric infrastructure around us. It's just the world in which we're swimming—or driving. The trick, then, is to make the water visible to the fish.

That's exactly what a small band of artists and urbanists attempted to do in San Francisco back in 2005. On a crisp fall morning, John Bela, Matthew Passmore, and Blaine Merker—members of an art and design firm called Rebar—stopped their pickup truck next to an empty sliver of curbside on the sunny side of Mission Street between First and Ecker. Bela hopped out of the truck and fed the meter a fistful of quarters. Then, instead of parking their truck in the space they had just paid for, they began unloading it.

First, they spread a tarp over the black asphalt. Atop the tarp they unrolled a mat of sod. On top of the green grass, they placed a park bench. Opposite the bench they put down a fifteen-foot-tall potted tree to provide a bit of shade. They surrounded their tiny park on three sides with a fence made of plastic bollards connected by rope, leaving it open on the side facing the sidewalk. In about fifteen minutes and with less than $500 worth of materials, the trio had transformed an on-street parking spot into a small public park.

According to Bela, he and his colleagues were interested in "interrogating the idea of 'the right to the city'" and the "internalized assumptions that are built into how we think about the use of space, the politics of space, and who has access." How do we collectively decide who gets to use public space, and for what purposes?

Bela, Passmore, and Merker had been looking around San Francisco for "unscripted pieces of land" where they could conduct a real-life experiment in urban transformation. They settled upon the metered parking spot as the ideal laboratory. One thing that intrigued them about parking was the extraordinary discrepancy between the price of public and private land. "You've got commercial real estate just next door that's worth hundreds of dollars per square foot," Bela said. "But for just a couple of dollars an hour, any person with a car can lease this patch of public space in this heavily contested, high-value terrain." Why could private automobile users pay so little to use this desirable curbside real estate? It just didn't make sense.

As far as the three partners understood, there was no rule or regulation mandating that only cars could be left at metered spots. "We decided to explore the boundaries of that short-term lease," Bela said. "Rather than parking a car, we would be park-making." The tree, bench, and real grass created a clear and legible invitation for people to use the space like any urban park, albeit a very small one, without it appearing like they were participating in some kind of "political protest or artistic intervention," Bela said.

After setting up their parking space–size park, the collaborators went to the roof of a building across the street to observe how the experiment unfolded, a little nervous that their understanding of the city's parking code might have been incorrect. "We all had suits in our car in case we got arrested," Bela said. They were also concerned that busy pedestrians might not even notice the grass-covered space. If they did, would they understand what it was for?

Within a few minutes, a man walking down Mission Street stopped, sat down on the bench, unwrapped a slice of pizza, and began to eat. Another man sat down on the edge of the potted tree, opened a newspaper, and began to read. Pretty soon, the two were chatting. Then they were laughing. Before long, Bela and his colleagues, watching from afar and snapping photos, realized they were not going to need to put on coats and ties for an arraignment that day. More and more people stopped by the grassy space to look at it, use it, and talk about it. "We created a social space," said Bela. "We created an invitation for public life, for socializing in a place that was previously just used for storing cars, for storing metal boxes."

When the time ran out on the parking meter, Bela said, "We just packed it up, rolled it away, swept up, and disappeared." Just like that, the space transformed back into a nondescript slab of asphalt for storing one private automobile.

Photos of people using the parking space spread across the blogs and websites of the early aughts, an era before social media, You-Tube, and even widely available smartphones. To some, the pictures were little more than the internet novelty of the day. But to people who had been making the case against cars and fighting for more livable communities for ages, Rebar's experiment felt like a revelation. It not only was a brilliant illustration of how small changes to a street could make a big difference to people's happiness, but also invited individuals to participate and take action themselves. They didn't have to protest or wait for people in power to change the status quo. They could be the change they wished to see in their cities, one parking space at a time.

Within a few weeks, Rebar was inundated with requests from people in cities all over who wanted to do their own versions of this parking-size experiment. In response, Rebar produced an illus-trated how-to manual, modeled on the simple assembly instructions that come with IKEA furniture, and posted it online as a free down-load. "Improve your neighborhood. Improve this street with this type of space," the instruction manual urged. "You don't need to hire an architect or a designer or work with the city. Just do it your-self." They called their concept Park(ing).

Rebar had one more big idea. Recognizing that taking over on-street parking might be legally risky depending on the city—and that it might expose people to physical harm from angry drivers—Rebar announced that starting in 2006, the third Friday of September would henceforth be known as Park(ing) Day, a day when people in cities around the world would take over metered, on-street parking spots and creatively transform them into tiny public parks. Making Park(ing) a special, annual event "provided people with this political cover, that other people are doing the same thing around the world on the same day," Bela said. Park(ing) Day participants wouldn't just be out there on their own, doing some weird project and preventing motorists from snagging the perfect parking spot. "You're part of a movement to reclaim streets," he said. Mixing simplicity with creativity and holding fast to the tactical urbanism spirit of short-term actions for long-term change, Park(ing) Day draws in people who might never have given much thought to how street space is used, altering their perspective in the process. "It's not an overt protest," Bela noted. "It is demonstrating an alternative to automobile dominance."

The first official Park(ing) Day resulted in forty-seven mini-parks in thirteen cities in three different countries. Eighteen years later, there were at least one hundred seventy-eight Park(ing) spots in dozens of cities across five continents, with Bela estimating that anywhere from twenty to thirty thousand people participated in one form or another. These installations now go beyond greenery and park benches; groups have transformed on-street parking spots into mini-playgrounds, yoga studios, chess clubs, farm stands, pollinator gardens, hammocks for napping, café seating, and just about every possible use of public space imaginable. Wherever it happens, Park(ing) Day is wildly creative, elaborate, and joyous. It demonstrates that, if given the opportunity to cut through or circumvent the typical bureaucracy, it is quite easy to create space for people, not cars.

What a City Can Do

What are the most effective catalysts to push cities toward quick, positive change—to ignore standard operating procedure, cut through the red tape, and act to fix its streets? It's not always easy to know. A pothole after one driver complains? Absolutely. A series of pedestrian and cyclist fatalities? Sometimes. The climate crisis? Sadly, not yet. But every now and then something big happens that proves that where there's a worldwide crisis, there's a way.

When COVID hit in early 2020, bars and restaurants were instantly thrown into an existential emergency. As they closed their doors to stop the spread of a contagious virus, countless jobs and small businesses were at risk of being lost for good. That's when all eyes turned toward the curb—and even the surface parking lot. All that outdoor space suddenly became visible in a whole new way, this time to people who had for the most part never given any thought to how it was traditionally used.

By summer 2020, cities from Sarasota to Sacramento rewrote old outdoor dining guidelines or crafted completely new ones, reducing or eliminating permitting fees for serving food and alcohol al fresco. Lengthy public hearing requirements—which too often gave veto power to cranky community members with abundant time and resources to oppose all forms of change, especially those that take parking—were suddenly scrapped. If a business had space outside and wanted to use it to host customers instead of store cars, it could.

Despite a smattering of complaints, outdoor dining was, by every measure, an overwhelming success everywhere it was instituted. In Los Angeles, 81 percent of businesses reported that they would have closed permanently had it not been for the city's emergency L.A. Al Fresco program. A New York City Department of Transportation survey showed that 84 percent of people in Manhattan supported using street space for outdoor dining to save restaurants. Milwaukee, Wisconsin, which originally planned to shut down its temporary Active Streets for Businesses program before winter set in, extended the program repeatedly; a survey of downtown customers showed that two thirds would dine outdoors all year so long as heaters were available. In Iowa, the owner of a Des Moines steak and seafood restaurant set up tables and chairs in the parking lot behind her building; even after she reopened her indoor dining room, most of her customers still requested to sit outside. The setup helped keep the fifty-eight-year-old restaurant afloat.

Pandemic-era outdoor dining programs saved jobs, provided a COVID-weary populace with an opportunity to forget their worries at least for a moment, and had the knock-on effect of creating an entirely new constituency for better and higher uses of public space. Almost overnight, the people who supported rethinking how cities and towns manage parking weren't just fanatical anti-car advocates or Brooklyn-based podcast hosts. They were conservative mayors applying their market-oriented philosophy to help the local economy. They were small business owners of all political stripes, many of whom would have previously scoffed at losing so much as a single parking space in front of or behind their establishments. Perhaps best of all, they were the countless restaurant patrons in cities and suburbs alike who suddenly understood that in the space it takes to store one or two cars, a dozen or more people can enjoy a meal. It would have been nice if it hadn't taken a global pandemic, but just like the passersby who witnessed the first Park(ing) Day, the fish finally saw the water.

How Far Is Too Far?

The question with tactical urbanism, especially when it's taken up by individuals working outside the permission structure of city government, is how far is too far? There are lots of ways to wake people up to the problems caused by cars and the ease with which they can be solved. Some, like traffic cones topped with flowers or toilet plungers stuck to the pavement, grab people's attention with whimsy and humor while also telling them they should "demand more" of their city's leaders, to use a catchphrase that's common among tactical urbanists like Jonathan Fertig. Typically, these are low-risk actions for the people who undertake them. Others, though, can expose activists to a boatload of legal and financial trouble. LA officials have told Crosswalk Collective that it could be on the hook for the cost of removing rogue crosswalks, as well as subject to various other fines and even criminal citations. Still other actions can stir up a lot of anger and controversy, especially when they're taken directly to the drivers of some of the most harmful vehicles on the road.

In March 2021, SUV owners in a handful of cities in the UK went outside one morning to find that the air had been let out of one or more of their vehicles' tires. On the windshield of each deflated SUV was a leaflet from an anonymous group that claimed responsibility: the Tyre Extinguishers. "ATTENTION—your gas guzzler kills" was the headline. The flyers went on to explain that the SUVs had been targeted because "driving around urban areas in your massive vehicle has huge consequences for others." Not least among these consequences was climate change. "We need emergency action to reduce emissions immediately," read the leaflet. "We're taking actions into our own hands because our governments and politicians will not." Even hybrid and electric SUVs weren't spared. As the leaflet explained, the vehicles were still too big for urban environments and caused just as much congestion and danger as those powered by gas. If the car owners were inconvenienced, too bad. "You will have no difficulty getting around . . . with walking, cycling or public transport," said the leaflet.

The Tyre Extinguishers went on to deflate the tires of at least a thousand vehicles in the next two weeks alone, targeting wealthy urban neighborhoods where SUVs are not used for practical purposes such as transporting lumber or bales of hay, but for flaunting wealth and status. The Tyre Extinguishers struck under cover of darkness, inserting lentils or other small objects inside a tire's valves, which has the effect of letting the air out quietly and slowly. That allowed the activists to slip away long before anyone noticed their tires had been flattened.

Like the Rebar group, the Tyre Extinguishers took an open-source approach to their activism, creating a how-to manual so anyone around the world could participate. It's available online as a free download in seventeen languages. So far, in addition to the UK, drivers in Germany, Switzerland, the Netherlands, New Zealand, and parts of the US have woken up to find their vehicles' tires deflated and a leaflet on their windshields, all thanks to people who are affiliated only by their mutual hatred of SUVs.

"We've chosen SUVs for a number of reasons," an anonymous member of the Tyre Extinguishers told us in an interview. According to the International Energy Agency, if SUV drivers were a country, they would be the fifth-largest carbon emitter in the world. Then, of course, there are the more immediate health effects of ground-level pollution from cars: heart attacks, strokes, cancer, lung disease, miscarriages, cognitive decline, and even possibly erectile dysfunction (as we learned in chapter 5). As the Tyre Extinguishers rep told us, the sheer scale of the damage SUVs cause made them fair game. "If someone was walking along the streets spraying poisonous fumes into people's faces, they'd be arrested and probably locked up. But if you spray those fumes into people's faces using a car, it's somehow legal." Motonormativity at its finest.

Who decides to download a leaflet, grab a bag of lentils, and venture out into the night to deflate SUV tires? The decentralized and secretive nature of the Tyre Extinguishers makes it difficult to say. "Some participants are people who live near busy polluted roads, slowly choked by gas guzzlers. Others are cyclists who have been nearly killed by an SUV too many times," we were told. Essentially, anyone around the world who is fed up with SUVs and their government's inability to rein them in can participate, alone or in a group. "That's part of the strength of this," said the Tyre Extinguishers rep. "It makes us very difficult to detect or catch, because even the people at the center of this have no idea of the identities of the many people involved."

And while the action may not be technically victimless, the relative privilege of the vehicle owners affected—and the lack of any real utility in so-called sport utility vehicles—is part of why the activists single them out. "SUVs are an attractive target because they are such an appalling example of totally unnecessary luxury emissions," the rep told us. "Anyone who has bought a gas-guzzling SUV in a climate crisis has made a choice to say they don't care about the impact their choices make. So although we shouldn't focus on individual actions generally, there are some actions, like buying an SUV, that are so egregious they must be stopped," they said. "What matters is making it impossible to own an SUV in an urban area."

There's another way in which the Tyre Extinguishers have something in common with Park(ing) Day and other tactical urbanists: They are focusing on a ubiquitous problem. Just like the underpriced parking spaces that inspired Rebar or the unprotected bike lanes that Jonathan Fertig made safer with appropriated traffic cones, SUVs are all around us. "They're absolutely everywhere," the rep told us. That creates ample opportunity for action, but it also shows what the world is up against.

Making a street safer by installing a bike lane or requesting a stop sign requires jumping through countless hoops, from calling city officials to organizing fellow community members. Meanwhile, a combination of regulatory loopholes, cheap gas, and auto industry propaganda have created an ever-escalating proliferation of SUVs, all without any input from the public or governmental reckoning with their effects. Anyone with money in their bank account or the ability to get a loan can go to a car dealer, purchase a giant SUV, and drive and park it where they please. This behavior is encouraged with free parking, tax breaks, subsidized highways, and the political imperative to keep gas prices low. It's no wonder many activists and concerned citizens feel that they have little recourse through official channels.

So, if policy is no match for these machines, is sabotage—especially a form that does not damage the vehicle but instead temporarily inconveniences the driver—an appropriate and proportional response? The Tyre Extinguishers think so. "For decades we've been asking for change and not getting it," said the person we interviewed. "By taking part, you'll be swapping words for action, and that's what we need."

Taking Action

Swapping words for action can mean lots of different things depending on your comfort level. Deflating SUV tires is a legal gray area, and drivers can get awfully touchy about people who mess with their cars. For those who don't want to go that far, or who don't feel like playing Bikesy and hacking road signs, less risky opportunities abound.

Simply dropping an orange traffic cone on your corner to slow down turning drivers, or putting a park bench and a flowerpot in a parking space when you feed the meter, can be an effective way to advocate for change where you live and inspire others to see the world around them differently. Calling an elected official to request they fix a dangerous street might be your first step on the long road to activism. Organizing a bike bus or showing up at a PTA meeting to ask people to support changes that would make walking to school safer might connect you with other, like-minded citizens and foster action that will make your community happier, healthier, and more accessible for people of all ages, abilities, and backgrounds. Talking with your friends and neighbors, donating to or volunteering with local nonprofits, and supporting candidates and political parties who recognize traffic violence as an epidemic like any other and climate change as an existential threat—all those are important actions, too.

A world built for cars and a culture of car dependency doesn't work. It certainly doesn't work for people who want to walk, roll, bike, or take transit or otherwise avoid the many harms, inconveniences, and expenses of driving for every trip. Our current system doesn't work for drivers either. The freedom of the open road isn't so free when the road is jammed with traffic, you can never be quite sure how much gas is going to cost from one month to the next, and there's no sidewalk or bike lane that might at least give you the option of choosing a different way.

That's why individual action, however you define it, is so crucial. It is exactly what will lead to institutional change. Even if you do it yourself, you won't be alone for long.

Conclusion

Moving Toward a Life After Cars

In his 1951 short story "The Pedestrian," the American science fiction author Ray Bradbury paints a chilling picture of a car-dominated city of three million people in the year 2053, a city where only one man, Leonard Mead, regularly ventures out of his house to go for a walk.

The story begins with a description of the pleasure Mead, with no particular destination in mind, still takes in the simple act of putting one foot in front of the other:

> To enter out into that silence that was the city at eight o'clock of a misty evening in November, to put your feet upon that buckling concrete walk, to step over grassy seams and make your way, hands in pockets, through the silences, that was what Mr. Leonard Mead most dearly loved to do.

These evening constitutionals afford Mead another pleasure: silence. Bradbury describes daytimes in this city of the future as filled with the "thunderous surge of cars." At night, however, his fellow citizens are also nowhere to be found. Everyone sits at home watching the entertainment screens in their living rooms. As Bradbury writes, in ten years, Mead "had never met another person walking."

In Bradbury's dystopian vision, which was first published in an anti-fascist magazine, Mead's desire to walk is viewed by the car-centric panopticon society around him as being so aberrant that it must be punished. One night, an autonomous police vehicle suddenly approaches this man who dares to move about on his own power, and Mead soon finds himself "fixed like a museum specimen," as Bradbury writes, in the searchlight of the empty cop car, which seems almost sentient. Then a robotic voice emanates from the vehicle, questioning Mead's motivation for being out of his house.

"What are you doing out?"

"Walking," said Leonard Mead.

"Walking!"

"Just walking," he said simply, but his face felt cold.

"Walking, just walking, walking?"

"Yes, sir."

"Walking where? For what?"

"Walking for air. Walking to see."

That answer doesn't satisfy the menacing, all-seeing vehicle. The voice commands him to get in the back seat. And then, controlled by some invisible hand, the car rolls off, taking Mead to the Psychiatric Center for Research on Regressive Tendencies. Walking? Just walking? In the year 2053? That's insane.

Bradbury's vision was not pulled out of thin air. The writer had himself been stopped by the police in Los Angeles in 1949 when out for a stroll with a friend one night on Wilshire Boulevard. He later described the incident in an interview:

> A police car pulled up, and the police inquired why we were walking on the sidewalk. And I said, "Well, we're putting one foot in front of the other." Well, that was the wrong answer, and the policeman was very suspicious of us for walking in an area where there were no pedestrians. . . . He told us to go home and not to walk anymore. So I said, "Yes, sir, I'll never walk again."

Bradbury's story was written about three quarters of a century ago. The future he imagined then is still some decades away. Yet in many regards we are frighteningly close to his fiction becoming our reality. In many places, where walking is rare and even looked at suspiciously, it practically has. It is up to us whether we accept this reality, or whether we resist and fight for change.

We are standing at a crossroads. Go one way, and we stand a chance of rebuilding the fabric of our towns, cities, and societies at a sustainable human scale and beginning to repair the damage done to our health, our environment, and our sanity by the automobile. We can create a world in which cars are not necessary for full enfranchisement in the community. A world where those who truly need to use cars and trucks—workers delivering heavy loads, residents of rural areas, some people with mobility disabilities—can do so without competing for space and resources with people whose use of personal motor vehicles is unnecessary, wasteful, and inefficient. A world in which walking is no longer stigmatized or dangerous; in which public transit is frequent and abundant; in which hopping on a bike to go to school or work or the grocery store is safe and easy.

It's a beautiful world, this one. A quieter, greener world that is more sustainable both environmentally and economically. It's also a happier world, where people are more likely to let their children roam free, to know and trust their neighbors, or to have spontaneous interactions with friends they bump into on a sidewalk. This is what life after cars could look like.

If we take the other branch at the crossroads, we double down on the catastrophic car-brained choices of the last 125 years. That path leads to wider and wider freeways that fill up with cars as soon as they are completed, draining the financial resources of our states and municipalities, and demolishing any semblance of places that are worth driving to anyway. That choice would require sending individuals deeper into debt as they participate in the SUV arms race in a desperate scramble to keep themselves and their families safe on roads—paradoxically making them less safe, given that there's no end in sight to the escalation. That course means accepting the continued automotive carnage that kills more than a million people every year around the globe. It means embracing the decimation of the natural world that cars inevitably require, no matter how they are powered. It would signal our acquiescence in the ongoing car-perpetuated atrophy of our social networks and our bodies.

Some people say that this future car-centered world will be just fine if it is all electric. Some people say that if we just make cars autonomous, the automotive utopia will be so much safer than the status quo that we won't have to worry about a thing.

And let's be clear: Both electrification and self-driving tech have real potential to change things for the better. Electric cars, in particular, eliminate tailpipe emissions, which will mean a radical improvement of air quality wherever they are used, especially in denser urban and suburban environments. And they are much quieter than gas-powered vehicles, although they still produce tire noise and toxic tire dust—more of both, in some cases, because their batteries make them heavier than legacy cars. But they still require vast networks of roads and huge amounts of parking, eating up green space and blighting communities. And they can still kill and maim people with the same force of any gas-powered car. No one who was ever hit by the driver of an electric car thought to themselves, "Sure, I'm severely injured, but at least the driver cares about climate change."

Electric cars must still be powered, too, and our grid is already strained by the incessant new demands we are making on it. The batteries for electric cars require rare minerals, and the rush to control those natural resources looks pretty ugly already in terms of its impacts on what unspoiled places remain on the planet, and the people who live in those places (not to mention the ocean floor, a place rich with mineral deposits but also countless species, many of them still undiscovered by humans). And how will we deal with electric batteries in the waste stream at scale?

These and many other problems with mass automotive electrification are only beginning to be imagined, much less solved. Other unintended consequences will inevitably arise—that's the nature of new technologies. That doesn't mean we shouldn't pursue electrification aggressively, but we should be focusing on reducing the need for car ownership in the first place, while also electrifying public transit and delivery vehicles rather than unquestioningly buying into yet another naive fantasy of harm-free personal motor vehicle transport as salvation.

As for autonomous vehicles, they may well prove to be much safer than human drivers—although the vision promoted by their boosters gets pushed further into the future each year and with each failure of the technology to even begin to match human perception and reaction. And AVs come with their own set of unintended consequences. Just ask the San Francisco neighbors of a parking lot where Waymo cars shuffled around all night, honking when they back up to let each other pass. Autonomous cars at scale will require highly regulated, predictable streetscapes—exactly the kind of life-crushing, soul-destroying road hells that make humans and other animals want to pass through at high speed rather than linger. Waste spaces stretching as far as the eye can see, with more and more land devoted to the robotic appetites of cars that circle endlessly, often empty, gathering data that will then be used to sell us things and to sell us as commodities to advertisers and marketers. Cars will monitor us wherever we go, controlled by unaccountable tech oligarchs or autocratic governments, influencing our consumer preferences, our politics, our ideologies, our very beliefs. Ray Bradbury would recognize the threat.

Cars are cars. The problem is cars. And the problem of cars can't be solved with different cars. To us, the choice is clear. If you've read this far, you probably feel the same. So what are we going to do about it?

We believe it is possible to take the better way, to sustain life without remaining dependent on cars, because we see individuals and governments making that choice more and more often. Humanity is not doomed to car dominance. It is no more fanciful to imagine a world in which the car is no longer king than it was to put this malevolent ruler on the throne in the first place.

How do we know it's possible? Well, for starters, we have seen so many cities and nations begin to turn the tide. Melissa and Chris Bruntlett, authors of *Curbing Traffic*, put it this way: "20th century urban planning changed the concept of a street from a place to pass time to a place to pass through. 21st century planning is about reversing that mindset and prioritizing people living in a city over cars driving through it."

Everywhere you look these days, people are fighting to create the post-car world we need.

In Madrid, plazas that were converted to car parks in the twentieth century are now back to being plazas, filled with conversation and flirtation and laughter, day and night. In Gainesville, Florida; South Bend, Indiana; Spokane, Washington; and dozens of other cities across North America, voters and planners have eliminated minimum parking requirements, meaning that housing for people is—finally!—once again getting priority over housing for cars. In New York City, whole blocks of the ancient Indigenous pathway now known as Broadway have been given back to people on foot.

Many cities, such as Milan, Brussels, Berlin, Barcelona, London, and Seoul, are enforcing zones in their dense centers where only low-emissions cars and trucks are admitted, or where those who burn gas must pay a toll to compensate for the damage they do, and to disincentivize drivers from entering at all. Germany—long a motor head's paradise—is encouraging the use of public transit over driving by offering the Deutschland-Ticket, which for just fifty-eight euros a month (as of 2025) allows unlimited access to local and regional public transport throughout the country—buses, trams, trains, subways, all of it. Other nations are studying the model. In US cities like Denver, Salt Lake City, Nashville, Austin, and Ann Arbor, rebates for electric bikes have proven so popular that people now sign up to be notified for the next round of releases the way they would for Taylor Swift tickets.

All this just goes to show that we can move to embrace and improve upon the proven transportation technologies that make for a better world. And we can do it in all kinds of places, from dense cities that were built before cars were invented to modern suburbs planned around mass motoring. It won't happen, however, without some old-fashioned hard work.

One of the most gratifying aspects of doing what we do has been connecting with people around the world who are also fighting for a better future. They are a diverse group, united in the belief that our streets can be places that nurture community rather than crushing it under the wheel. We've talked to Wes Marshall, a professor of civil engineering who called out his profession's destructive tendencies in his book *Killed by a Traffic Engineer*; Baruch Herzfeld, who is helping New York City delivery riders charge up their e-bikes safely and securely; Shabazz Stuart, a Brooklyn-based entrepreneur who is building the technology and infrastructure to help cities provide secure bicycle parking facilities; Patty Wiens, Winnipeg's bike mayor, who is tirelessly organizing riders in one of the most car-centric cities in North America; Jonathon Stalls, the pedestrian activist and "walking artist" who leads elected officials on walks to help them see just how hostile automobile infrastructure can be for the people they serve; the late Donald Shoup, the economist and professor who wrote the definitive text on how free parking distorts and degrades our cities; Cyprine Odada, who leads Critical Mass bike rides in Nairobi to build support for better bike infrastructure in one of Africa's largest cities; and dozens of others.

It's the countless ordinary people around the world who give us the most hope, though. From New Zealand to Argentina, from Norway to Mexico, in Ireland and France and in every corner of the United States, these are the people who are making change for the better. People who might not consider themselves experts or activists, but who, each in their own way, are turning us toward the better path, the more human and sustainable future.

How can you be a part of it?

Here are a few steps we can take together toward a car-free future.

Learn to *see* cars. As big as they are, cars have become essentially invisible to us because they are such a deeply ingrained feature of the modern world. So start looking harder. Try walking in a place you would normally only consider driving through (carefully!) and allow yourself to feel the magnitude of the damage cars cause. Sit in a park, close your eyes, and start to listen—chances are your ears will never be free of the sound of passing cars not far away. Look at the car storage along the curb on your street and imagine what that space could be used for if those gigantic hunks of metal weren't there. (And start calling it car storage, not parking. Speaking is its own form of seeing.) Leave your car at the edge of the lot at the big-box store, walk across the asphalt, and ask yourself whether this can be considered a place worth being in, and if this is the best use of our precious land. Once you see the true nature of cars, you won't be able to unsee it.

Engage with local government. Go to those planning meetings about the new bike lane or the highway widening or the street redesign, if you can get there. If you can't, send written comment.

Call your local representatives and explain how you feel about the jerks who speed down your street. Get to know which elected officials in your area are open to a less autocentric way of life and tell them you support them when they take a stand. Local government can be very responsive to squeaky wheels. You can help to make sure that the squeaks aren't coming just from car wheels.

Find your people. Social media networks come and go, and none of them is perfect, but they have their uses. If you're on one of these platforms, start following like-minded folks to learn about what is going on nationally and internationally so you can bring those ideas home. If you're not into social media, go to your local bike store and ask about group rides. Join a local pedestrian, cycling, or transit advocacy group or local parks conservancy. You'll almost certainly meet some people who "get it"—and who will be there for you and with you when it's time to get something done. It can be a real relief to connect with others and confirm that the problem isn't with you—it's with the cars.

Preach to the unconverted. Most people have an intuitive sense that a life without cars, or with at least a lot fewer of them, is better. Think of where people choose to go on vacation: strolling the Marais in Paris, biking the streets of Amsterdam. Not even your friend with the Ford F-250 in the garage that he uses to haul nothing more than a few bags of groceries thinks those places would be better with cars. Talking about and sharing the relatable joy we find in societally approved car-free or car-light spaces like European cities or theme parks can be the beginning of that guy becoming less oblivious to the harm cars do. Use every opportunity to sneak in the idea that maybe, just maybe, we don't have to organize our lives around the care and feeding of automobiles. Hear a loved one complaining about gas prices? Maybe that can open the door to a discussion about how we got to a place where we can't go anywhere without paying at the pump.

Believe change is possible. This is not a sequential series of steps. It's a cycle in which we continually rediscover the inspiration that can keep us going. It's a way of life, in which we have to keep renewing and refreshing our belief that things can be different and better. Look to the examples of positive change that are popping up every day around the world and around your own community. As the Danish architect Jan Gehl said about the transformation of Copenhagen, "I think this is the most important thing: Every morning when you wake up, you have to feel that your city is a little better than the day before. That is a nice feeling, because it gives you hope for the generations to come." You don't have to limit yourself to Copenhagen to find the kinds of vibes that will remind yourself of the potential for positive change.

Above all, remember this: You're not alone in wanting a better world, one in which cars are relegated to their proper use. Cars are tools that can be useful at certain times and places. They are not gods. They are not the foundation of our society. They should serve us. We should not serve them.

You're not alone in thinking that change is possible. Indeed, it is necessary.

There *can* be life, a world, after cars—and for ourselves, our neighbors, our children, we must keep moving toward it, one step at a time.

Acknowledgments

Taking on the forces of car culture is never easy, and we wouldn't have been able to do it without the confidence and support of countless people, all of whom left an indelible mark on this book.

Chief among them is our brilliant editor at Thesis, Megan McCormack, who has believed in and advocated for us since day one. Her suggestions and notes made our writing better every step of the way, and we're grateful for her creativity, vision, and enthusiasm. We also extend our sincere gratitude to Adrian Zackheim, Niki Papadopoulos, and the entire team at Penguin Random House for their unwavering faith in the project.

Our agents at Stonesong, Emmanuelle Morgen and Kim Lindman, were early champions of this book and guided us through the entire process with grace, kindness, intelligence, and a shared passion for safe streets. We thank you from the bottom of our hearts.

Ali Lemer, our excellent audio editor, kept the podcast running behind the scenes while we wrote the book. Her talent, technical chops, and sound editorial judgment always make us sound great. Thank you, Ali, for being the secret weapon of *The War on Cars*. We are also thankful to Josh Wilcox at the Brooklyn Podcasting Studio.

Beyond providing a home to record the podcast, Josh has long been a de facto producer whose contributions make each episode better. Curtis Fox, our first producer and editor, deserves a lot of credit and recognition for helping us launch the podcast and giving it the tone and style it has to this day. And Dani Finkel designed the logo that we have used since the first episode.

Life After Cars drew on many different sources, and a bibliography is included, but if you read one book after this one, we hope it's *Fighting Traffic: The Dawn of the Motor Age in the American City* by Peter Norton. It is an indispensable resource for anyone seeking to learn from history so as not to repeat it. No one has influenced our understanding of these issues more than Peter, and we are deeply appreciative of his scholarship and friendship. We'd also like to thank all of the advocates, journalists, researchers, and many others who took us along for the ride in the book and on the podcast: the volunteer leaders of the Montclair Bike Bus, Andy Hawkins, Sam Balto, John Bela, Jonathan Fertig, Patty Wiens, Filip Watteeuw, John Bauters, Michael Janz, Vignesh Swaminathan, Tom Flood, Gary Fisher, Alicia Kennedy, Peter Walker, Ed Niedermeyer, Aaron Gordon, Beth Osborne, Wes Marshall, Alissa Walker, Michael Hobbes, Jonathon Stalls, Jaume Balmes, Guille Lopez, Rosa Suri, Genis Dominguez, Mindy Roberts, Ian Walker, Tara Goddard, Angie Schmitt, Anna Zivarts, Charles T. Brown, Greg Shill, David Zipper, Gretchen Sorin, Sarah Seo, Jessica Valenti, Bob Sorokanich, Kendra Pierre-Louis, Marley Blonsky, George Hahn, Dan Savage, Donald Shoup, Cory Doctorow, Nitish Pahwa, Bernie Wagenblast, Amy Westervelt, Jamelle Bouie, David Roberts, Anil Dash, Adam Conover, Rick Steves, Derek Guy, Rollie Williams, Nicole Conlan, Bill

McKibben, Ed Begley Jr., Nick Offerman, and Adam McKay. We also owe a tremendous debt of gratitude to the late professor Donald Shoup, for his wit, wisdom, and the ability to make the invisible visible.

Thank you to Susan Mocarski and the entire Cleverhood crew in Providence, Rhode Island, for their longtime sponsorship of the podcast. Thanks also to Steve Bercu and the Helen and William Mazer Foundation.

Perhaps most important, we want to extend our immense appreciation to our community of listeners all over the world who are working to make their communities safer, more sustainable, and more equitable, often in the face of tremendous odds. Thank you for all you do.

Sarah's Acknowledgments

Much of this book was written and researched in the Wertheim Study at the main branch of the New York Public Library, part of the Vartan Gregorian Center for Research in the Humanities. It was a privilege and an inspiration to work alongside the other writers, scholars, and artists in residency in that historic building, one of New York City's essential public treasures. I would like to thank everyone who works there for their indispensable help, which immeasurably broadened and deepened the scope of this book. (Thanks to Lauren Sandler for the tip.)

I would also like to thank everyone at Moulin à Nef, the Virginia Center for the Creative Arts' residency in Auvillar, France. Thanks especially to Fatiha Boukhris, Géraldine Chevallier, Cheryl Fortier, and Sabine van den Bergh for welcoming me onto the team there.

Gratitude, also, to fellow writer in residence Lex Shramko, who helped keep me on track in the final hectic days of completing the manuscript.

Thanks also to all my friends, especially Heather Millar and Sam Maser, and of course my Wednesday Brearley crew: Emily Chase, Joanna Delson, Katharine Hellman, Rozella Kennedy, Emily O'Connor, and Claudia Silver. Special thanks to my Suffragette Kitty bandmates, Nikolaus Schuhbeck, Aricka Martinez, and Tanya Lofgren, who helped me employ rock and roll as a stress management technique. (It works.)

To my mother, Clelia Garrity, thank you for showing me how to work hard and not give up.

Thanks to my stepmother, Carmen Echavarren, for believing in me.

And merci beaucoup to my uncle Sam Goodyear, a faithful listener to the podcast, for truly *getting it.*

My father, Dick Goodyear, always encouraged me to read and learn everything I wanted to, and to think and to argue for what I believe. Sadly, he didn't live long enough to see this book, but he would have gotten such a kick out of it. Thanks for everything, Dad.

Finally, eternal gratitude to my beloved wife, Laura Conaway, and my dear son, Nathaniel Goodyear. Couldn't have done it without you.

Doug's Acknowledgments

When I first got involved with advocacy, I could not have imagined where it would take me, nor that I would have the good fortune to fight for safe streets alongside the best leaders and advocates in New

York or any city. Thank you to Jon Orcutt, Dani Simons, Brad Lander, Paul Steely White, Eric McClure, Charlie Komanoff, Steve Vaccaro, Adam White, Danny Harris, Ben Furnas, Caroline Samponaro, Tom DeVito, Joe Cutrufo, Jessie Singer, Kathy Park Price, Rob Price, Clarence Eckerson Jr., Shabazz Stuart, Ben Kabak, Sarah Kaufman, Laura Fox, Gersh Kuntzman, Ben Fried, Dave Colon, David Meyer, Stephen Miller, Brad Aaron, Hayes Lord, Vincent Barone, Ya-Ting Liu, Melinda Hanson, Adam Mansky, Mike Epstein, Rich Miller, Mike Racioppo, Joanna Oltman Smith, Dave "Paco" Abraham, Ken Coughlin, Janet Liff, Hilda Cohen, Juan Restrepo, Lisa Orman, Sara Lind, Jackson Chabot, Noel Hidalgo, Jehiah Czebotar, Mike Lydon, and Charlie Todd. I am lucky to count you all as colleagues, mentors, and, most important, friends. I'd especially like to recognize Amy Cohen and Gary Eckstein and all the members of Families for Safe Streets for their tireless and selfless activism. And particular gratitude to Janette Sadik-Khan and Seth Solomonow, whose *Street Fight* paved the way for *Life After Cars*.

I'd also like to thank the people who have welcomed me into what is truly a national and international movement, including Melissa and Chris Bruntlett, Mark Wagenbuur, Saskia Kluit, Marco te Brömmelstroet, Meredith Glaser, Lucas Harms, Henry Cutler at WorkCycles in Amsterdam, Michael Schneider of Streets for All in Los Angeles, Veronica O. Davis, Becca Wolfson, Tony Jordan, Rob Toftness, Jason Slaughter, Ray Delahanty, Grant Ennis, Steven Vance, Kevin Hardman, Jonathan Maus, John Simmerman, Hirra Khan, Andrew Simms, Leo Murray, Cathy Lamri, Briana Van Note at the Netherlands Board of Tourism & Conventions, Wies Callens at the Fietsersbond in Brussels, everyone at the European Cyclists' Federation and the Velo-city festival, and Giacomo Biraghi, Luca

Ballarini, Laura Martini, and the entire staff at Stratosferica and the Utopian Hours festival in Turin, Italy.

I did most of my research and writing for the book at Playground Brooklyn in Gowanus. Thank you to Joonhyun Hwang and the staff there for providing the perfect environment for creative professionals.

My parents Neil Gordon and Sally Gordon raised me to stick up for what is just and right and were an incredible source of encouragement during the writing of this book, as they always have been. Thanks also to my sister, Rebecca Gordon, one of my biggest cheerleaders. We have always been there for each other, and always will be. I also want to remember my grandmother Miriam Gordon. She was an avid reader and I know she would have enjoyed sharing this book with everyone.

I happened to have married into an exceptionally warm and supportive family and am so fortunate to have Jerry and Paula Kaye and Michelle, Alan, Aviva, and Charlie Silverman in my life.

Lastly, words cannot fully express my appreciation and love for my wonderful wife, Leora Kaye, who is my light and my support, and my amazing kids, Galit and Zeb. I adore you all.

—March 7, 2025

Notes

INTRODUCTION

xii **GM alone shelled out:** Julia Faria, "General Motors Company's Advertising Spending in the United States from 2007 to 2022," Statista, September 10, 2024, statista.com/statistics /261531/general-motors-advertising-spending-in-the-us.

xiv **Paul Fairie, a researcher:** Paul Fairie (@paulisci.bsky.social), "A Brief History of the War on Cars," Bluesky, October 11, 2023, bsky.app/profile/paulisci.bsky.social/post /3kbjanmaowa2h.

xiv **In 2002, *The Economist* published a story:** "The War Against the Car," *The Economist*, May 30, 2002, economist.com/britain/2002/05/30/the-war-against-the-car.

xv **Roads, he declared:** Jason Margolis, "Cyclists Accuse Toronto Mayor Ford of 'War on Bikes,'" BBC News, May 3, 2012, bbc.com/news/magazine-17914504.

xv **"Ladies and gentlemen, the war":** Tess Kalinowski and David Rider, "'War on the Car Is Over': Ford Moves Transit Underground," *Toronto Star*, December 2, 2010, thestar.com /news/gta/city-hall/war-on-the-car-is-over-ford-moves-transit-underground/article _20fe19e7-fe10-5260-a7b0-b8aff127efcd.html.

xv **The *New York Post* published:** Melissa Klein, "NYC's War on Cars Has Eliminated 6,100 Parking Spots in Two Years," November 9, 2019, *New York Post*, nypost.com/2019/11/09/ nycs-war-on-cars-has-eliminated-6100-parking-spots-in-two-years.

xvii **Global carbon emissions:** Laura Cozzi, Apostolos Petropoulos, Leonardo Paoli, Mathilde Huismans, and Amrita Dasgupta, "As Their Sales Continue to Rise, SUVs' Global CO2 Emissions Are Nearing 1 Billion Tonnes," International Energy Agency, February 27, 2023, iea.org/commentaries/as-their-sales-continue-to-rise-suvs-global-co2-emissions-are -nearing-1-billion-tonnes.

xvii **Nearly 43,000 people were killed by cars:** "NHTSA Estimates for 2022 Show Roadway Fatalities Remain Flat After Two Years of Dramatic Increases," US Department of Trans-portation, April 20, 2023, transportation.gov/briefing-room/nhtsa-estimates-2022-show -roadway-fatalities-remain-flat-after-two-years-dramatic.

xvii **pedestrian fatalities were the highest they had been:** Amanda Holpuch, "U.S. Pedes-trian Deaths Are at Highest Level in 41 Years, Report Says," *New York Times*, June 27, 2023, nytimes.com/2023/06/27/us/pedestrian-deaths-2022.html.

xvii **42 percent of American children:** Sandra A. Ham, Sarah Levin Martin, and Harold W. Kohl III, "Changes in the Percentage of Students Who Walk or Bike to School—United

States, 1969 and 2001," *Journal of Physical Activity and Health* 5, no. 2 (2008): 205–15, doi.org/10.1123/jpah.5.2.205.

xvii **that number was 11 percent:** Eleftheria Kontou, Noreen C. McDonald, Kristen Brookshire, Nancy C. Pullen-Seufert, and Seth LaJeunesse, "U.S. Active School Travel in 2017: Prevalence and Correlates," *Preventive Medicine Reports* 17 (March 2020): 101024, doi .org/10.1016/j.pmedr.2019.101024.

xviii **Gen Z has been slower to embrace driving:** Peter Weber, "Gen Z Is Historically Slow Getting Driver's Licenses. Boomers Aren't Letting Theirs Go," *The Week*, February 14, 2023, theweek.com/transportation/1020962/gen-z-is-historically-slow-getting-drivers-licenses -boomers-arent-letting.

CHAPTER ONE: A BRIEF HISTORY OF THE WAR ON CARS

3 **Metropolis has "one of the worst":** Technically, Metropolis wasn't mentioned by name until *Action Comics* #16, which was released in September 1939.

5 **In 1914—the year Jerry Siegel and Joe Shuster:** "Jerry Siegel, Superman's Creator, Dies at 81," *New York Times*, January 31, 1996, nytimes.com/1996/01/31/us/jerry-siegel-superman -s-creator-dies-at-81.html; and "Joseph Shuster, Cartoonist, Dies; Co-Creator of 'Superman' was 78," *New York Times*, August 3, 1992, nytimes.com/1992/08/03/arts/joseph-shuster -cartoonist-dies-co-creator-of-superman-was-78.html.

5 **approximately 4,700 people:** National Safety Council, "Car Crash Deaths and Rates," Injury Facts, injuryfacts.nsc.org/motor-vehicle/historical-fatality-trends/deaths-and-rates.

6 **on the evening of September 13, 1899:** Keith Williams, "Who Was the First Person Killed by a Car in New York?," *New York Times*, March 30, 2018, nytimes.com/2018/03 /30/nyregion/who-was-the-first-person-killed-by-a-car-in-new-york.html.

6 **He was rushed to Roosevelt Hospital:** "Automobile Victim Dead. Henry H. Bliss Succumbs to His Injuries in Roosevelt Hospital," *New York Times*, September 15, 1899, timesmachine.nytimes.com/timesmachine/1899/09/15/100451056.html.

7 **Given his status as patient zero:** Andrew McFarlane, "How the UK's First Fatal Car Accident Unfolded," *BBC News*, August 17, 2010, bbc.com/news/magazine-10987606. The first pedestrian killed by a motor vehicle in Great Britain, and probably the world, was Bridget Driscoll, who was run over by a gas-powered Benz motorcar at London's Crystal Palace on August 17, 1896. An employee of the Anglo-French Motor Company was driving the car as a demonstration of this innovation at four miles per hour when he hit Driscoll, fracturing her skull. The coroner who conducted the inquest hoped Driscoll's death "would be the last" of its kind. Even earlier, in 1869, Mary Ward, an "Anglo-Irish naturalist, astronomer and author" was killed by a steam-powered car built by her cousins. Nevertheless, we focus on Bliss here because of the United States' more central role in automobile manufacturing and exporting of car culture around the world.

8 **At least twenty-five more people:** US Department of Transportation, "Motor Vehicle Traffic Fatalities and Fatality Rates."

8 **In 1920, it was 12,155:** US Department of Transportation, "Motor Vehicle Traffic Fatalities and Fatality Rates."

8 **The crisis was so obvious:** "Nation Roused Against Motor Killings: Secretary Hoover's Conference Will Suggest Many Ways to Check the Alarming Increase of Automobile Fatalities.—Studying Huge Problem," *New York Times*, November 23, 1924, timesmachine .nytimes.com/timesmachine/1924/11/23/104162618.html.

9 **"on any day in which":** Peter D. Norton, *Fighting Traffic: The Dawn of the Motor Age in the American City* (Cambridge, MA: MIT Press, 2008), 40.

9 **"squarely on the shoulders":** Norton, *Fighting Traffic*, 40.

10 **In 1926, automobiles killed:** "Autos Killed 1,066 Here in '26 408 Children Among Victims," *New York Times*, January 12, 1927, https://timesmachine.nytimes.com/timesmachine /1927/01/12/101684343.html?pageNumber=19.

10 **60 percent of automobile fatalities:** Bill Loomis, "1900–1930: The Years of Driving Dangerously, *Detroit News*, April 26, 2015, detroitnews.com/story/news/local/michigan-history /2015/04/26/auto-traffic-history-detroit/26312107/.

10 **"a little girl, crushed between two colliding automobiles":** Norton, *Fighting Traffic*, 43.

10 **"had four plaster reliefs":** Peter Norton, "When Cities Made Monuments to Traffic Deaths," *Bloomberg*, June 10, 2022, bloomberg.com/news/features/2022-06-10/how-cities-responded -to-traffic-deaths-100-years-ago.

10 **Newspapers frequently labeled:** Loomis, "1900–1930: The Years of Driving Dangerously."

10 **"darting into the street":** Norton, "When Cities Made Monuments to Traffic Deaths."

10 **"death car drivers":** J. W. Barrall, *Pioneer News*, January 5, 1923.

11 **"reckless and vicious drivers":** Norton, *Fighting Traffic*, 28.

11 **more modern crisis of gun violence:** Garry Wills, "Our Moloch," *New York Review of Books*, December 15, 2012, nybooks.com/online/2012/12/15/our-moloch.

11 **In late 1920s Harlem:** Stephen Robertson, "Traffic Accidents in 1920s Harlem," *Digital Harlem Blog*, April 1, 2010, drstephenrobertson.com/digitalharlemblog/maps/traffic-accidents -in-1920s-harlem.

11 **dubbed the "Death-O-Meter":** "Death-O-Meter Dedicated," *Brooklyn Daily Eagle*, May 14, 1927, bklyn.newspapers.com/image/83391759/?terms=%22death-o-meter%22.

11 **"municipal murder maps":** "City 'Murder Map' Lists Killings: Shows Where 154 Children Were Victims of Traffic in Manhattan in 1927. More Playgrounds Urged: City Club Says Establishment of Parks on East Side Would Save Many Lives," *New York Times*, June 25, 1928, timesmachine.nytimes.com/timesmachine/1928/06/25/91530612.html.

12 **approximately 110 people who are killed:** National Highway Traffic Safety Administration, "Early Estimate of Motor Vehicle Traffic Fatalities in 2023," in "Traffic Safety Stats: CrashStats," April 2024, crashstats.nhtsa.dot.gov/Api/Public/ViewPublication/813561.

12 **"The reason the word":** Sarah Goodyear, Doug Gordon, and Aaron Naparstek, hosts, *The War on Cars*, podcast, episode 80, "There Are No Accidents with Jessie Singer," February 15, 2022, thewaroncars.org/2022/02/15/there-are-no-accidents-with-jessie-singer.

13 **"If reasonable safety of life and limb":** Norton, *Fighting Traffic*, 65.

13 **A pedestrian struck by a driver at:** "Impact Speed and a Pedestrian's Risk of Severe Injury or Death," AAA Foundation for Traffic Safety, September 2011, aaafoundation.org /impact-speed-pedestrians-risk-severe-injury-death.

14 **In 1923, the public outcry:** Norton, *Fighting Traffic*, 96–99.

15 **"Great Wall of China Against Progress":** Norton, *Fighting Traffic*, 98.

15 **"never returned to a peacetime footing":** Norton, *Fighting Traffic*, 99.

16 **Jaywalking, a word people use:** Norton, *Fighting Traffic*, 72–75.

17 **people dressed as giant eyeballs:** Andy Bosselman, "Eyes on the Street: There Are Literally Giant Eyeballs on the Street," *Streetsblog Denver*, September 4, 2019, denver.streetsblog .org/2019/09/04/eye-on-the-street-there-are-literally-eyeballs-on-the-street.

17 **"Speeding Catches Up with You":** Traffic Safety Marketing, "Speeding Catches Up with You," National Highway Traffic Safety Administration, accessed March 2, 2025, traffic safetymarketing.gov/safety-topics/speeding/speeding-catches-up-with-you.

18 **"examines how transportation":** "America on the Move," Smithsonian National Museum

of American History, accessed March 2, 2025, americanhistory.si.edu/explore/exhibitions/america-on-the-move.

18 **"If there is an official history of the automobile"**: Peter Norton, "Autonomous Vehicles: A Powerful Tool If You Can Get the Problem Right," Robohub, June 25, 2014, robohub.org/autonomous-vehicles-a-powerful-tool-if-you-can-get-the-problem-right.

18 **"The automobile has won"**: E. B. White, "One Man's Meat," *Harper's Magazine*, February 1942.

19 **it displaced an estimated 475,000 households:** Farrell Evans, "How Interstate Highways Gutted Communities—and Reinforced Segregation," History, updated September 21, 2023, history.com/news/interstate-highway-system-infrastructure-construction-segregation.

19 **"gouged across a city":** Robert A. Caro, *The Power Broker: Robert Moses and the Fall of New York* (Vintage Books, 1975), 839.

19 **In 1959, the construction:** "The I-81 Story," NYCLU, March 12, 2021, nyclu.org/resources/campaigns-actions/campaigns/i-81-story.

20 **As of this writing, Texas:** Kelsey Thompson, "How Much Will Each Phase of Austin's $4.5B I-35 Expansion Cost?," KXAN, September 17, 2024, kxan.com/traffic/traffic-projects/i-35-expansion-project/how-much-will-each-phase-of-austins-4-5b-i-35-expansion-cost; Bryan C. Parker, "I-35's Massive Overhaul Will Displace Dozens of Businesses and Last Nearly a Decade," *Austin Monthly*, March/April 2024, austinmonthly.com/i-35s-massive-overhaul-will-displace-dozens-of-businesses-and-last-nearly-a-decade.

21 **More than 20 percent of residents:** Jonmaesha Beltran, "How Would Widening Milwaukee's I-94 Affect Residents Near the Highway?," *Wisconsin Watch*, May 23, 2023, wisconsinwatch.org/2023/05/how-would-widening-milwaukees-i-94-affect-residents-near-the-highway.

22 **appeared in a 1957 Chevrolet ad:** Emily Badger, "The Myth of the American Love Affair with Cars," *Washington Post*, January 27, 2015, washingtonpost.com/news/wonk/wp/2015/01/27/debunking-the-myth-of-the-american-love-affair-with-cars; and Doug Gordon, host, *The War on Cars*, podcast, episode 50, "America's Love Affair with Cars," October 14, 2020, thewaroncars.org/2020/10/14/americas-love-affair-with-cars.

22 **In the special, Groucho says:** "Merrily We Roll Along," NBC, October 21, 1961, youtube.com/watch?v=-i8brz9nE1E.

23 **the Uber driver who obstructed Lyden's path:** David Meyer, "20th Precinct Chief Wanted to Arrest Taxi Driver Who Killed Madison Lyden—but Cy Vance Said No," *Streetsblog NYC*, September 5, 2018, nyc.streetsblog.org/2018/09/05/20th-precinct-chief-wanted-to-arrest-taxi-driver-who-killed-madison-lyden-but-cy-vance-said-no.

24 **released with just a $1,000 fine:** Emily Olson, "New York Truck Driver Fined $US1,000 over Crash That Killed Australian Tourist Madison Lyden," ABC, January 16, 2019, abc.net.au/news/2019-01-17/new-york-truck-driver-who-killed-tasmanian-cyclist-fined/10721716.

24 **The full stretch, running fifty-one blocks:** Gersh Kuntzman, "City to Begin Finishing Central Park West Bike Lane in Mere Weeks," *Streetsblog NYC*, July 9, 2020, nyc.streetsblog.org/2020/07/09/city-to-begin-finishing-central-park-west-bike-lane-in-mere-weeks.

24 **that same paper published:** James Barron, "The People of Central Park West Want Their Parking Spaces (Sorry, Cyclists)," *New York Times*, August 18, 2019, nytimes.com/2019/08/18/nyregion/cars-cyclists-bike-lanes-.html.

24 **Since Henry Bliss was hit by that taxi:** Patrick Miner, Barbara M. Smith, Anant Jani, Geraldine McNeill, and Alfred Gathorne-Hardy, "Car Harm: A Global Review of Automobility's Harm to People and the Environment," *Journal of Transport Geography* 115 (February 2024): 103817, doi.org/10.1016/j.jtrangeo.2024.103817.

25 **"Hope is a discipline":** Mariame Kaba, "Hope Is a Discipline," interview by Brian Sonenstein and Kim Wilson, *Toward Freedom*, September 17, 2020, towardfreedom.org/story/archives/activism/hope-is-a-discipline.

CHAPTER TWO: CAR CULTURE AND BIKELASH

27 **In March 2018, a driver allegedly suffered:** Al Baker and Sean Piccoli, "2 Children Killed by Driver in Brooklyn Intersection," *New York Times*, March 5, 2018, nytimes.com/2018/03/05/nyregion/park-slope-children-killed-by-driver.html.

28 **Not everyone was pleased:** Colin Mixson, "Slope's New Ninth Street Bike Lanes Make Road No Safer for Pedestrians, Residents Say," *Brooklyn Paper*, January 28, 2019, brooklyn paper.com/slopes-new-ninth-street-bike-lanes-make-road-no-safer-for-pedestrians-residents-say.

29 **The owner of a funeral home:** Anna Quinn, "Bike Lane Has Made 9th Street 'Almost Lawless,' Residents Say," *Park Slope Patch*, January 29, 2019, patch.com/new-york/parkslope/bike-lane-has-made-9th-street-almost-lawless-residents-say.

29 **They plastered flyers:** Julianne Cuba, "FDNY: Traffic—Not Bike Lanes—Is to Blame for Increased Response Times," *Streetsblog NYC*, September 19, 2019, nyc.streetsblog.org/2019/09/19/fdny-traffic-not-bike-lanes-is-to-blame-for-increased-response-times.

29 **Things got weird fast:** Doug Gordon, Sarah Goodyear, and Aaron Naparstek, hosts, *The War on Cars*, podcast, episode 28, "The Problem with Public Meetings, Part 2," October 4, 2019, thewaroncars.org/2019/10/04/the-problem-with-public-meetings-part-2.

30 **a local reporter later offered this play-by-play:** Jake Offenhartz, "Battle Over Park Slope Bike Lane Gets Physical: 'You Wanna Clown Around with Me?,'" *Gothamist*, September 26, 2019, gothamist.com/news/battle-over-park-slope-bike-lane-gets-physical-you-wanna-clown-around-me.

31 **One of the earliest:** David Jackson, "Bike-Lash!," *New Republic*, March 25, 2010, newrepublic.com/article/74052/bike-lash.

31 ***New York* magazine used the term:** Matthew Shaer, "Not Quite Copenhagen," *New York*, March 18, 2011, nymag.com/news/features/bike-wars-2011-3.

33 **"As a former federal prosecutor":** Ben Fried, "Good Riddance to the Prospect Park West Bike Lane Lawsuit," *Streetsblog NYC*, September 22, 2016, nyc.streetsblog.org/2016/09/22/good-riddance-to-the-prospect-park-west-bike-lane-lawsuit.

34 **In the 1950s, following the lead:** Athlyn Cathcart-Keays and Tim Warin, "Story of Cities #36: How Copenhagen Rejected 1960s Modernist 'Utopia,'" *The Guardian*, May 5, 2016, theguardian.com/cities/2016/may/05/story-cities-copenhagen-denmark-modernist-utopia.

34 **This idea came to a head in 1962:** "'Copenhagenizing' the World, One City at a Time," *Copenhagen Post*, November 10, 2012, cphpost.dk/2012-11-10/general/copenhagenizing-the-world-one-city-at-a-time.

34 **"We're not Italians":** "'Copenhagenizing' the World," *Copenhagen Post*.

34 **pedestrian volumes increased by 35 percent:** Global Designing Cities Initiative, "Pedestrian Only Streets: Case Study | Stroget, Copenhagen," in Global Street Design Guide, 2024, globaldesigningcities.org/publication/global-street-design-guide/streets/pedestrian-priority-spaces/pedestrian-only-streets/pedestrian-streets-case-study-stroget-copenhagen.

35 **eighty thousand people who visit:** "Case Studies: Great Public Spaces," Project for Public Spaces, April 15, 2015, pps.org/places/stroget.

35 **"If you're in New Zealand":** Pippa Coom, interview with Doug Gordon, recorded June 20, 2024.

36 **During a 2019 episode of *The View*:** Sarah Goodyear, Doug Gordon, and Aaron Naparstek, hosts, *The War on Cars*, podcast, episode 10, "Whoops! The Liberal Blind Spot for Cars," January 21, 2019, thewaroncars.org/2019/01/21/whoops-the-liberal-blind-spot -for-cars.

37 **"I also question whether":** John Cassidy, "Battle of the Bike Lanes," *New Yorker*, March 8, 2011, newyorker.com/news/john-cassidy/battle-of-the-bike-lanes.

38 **"as fast as the city":** "New York Bike Lanes Create Controversy," *Outside*, March 10, 2011, outsideonline.com/outdoor-adventure/biking/new-york-bike-lanes-create-controversy.

38 **"streets will become essentially impassable":** Ezra Klein, "Love Driving? Buy Your Neighbor a Bike," *Washington Post*, March 11, 2011, washingtonpost.com/blogs/ezra-klein/ post/love-driving-buy-your-neighbor-a-bike/2011/03/08/AB7JHfP_blog.html.

38 **"As things stand, given that":** R. A., "The World Is His Parking Spot," *The Economist*, March 9, 2011, economist.com/free-exchange/2011/03/09/the-world-is-his-parking-spot.

38 **a leading pedestrian interval (LPI):** Doug Gordon, "Let Cyclists Go on LPIs. (They're Doing it Anyway)," *Brooklyn Spoke*, September 24, 2015, brooklynspoke.com/2015/09 /24/let-cyclists-go-on-lpis-theyre-doing-it-anyway.

39 **Dershowitz wrote in an editorial:** Alan M. Dershowitz, "Pedestrians and Bicyclists, At Odds. Time to Stop the Rampant Running of Red Lights and Change the Culture of Cycling in NYC," *New York Daily News*, April 8, 2018, nydailynews.com/2016/12/03/pedestrians -and-bicyclists-at-odds-time-to-stop-the-rampant-running-of-red-lights-and-change-the -culture-of-cycling-in-nyc.

39 **Michael Hobbes, a journalist:** Doug Gordon, Aaron Naparstek, and Sarah Goodyear, hosts, *The War on Cars*, podcast, episode 72, "You're Wrong About Bikes with Michael Hobbes," November 8, 2021, thewaroncars.org/2021/11/08/youre-wrong-about-bikes-with -michael-hobbes.

40 **researchers at the University of South Florida:** Angie Schmitt, "Study: Cyclists Don't Break Traffic Laws Any More Than Drivers Do," *Streetsblog USA*, January 3, 2018, usa .streetsblog.org/2018/01/03/study-cyclists-dont-break-traffic-laws-any-more-than -drivers-do.

40 **A 2007 study by Transport for London:** Road Network Performance & Research Team, Proportion of Cyclists Who Violate Red Lights in London (Transport for London, RNPR Traffic Note 8, June 2007), content.tfl.gov.uk/traffic-note-8-cycling-red-lights.pdf.

41 **"nearly everyone has jaywalked":** Wesley E. Marshall, Daniel Piatkowski, and Aaron Johnson, "Scofflaw Bicycling: Illegal but Rational," *Journal of Transport and Land Use* 10, no. 1 (2017): 805–36, doi.org/10.5198/jtlu.2017.871.

41 **analysis of Brooklyn's Prospect Park:** Jonathan Soma, "The Important Numbers on the PPW Bike Lane," accessed March 2, 2025, jonathansoma.com/ppw.

42 **"it will change culture":** Jon Orcutt, Twitter, (now X), January 18, 2015, https://x.com /jonorcutt/status/556844177376681984.

43 **"cycle lanes present fundamental challenges":** Kirsty Wild, Alistair Woodward, Adrian Field, and Alex Macmillan, "Beyond 'Bikelash': Engaging with Community Opposition to Cycle Lanes," *Mobilities* 13, no. 4 (2018): 505–19, doi.org/10.1080/17450101.2017 .1408950.

44 **Bloomberg's approval rating:** "The Latest New York Times Polling Results," *New York Times*, August 16, 2013, archive.nytimes.com/www.nytimes.com/interactive/2013/08/18 /nyregion/bloomberg-poll-results.html.

44 **Even as far back:** Doug Gordon, "Culture. Policy. Breakfast," *Brooklyn Spoke*, January 19, 2015, brooklynspoke.com/2015/01/19/culture-policy-breakfast.

45 **The American economist:** Lant Pritchett, "Is Migration Good for Development? How Could You Even Ask?," presentation at Columbia University, February 13, 2009, accessed March 6, 2025, scribd.com/presentation/13110177/Is-Migration-Good-for-Development -columbia#page=22.

45 **Seat belts are:** "Seat Belts," Governors Highway Safety Association, accessed March 4, 2025, ghsa.org/issues/seat-belts.

45 **In 1980, when:** Daniel Ackerman, "Before Face Masks, Americans Went to War Against Seat Belts," *Business Insider*, May 26, 2020, businessinsider.com/when-americans-went-to -war-against-seat-belts-2020-5.

CHAPTER THREE: CARS RUIN CHILDHOOD

50 **Households own an average of two cars:** Data USA, "Upper Montclair, NJ," accessed March 2, 2025, datausa.io/profile/geo/upper-montclair-nj.

50 **"[When] they come to school":** Sarah Goodyear, host, Doug Gordon, interviewer, *The War on Cars*, podcast, episode 110, "Back to School with the Bike Bus," September 5, 2023, thewaroncars.org/2023/09/05/111-back-to-school-with-the-bike-bus.

51 **The world's first organized bike bus:** Jordi Honey-Rosés, "The Global Bike Bus Movement," City Lab Barcelona, January 9, 2024, citylabbcn.org/the-global-bike-bus-movement.

52 **"When you see the children":** Goodyear, "Back to School with the Bike Bus."

54 **"There's a tremendous unmet demand":** Sam Balto, interview with Sarah Goodyear, May 2023.

55 **American psychologist Louise Bates Ames:** Lenore Skenazy, "What '70s Kids Did That Today's Kids Don't," *Times-Republican*, June 11, 2024, timesrepublican.com/opinion /columnists/2024/06/what-70s-kids-did-that-todays-kids-dont.

55 **Ames included a list:** Louise Bates Ames, PhD and Frances L. Ilg, MD, *Your Six Year Old: Loving and Defiant* (Dell Publishing, 1979), Kindle, 65.

55 **Modern parenting happens:** Markella B. Rutherford, *Adult Supervision Required: Private Freedom and Public Constraints for Parents and Children* (Rutgers University Press, 2011).

56 **According to the FBI:** "2022 National Crime Information Center (NCIC) Missing Person and Unidentified Person Statistics Pursuant to the Requirements of the Crime Control Act of 1990, Pub. L. No. 101-647, 104 Stat. 4789," February 2, 2023, fbi.gov/file-repository /2022-ncic-missing-person-and-unidentified-person-statistics.pdf.

56 **In contrast, 1,129 children:** National Highway Traffic Safety Administration, "Traffic Safety Facts: 2022 Data," National Highway Traffic Safety Administration, June 2024, crashstats.nhtsa.dot.gov/Api/Public/ViewPublication/813575.

56 **researchers with the Centers for Disease Control and Prevention:** John D. Omura, Eric T. Hyde, Kathleen B. Watson, Sarah Sliwa, Janet E. Fulton, and Susan A. Carlson, "Prevalence of Children Walking to School and Related Barriers—United States, 2017," Centers for Disease Control and Prevention, stacks.cdc.gov/view/cdc/151601/cdc_151601_DS1.pdf.

57 **Using evidence from pediatricians:** Tiffany Lam, "Too Far to Walk?," *Safe Routes Partnership*, May 22, 2018, saferoutespartnership.org/blog/too-far-walk.

57 **In 1969, 41 percent:** Safe Routes to School, "The Decline of Walking and Bicycling," in Safe Routes to School Guide Online, guide.saferoutesinfo.org/introduction/the_decline _of_walking_and_bicycling.cfm.

57 **In Canada, only 47 percent:** "Active Transportation—How Are Children Getting to School?," Government of Canada, last modified January 13, 2023, canada.ca/en/public -health/services/publications/healthy-living/active-transportation-how-children-getting -school.html.

58 **According to the US Department of Transportation:** "Improving Safety for Walking, Biking, and Rolling," US Department of Transportation, last updated January 17, 2025, www.transportation.gov/pedestrian-bicycle-safety.

58 **The National Poll on Children's Health:** Parent Traffic Hazardous to Student Safety," *Mott Poll Reports* 41, no. 4 (August 15, 2022), mottpoll.org/reports/parent-traffic-hazardous-student-safety.

58 **An analysis of nearly one million car crashes:** Jesse Coburn, "'Always Scared': Dangerous Streets Outside City Schools Threaten Children," *Streetsblog NYC*, May 24, 2022, nyc.streetsblog.org/2022/05/24/danger-zones-chaotic-school-streets-threaten-city-children.

58 **A 2016 study in Toronto:** Linda Rothman, Andrew Howard, Ron Builung, Colin Macarthur, and Alison Macpherson, "Dangerous Student Car Drop-Off Behaviours and Child Pedestrian-Motor Vehicle Collisions: An Observational Study," Traffic Injury Prevention, January 13, 2016, news.yorku.ca/files/driver-behaviour.pdf.

59 **For decades, motor vehicle:** Dustin Jones, "Firearms Overtook Auto Accidents as the Leading Cause of Death in Children," NPR, April 22, 2022, npr.org/2022/04/22/1094364930/firearms-leading-cause-of-death-in-children.

59 **Despite this macabre dethroning:** National Highway Traffic Safety Administration, "Traffic Safety Facts: 2022 Data."

59 **one hundred thousand adolescents died:** "Adolescent and Young Adult Health," World Health Organization, November 26, 2024, who.int/news-room/fact-sheets/detail/adolescents-health-risks-and-solutions.

59 **According to the CDC, only 24 percent:** "Physical Activity Facts," CDC, June 25, 2024, cdc.gov/physical-activity-education/data-research/facts-stats.

59 **A 2024 study by researchers at Polytechnique Montréal:** Zaha Tavakoli, Shabnam Abdollahi, E. Owen D. Waygood, Antonio Páez, and Geneviève Boisjoly, "Traffic Danger's Potential Impact on Children's Accessibility," Transportation Research Part D: Transport and Environment 135 (October 2024): 104370, doi.org/10.1016/j.trd.2024.104370.

60 **Bruce Appleyard, an urban designer:** Sarah Goodyear, "Kids Who Get Driven Everywhere Don't Know Where They're Going," *CityLab, Bloomberg*, May 7, 2012, bloomberg.com/news/articles/2012-05-07/kids-who-get-driven-everywhere-don-t-know-where-they-re-going. Bruce Appleyard is the son of renowned urbanist researcher Donald Appleyard, whose work is featured in chapter 6.

63 **3,300 annual traffic fatalities:** Gary Toth, "Exiting the 'Forgiving Highway' for the 'Self Explaining Road," Project for Public Spaces, August 6, 2009, pps.org/article/what-can-we-learn-from-the-dutch-self-explaining-roads; and Ben Fried, "The Origins of Holland's 'Stop Murdering Children' Street Safety Movement," *Streetsblog USA*, February 20, 2013, usa.streetsblog.org/2013/02/20/the-origins-of-hollands-stop-murdering-children-street-safety-movement.

64 **Five hundred of:** "Stop Killing Our Children," ETA, September 20, 2019, 39 min., 31 sec., vimeo.com/361286029; and Fried, "The Origins of Holland's 'Stop Murdering Children' Street Safety Movement."

64 **One of those children was:** Adam Tranter, "On This Day in 1971: How the Dutch Reclaimed Their Streets for Children," LinkedIn, October 14, 2014, linkedin.com/pulse/day-1971-how-dutch-reclaimed-streets-children-adam-tranter-hhf1e.

64 **He called for the formation:** Vic Langenhoff, "Pressiegroep Stop de kindermoord," *De Tijd*, September 20, 1972.

64 **"The car has disrupted our way of living":** *Together We Cycle*, written by Gertjan Hulster, directed by Arne Gielen (Nieuw & Verbeterd, 2020), togetherwecycle.eu.

64 **Some kids held signs:** Mark Wagenbuur, "Amsterdam Children Fighting Cars in 1972," *Bicycle Dutch* (blog), December 12, 2013, bicycledutch.wordpress.com/2013/12/12/amsterdam-children-fighting-cars-in-1972.

65 **In 1975, the traffic fatality:** Fried, "The Origins of Holland's 'Stop Murdering Children' Street Safety Movement."

65 **Sean Kenney, an artist:** Sean Kenney, email interview with Doug Gordon, September 3, 2024.

66 **"The best park for kids":** Sarah Goodyear, Doug Gordon, and Aaron Naparstek, hosts, *The War on Cars*, podcast, episode 20, "Self-Driving Kids," produced by Matt Cutler, June 26, 2019, thewaroncars.org/2019/06/26/self-driving-kids.

67 **According to UNICEF:** Anna Gromada, Gwyther Rees, and Yekaterina Chzhen, *Worlds of Influence: Understanding What Shapes Child Well-Being in Rich Countries, Innocenti Report Card 16* (UNICEF Office of Research, 2020), unicef.org/innocenti/media/1816/file/UNICEF-Report-Card-16-Worlds-of-Influence-EN.pdf.

CHAPTER FOUR: CARS RUIN NATURE

71 **The conservancy posted:** Central Park (@CentralParkNYC), "It's with a heavy heart we share that a barred owl, a beloved Central Park resident, passed away early this morning," Twitter (now X), August 6, 2021, x.com/CentralParkNYC/status/1423698784836521984.

72 **Rat poison may have contributed:** Katie Honan, "Barry the Owl Was Poisoned Before Central Park Truck Hit Her," *The City*, September 21, 2021, thecity.nyc/2021/09/21/barry-the-owl-was-poisoned-before-central-park-truck-hit-her.

72 **finally banning it in 2018:** Jeffery C. Mays, "Central Park's Scenic Drives Will Soon Be Car-Free," *New York Times*, April 20, 2018, nytimes.com/2018/04/20/nyregion/central-park-car-ban.html.

72 **"Just say your van":** Steve O. (@eveostay), "Just say your van killed the owl—and then announce that you're going to remove motor vehicles from the park FOR REAL," Twitter (now X), August 6, 2021, x.com/eveostay/status/1423741318736617473. Twitter account locked by user, confirmed by the author, November 6, 2024.

72 **"Her arrival during":** Michiko Kakutani, "Barry the Owl Brought Us Together. What Will We Do Without Her?," *New York Times*, August 11, 2021, nytimes.com/2021/08/11/science/barry-central-park-owl.html.

72 **according to the Barn Owl Trust:** "Barn Owl Hazards: Major Roads," Barn Owl Trust, accessed February 27, 2025, barnowltrust.org.uk/hazards-solutions/barn-owls-major-roads.

73 **The first people to document:** Ben Goldfarb, *Crossings: How Road Ecology Is Shaping the Future of Our Planet* (W. W. Norton, 2023), 15.

73 **They didn't call it roadkill:** Goldfarb, *Crossings*, 16.

73 **"On a summer motor":** Dayton Stoner, "The Toll of the Automobile," *Science* 61, no.1568 (1925): 56–57, doi.org/10.1126/science.61.1568.56.

74 **In his 2023 book, *Traffication*:** Paul F. Donald, *Traffication: How Cars Destroy Nature & What We Can Do About It* (Pelagic, 2023), 51.

76 **"Before you can log":** Goldfarb, *Crossings*, 12.

77 **"within two miles of a road":** Sarah Goodyear, host, *The War on Cars*, podcast, episode 108, "Traffication with Paul Donald," July 18, 2023, thewaroncars.org/2023/07/18/108-traffication-with-paul-donald.

78 **335,000 hedgehogs a year perish:** Donald, *Traffication*, 51.

78 **In Indonesia, the government:** A. Muh. Ibnu Aqil, "Indonesia to Build More Wildlife Crossings in Infrastructure Development," Jakarta Post, January 10, 2023, asianews.network /indonesia-to-build-more-wildlife-crossings-in-infrastructure-development.

78 **"Elk scat lay everywhere":** Goldfarb, *Crossings*, 300.

79 **This pink-fleshed fish:** Kale Williams, "The Decline of Pacific Salmon Is 'Death by a Thousand Cuts,' Expert Says," KGW8, December 13, 2023, kgw.com/article/news/local /the-story/pacific-northwest-salmon-columbia-river-endangered-species-act/283 -7bebbb73-8439-4430-a672-6d94c31c6bc9.

79 **"I first started hearing":** Mindy Roberts, interview by Sarah Goodyear, December 7, 2023.

80 **If you've been wondering:** Charles Slack, *Noble Obsession: Charles Goodyear, Thomas Hancock, and the Race to Unlock the Greatest Industrial Secret of the Nineteenth Century* (Hyperion, 2002), 83.

81 **Charles himself had died:** Slack, *Noble Obsession*, 231.

81 **doggedly sifted through the dozens of chemicals:** Sarah McQuate, "Tire-Related Chemical Is Largely Responsible for Adult Coho Salmon Deaths in Urban Streams," UW News, December 3, 2020, washington.edu/news/2020/12/03/tire-related-chemical -largely-responsible-for-adult-coho-salmon-deaths-in-urban-streams.

82 **three Indigenous tribes:** "U.S. Regulators Will Review Car-Tire Chemical That Kills Salmon, Upon Request from West Coast Tribes," CBS News, November 5, 2023, cbsnews .com/sacramento/news/u-s-regulators-will-review-car-tire-chemical-that-kills-salmon -upon-request-from-west-coast-tribes-2.

83 **"When exposed to prolonged":** Donald, *Traffication*, 93.

84 **"Birds raised in the presence":** Donald, *Traffication*, 95.

84 **"The great majority of species,"** Goodyear, "Traffication with Paul Donald."

85 **"Pavement itself blankets":** Goldfarb, *Crossings*, 4.

87 **in memory of P-22:** National Park Service, "Puma Profiles: P-22," nps.gov/articles /000/puma-profiles-p-22.htm.

87 **"Traffication is backed":** Goodyear, "Traffication with Paul Donald."

88 **On Reddit, the savior dude:** throwyMcTossaway, "Sea Turtle Jesus keeps being resurrected every 25-35 minutes!!," in r/CommercialsIHate, Reddit, May 17, 2022, reddit.com /r/CommercialsIHate/comments/uremve/sea_turtle_jesus_keeps_being_resurrected _every.

89 **"You can't see *anything* from a car":** Edward Abbey, *Desert Solitaire: A Season in the Wilderness* (Touchstone Books, 1990), xiv.

89 **"The paradox of roads":** Sarah Goodyear, host, *The War on Cars*, podcast, episode 116, "Road Ecology with Ben Goldfarb," thewaroncars.org/2023/12/19/116-road-ecology-with -ben-goldfarb.

90 **Adfree Cities won a ban:** Clea Skopeliti, "Toyota SUV Adverts Banned in UK on Environmental Grounds," *The Guardian*, November 21, 2023, theguardian.com/media/2023 /nov/22/toyota-suv-adverts-banned-in-uk-on-environmental-grounds.

91 **"a sense of responsibility to society":** Advertising Standards Authority, "ASA Ruling on Toyota (GB) plc," November 22, 2023, asa.org.uk/rulings/toyota—gb—plc-a23-1191673 -toyota—gb—plc.html.

91 **In 2021, Japan recorded:** World Health Organization, Global Status Report on Road Safety 2023 (World Health Organization, 2023), who.int/teams/social-determinants-of-health /safety-and-mobility/global-status-report-on-road-safety-2023.

92 **"Atsushi Hosokawa, an animal":** Hisako Ueno and Yan Zhuang, "A Tokyo Taxi Driver Is Charged with Running Down a Pigeon," *New York Times*, December 22, 2023, nytimes .com/2023/12/22/world/asia/driver-arrested-pigeon-japan.html.

CHAPTER FIVE: CARS ARE KILLING US

95 **"A 1959 Department of Commerce":** Ralph Nader, *Unsafe at Any Speed: The Designed-In Dangers of the American Automobile* (Grossman, 1965), vii.

95 **By 1966, the number of Americans killed:** National Safety Council, introduction, Injury Facts, injuryfacts.nsc.org/motor-vehicle/overview/introduction.

96 **In 2022, 46,027 people:** National Safety Council, "Pedestrians," Injury Facts, injuryfacts .nsc.org/motor-vehicle/road-users/pedestrians.

97 **When Nader was writing:** United States Department of Transportation, "Motor Vehicle Traffic Fatalities and Fatality Rates, 1899–2022," Traffic Safety Facts Annual Report Portal, August 2024, cdan.dot.gov/tsftables/Fatalities%20and%20Fatality%20Rates.pdf.

97 **And the traffic death rate:** National Safety Council, "Car Crash Deaths and Rates," Injury Facts, injuryfacts.nsc.org/motor-vehicle/historical-fatality-trends/deaths-and-rates.

98 **No amount of statistical rationalization:** National Highway Traffic Safety Administration, "Overview of Motor Vehicle Traffic Crashes in 2022," revised June 2024, crashstats .nhtsa.dot.gov/Api/Public/ViewPublication/813560.

98 **Another 5.2 *million* people:** National Safety Council, introduction, Injury Facts.

98 **In the twenty-first century, wealthy nations:** World Health Organization, "Road Traffic Deaths: Data by Country," updated February 9, 2021, apps.who.int/gho/data/view.main .51310?lang=en.

98 **In France, the number of traffic deaths:** French Road Safety Observatory, "2023 Road Safety Annual Report," September 13, 2024, www.onisr.securite-routiere.gouv.fr/en/road -safety-performance/annual-road-safety-reports/2023-road-safety-annual-report.

98 **And in the Netherlands:** Annelies Schoeters, National Road Safety Profile—Netherlands (European Road Safety Observatory, 2023), road-safety.transport.ec.europa.eu/system /files/2023-02/erso-country-overview-2023-netherlands_0.pdf.

99 **Cognitive dissonance is defined:** *Merriam-Webster Dictionary*, "cognitive dissonance" accessed March 4, 2025, merriam-webster.com/dictionary/cognitive%20dissonance.

99 **every day, about 110 people:** National Safety Council, introduction, Injury Facts.

100 **"In 2017, there were 1.44 million years of potential life lost":** Tasnim Ahmed and Aya Elamroussi, "Guns Overtake Car Crashes as Leading Cause of US Trauma-Related Deaths, Study Says," CNN, February 23, 2022, cnn.com/2022/02/23/us/guns-leading -cause-of-trauma-related-deaths/index.html.

100 **"a person is more likely":** National Safety Council, "For the First Time, We're More Likely to Die from Accidental Opioid Overdose than Motor Vehicle Crash," January 14, 2019, https://www.nsc.org/in-the-newsroom/for-the-first-time-were-more-likely-to-die-from -accidental-opioid-overdose-than-motor-vehicle-crash.

100 **In 2022, 1,129 children:** National Highway Traffic Safety Administration, "Traffic Safety Facts: 2022 Data," National Highway Traffic Safety Administration, June 2024, crashstats .nhtsa.dot.gov/Api/Public/ViewPublication/813575.

101 **"Does the fact that our whole lifestyle":** Sarah Goodyear, host, *The War on Cars*, podcast, episode 48, "Right of Way," September 11, 2020, thewaroncars.org/2020/09/11/right -of-way.

101 **"maybe Grandma or Grandpa":** Bess Levin, "JD Vance Says the Solution to the Childcare Crisis Is to Have Grandparents Do It for Free," *Vanity Fair*, September 5, 2024,

vanityfair.com/news/story/jd-vance-solution-childcare-crisis-is-to-have-grandparents
-do-it-for-free.

102 **Air pollution is estimated:** Sumil K. Thakrar et al., "Reducing Mortality from Air Pollution in the United States by Targeting Specific Emission Sources," *Environmental Science
& Technology Letters* 7, no. 9 (2020): 639–45, doi.org/10.1021/acs.estlett.0c00424.

102 **According to the World Health Organization:** World Health Organization, "Ambient
(Outdoor) Air Pollution," October 24, 2024, who.int/news-room/fact-sheets/detail/ambient
-(outdoor)-air-quality-and-health.

102 **Air pollution created:** "Air Pollution and Asthma," Asthma and Allergy Foundation of
America, last reviewed April 2024, aafa.org/asthma/asthma-triggers-causes/air-pollution
-smog-asthma; Cameron Scott, "Study Links Air Pollution to Nearly 6 Million Preterm
Births Around the World," University of California, San Francisco, September 28, 2021,
ucsf.edu/news/2021/09/421471/study-links-air-pollution-nearly-6-million-preterm-births
-around-world; Jake Ellison, "UW Study Strengthens Evidence of Link Between Air Pollution and Child Brain Development," *UW News*, July 12, 2022, washington.edu/news
/2022/07/12/uw-study-strengthens-evidence-of-link-between-air-pollution-and-child
-brain-development; "Study Identifies Mechanism That Links Air Pollution to Heart Disease," Columbia University Irving Health Center, May 25, 2016, cuimc.columbia.edu
/news/study-identifies-mechanism-links-air-pollution-heart-disease; "Air Pollution Particles
Linked to Development of Alzheimer's," University of Technology, Sydney, March 1, 2024,
uts.edu.au/news/health-science/air-pollution-particles-linked-development-alzheimers;
Sushama R. Chaphalkar, "Air Pollution May Affect Male Reproduction via Oxidative
Stress, Says Study," *News Medical Life Sciences*, January 3, 2024, news-medical.net
/news/20240103/Air-pollution-may-affect-male-reproduction-via-oxidative-stress-says
-study.aspx.

102 **Everyone suffers from:** Holly Ober, "Clearing the Air (Inside Your Car)," *UC Riverside
News*, January 13, 2020, news.ucr.edu/articles/2020/01/13/clearing-air-inside-your-car.

103 **"the problem of reduced visibility":** Nader, *Unsafe at Any Speed*, 149.

103 **The automakers knew:** David R. Jones, "Auto Men Testify on Smog Devices," *New York
Times*, April 8, 1965, timesmachine.nytimes.com/timesmachine/1965/04/08/101536941
.html.

103 **in 1965, the same year that Nader:** Joseph C. Ingraham, "Physicians Picket Automobile
Show," *New York Times*, April 8, 1965, nytimes.com/1965/04/08/archives/physicians-picket
-automobile-show-safety-defects-in-new-cars.html.

104 **Scientists in California:** Rosanna Xia, "The Biggest Likely Source of Microplastics in
California Coastal Waters? Our Car Tires," *Los Angeles Times*, October 2, 2019, latimes
.com/environment/story/2019-10-02/california-microplastics-ocean-study.

104 **Particles from brake wear:** "Air Pollution Particles," University of Technology, Sydney.

104 **"massively serious health problem":** Sarah Goodyear, host, *The War on Cars*, podcast,
episode 108, "Traffication with Paul Donald," July 18, 2023, thewaroncars.org/2023/07
/18/108-traffication-with-paul-donald.

105 **has called physical inactivity:** World Health Organization, "WHO Highlights High Cost
of Physical Inactivity in First-Ever Global Report," news release, October 19, 2022, who
.int/news/item/19-10-2022-who-highlights-high-cost-of-physical-inactivity-in-first-ever
-global-report.

105 **Kimble interviewed one:** Megan Kimble, *City Limits: Infrastructure, Inequality, and the
Future of America's Highways* (Crown, 2024), 144–45.

106 **"I-35 is stop-and-go":** Sarah Goodyear, Doug Gordon, and Aaron Naparstek, hosts, *The*

War on Cars, podcast, episode 123, "The Texas Freeway Fight with Megan Kimble," April 2, 2024, thewaroncars.org/2024/04/02/123-the-texas-freeway-fight-with-megan-kimble.

106 **"Residents of peri-urban":** Chien-Yu Lin, Nyssa Hadgraft, Neville Owen, Takemi Sugiyama, and Manoj Chandrabose, "Proximity to City Centre and Cardiometabolic Risk in Middle-Aged and Older Australians: Mediating Roles of Physically Active and Sedentary Travel," *Journal of Transport and Health* 36 (May 2024): 101783, doi.org/10.1016/j.jth.2024.101783.

106 **Japanese researchers took:** Haruka Kato, Taisuke Ichihara, and Kenta Arai, "Health Expenditure Impact of Opening a New Public Transport Station: A Natural Experiment of JR-Sojiji Station in Japan," *Journal of Transport and Health* 36 (May 2024): 101808, doi.org/10.1016/j.jth.2024.101808.

107 **while three quarters of the world's:** World Health Organization, *Global Status Report on Physical Activity 2022* (World Health Organization, 2022), 53, iris.who.int/bitstream/handle/10665/363607/9789240059153-eng.pdf.

108 **In Wuhan, China, air pollution:** Lala Saha, Amit Kumar, Sanjeev Kumar, John Korstad, Sudhakar Srivastava, and Kuldeep Bauddh, "The Impact of the COVID-19 Lockdown on Global Air Quality: A Review," *Environmental Sustainability* 5, no. 1 (2022): 5–23, doi.org/10.1007/s42398-021-00213-6.

108 **the greatest global respiratory virus crisis:** X. Wu, R.C. Nethery, M. B. Sabath, D. Braun, and F. Dominici, "Air Pollution and COVID-19 Mortality in the United States: Strengths and Limitations of an Ecological Regression Analysis," *Science Advances* 6, no. 45 (2020): eabd4049, doi.org/10.1126/sciadv.abd4049.

109 **removing huge numbers of cars:** Sarah Goodyear, Doug Gordon, and Aaron Naparstek, hosts, *The War on Cars*, podcast, episode 39, "Riding Out the Pandemic," March 20, 2020, thewaroncars.org/2020/03/20/riding-out-the-pandemic.

109 **"During this pandemic as people":** Sarah Goodyear, Doug Gordon, and Aaron Naparstek, hosts, *The War on Cars*, podcast, episode 40, "Field Dispatches from Four Continents," March 29, 2020, thewaroncars.org/episode-40-field-dispatches-from-four-continents-final-web-transcript.

109 **"Is the world witnessing":** Sarah Goodyear, Doug Gordon, and Aaron Naparstek, hosts, *The War on Cars*, podcast, episode 43, "Victory?," May 22, 2020, thewaroncars.org/2020/05/22/victory.

110 **"More and more cities are taking on":** "Victory?," *The War on Cars*.

111 **the M14 won the dubious distinction:** Valeria Ricciulli, "Manhattan's M14A Is Officially the Slowest Bus Route in NYC," *Curbed New York*, July 30, 2019, ny.curbed.com/2019/7/23/20707130/nyct-mta-buses-nyc-routes-m14a-b15-manhattan-brooklyn.

112 **In Oslo, incentives for driving:** "Oslo Takes Bold Steps to Reduce Air Pollution, Improve Livability," UN Environment Programme, October 22, 2018, unep.org/news-and-stories/story/oslo-takes-bold-steps-reduce-air-pollution-improve-livability.

112 **In Hoboken, New Jersey, a commitment to:** City of Hoboken, "City of Hoboken Reaches New Vision Zero Milestone: Seven Consecutive Years Without a Traffic Death," January 31, 2024, hobokennj.gov/news/city-of-hoboken-reaches-new-vision-zero-milestone-seven-consecutive-years-without-a-traffic-death.

112 **In London, since 2019 drivers have been charged:** Maelyne Coggins, "ULEZ and Its Expansion," Institute for Government, September 22, 2023, instituteforgovernment.org.uk/explainer/ulez.

112 **53 percent in Central London:** "New Data Shows Mayor's ULEZ Expansion Is Working Better Than Expected, Bringing Cleaner Air to Five Million More Londoners," Mayor of

London's office, press release, July 25, 2024, london.gov.uk/media-centre/mayors-press
-releases/new-data-shows-mayors-ulez-expansion-working-better-expected-bringing
-cleaner-air-five-million-more.

112 **When proposing the expansion of the zone:** "Mayor Announces Bold Plans to Secure a Green, Clean Future for London," Mayor of London's office, press release, January 18, 2022, london.gov.uk/press-releases/mayoral/mayor-announces-bold-plans-for-a-greener -london.

113 **"Mr. Khan's much-hated road charge":** Dan Woodland, "Anti-ULEZ Protesters Clash with Met Police Officers as They're Prevented from Protesting Hated Low-Emission Scheme Outside Sadiq Khan's London Home in Heated Scenes," *Daily Mail*, April 9, 2024, dailymail.co.uk/news/article-13287679/Anti-ULEZ-protesters-Met-Police-officers -Sadiq-Khan-London-home.html.

113 **"We have too often seen measures":** Mayor of London's office, "Mayor Announces Bold Plans to Secure a Green, Clean and Healthy Future for London," press release, January 18, 2022, london.gov.uk/press-releases/mayoral/mayor-announces-bold-plans-for-a-greener -london.

113 **In May 2024, after the expanded ULEZ:** Yasmin Rufo, "Who Is the Conservative Mayoral Candidate Susan Hall?," BBC, April 19, 2024, bbc.com/news/articles/cd1qd770zlvo.

113 **"This is a huge step":** David Zipper, LinkedIn, September 9, 2024, linkedin.com/posts /david-zipper-6833006_my-initial-reaction-this-is-a-huge-step-activity-7239000961 992527875-CFTp.

113 **a law that would require intelligent speed assistance:** Amy Cohen, "California's Anti-Speeding Bill Can Be a Traffic Safety Breakthrough," *CityLab, Bloomberg*, September 17, 2024, bloomberg.com/news/articles/2024-09-17/california-s-anti-speeding-tech-can-be-a -traffic-safety-breakthrough.

114 **It's a promising trend:** "Seat Belts," Governors Highway Safety Association, accessed February 27, 2025, https://www.ghsa.org/issues/seat-belts.

CHAPTER SIX: CARS RUIN SOCIETY

115 **In 1969, San Francisco embarked:** Donald Appleyard, *Livable Streets* (University of California Press, 1981), xiii.

116 **"People are afraid":** Appleyard, *Livable Streets*, 22.

116 **"LIGHT street respondents":** Appleyard, *Livable Streets*, 22.

117 **"The protection and creation of livable streets":** Appleyard, *Livable Streets*, 9.

118 **including in a 2011 study:** Joshua Hart and Graham Parkhurst, "Driven to Excess: Impacts of Motor Vehicles on the Quality of Life of Residents of Three Streets in Bristol UK," *World Transport Policy & Practice* 17 (June 2011): 12–30, core.ac.uk/download/pdf /323897729.pdf.

118 **As Mimi Sheller writes:** Mimi Sheller, *Mobility Justice: The Politics of Movement in an Age of Extremes* (Verso, 2018), 23.

120 **Putnam names autocentric:** Robert D. Putnam, *Bowling Alone: The Collapse and Revival of American Community* (Simon & Schuster, 2000).

120 **The loneliness crisis:** "Our Epidemic of Loneliness and Isolation 2023: U.S. Surgeon General's Advisory on the Healing Effects of Social Connection and Community," hhs.gov /sites/default/files/surgeon-general-social-connection-advisory.pdf.

121 **"A longtime resident of Army Street":** Appleyard, *Livable Streets*, 126.

122 **"It has crept":** Sarah Goodyear, host, *The War on Cars*, podcast, episode 108, "Traffica-

tion with Paul Donald," July 18, 2023, thewaroncars.org/2023/07/18/108-traffication-with -paul-donald.

122 **vehicle miles traveled have soared:** Jeff Davis, "Trends in Per Capita VMT," Eno Center for Transportation, June 7, 2019, enotrans.org/article/trends-in-per-capita-vmt.

122 **The average length of commute:** "Census Bureau Estimates Show Average One-Way Travel Time to Work Rises to All-Time High," United States Census Bureau, press release, March 18, 2021, census.gov/newsroom/press-releases/2021/one-way-travel-time-to -work-rises.html.

122 **More people bought cars:** Charles Komanoff, "Komanoff Dissects New York City's Car Baby Boom," *Streetsblog NYC*, April 19, 2023, nyc.streetsblog.org/2023/04/19/komanoff -dissects-new-york-citys-car-baby-boom.

123 *Motor Mania* **was the title:** Jeff Lenburg, *The Encyclopedia of Animated Cartoons* (Checkmark Books, 1999), 86–87.

124 **The result is a paper:** Ian Walker, Alan Tapp, and Adrian Davis, "Motonormativity: How Social Norms Hide a Major Public Health Hazard," *International Journal of Environment and Health* 11, no. 1 (2023): 21–33, doi.org/10.1504/IJENVH.2023.135446.

124 **"We've all seen this":** Sarah Goodyear, Doug Gordon, and Aaron Naparstek, hosts, *The War on Cars*, podcast, episode 99, "Car Brain with Dr. Ian Walker," January 31, 2023, thewaroncars.org/2023/01/31/car-brain-with-dr-ian-walker.

126 **Other research has revealed:** Benjamin Preston, "The Rich Drive Differently, a Study Suggests," *Wheels* (blog), *New York Times*, August 12, 2013, archive.nytimes.com/wheels .blogs.nytimes.com/2013/08/12/the-rich-drive-differently-a-study-suggests.

126 **Mr. Wheeler is even more:** Carmel Lobello, "It's Not Your Imagination: BMW Drivers Are the Biggest Jerks," *The Week*, January 11, 2015, theweek.com/articles/461073/not -imagination-bmw-drivers-are-biggest-jerks.

126 **"how mobility behavior":** Harald Schuster, Jolanda van der Noll, and Anette Rohmann, "Orientation Towards the Common Good in Cities: The Role of Individual Urban Mobility Behavior," *Journal of Environmental Psychology* 91 (November 2023): 102125, doi .org/10.1016/j.jenvp.2023.102125.

127 **It provides millions:** "State of the U.S. Automotive Industry 2020," American Automakers AAPC, accessed March 5, 2025, americanautomakers.org/sites/default/files/AAPC%20 ECR%20Q3%202020.pdf.

127 **More than 90 percent:** Jack Caporal, "How Many Cars Are in the U.S.? Car Ownership Statistics 2024," *Motley Fool Money*, August 28, 2024, fool.com/money/research/car -ownership-statistics.

127 **the Obama administration pumped:** Mitchell Hartman, "What Did America Buy with the Auto Bailout, and Was It Worth It?," *Marketplace*, November 13, 2018, marketplace .org/2018/11/13/what-did-america-buy-auto-bailout-and-was-it-worth-it.

127 **"a man named Henry Ford":** Trump White House Archives, "Remarks by President Trump at Ford Rawsonville Components Plant," May 21, 2020, trumpwhitehouse .archives.gov/briefings-statements/remarks-president-trump-ford-rawsonville-components -plant.

127 **"Henry Ford was an antisemite":** Jonathan Greenblatt (@JGreenblattADL), "Henry Ford was an antisemite and one of America's staunchest proponents of eugenics. The President should apologize. If he doesn't know why, our backgrounder on Ford's legacy will help: https://adl.org/resources/back," Twitter (now X), May 21, 2020, x.com/JGreenblattADL /status/1263637636830412800.

128 **Ford published eighty-one:** "Henry Ford and Anti-Semitism: A Complex Story," the Henry Ford, accessed March 5, 2025, thehenryford.org/collections-and-research/digital -resources/popular-topics/henry-ford-and-anti-semitism-a-complex-story.

128 **From the Third Reich:** Matthew Wills, "Henry Ford's Anti-Semitism," *J-STOR Daily*, October 13, 2016, daily.jstor.org/henry-fords-anti-semitism.

128 **"Because *The Dearborn Independent*":** "Ford's Anti-Semitism," *American Experience*, PBS, accessed February 27, 2025, pbs.org/wgbh/americanexperience/features/henryford -antisemitism.

129 **"a bloodbath for the country":** Arit John, Kit Maher, and Alayna Treene, "Trump Warns of 'Bloodbath' for Auto Industry and Country If He Loses the Election," CNN, March 17, 2024, cnn.com/2024/03/16/politics/trump-bloodbath-auto-industry-election/index.html.

130 **Before he became Trump's:** Zack Budryk, "Vance Unveils Legislation Eliminating EV Tax Credits," *The Hill*, September 28, 2023, thehill.com/policy/energy-environment /4228180-vance-unveils-legislation-eliminating-ev-tax-credits.

130 **"my steaks and cheeseburgers":** Aaron Rupar (@atrupar), "Ted Cruz: 'Kamala can't have my guns. She can't have my gasoline engine. And she sure as hell can't have my steaks and cheeseburgers," Twitter (now X), July 24, 2024, https://x.com/atrupar/status/1816282 594008285377.

130 **"Are you ready for the government":** Diana Furchtgott-Roth, "The Government Wants to Take Away Your Car," Heritage Foundation, June 12, 2023, heritage.org/government -regulation/commentary/the-government-wants-take-away-your-car.

131 **"only 15 minutes of freedom":** Stuart Jeffries, "What Is Freedom? 15-Minute City Conspiracies Show Just How Little Some Understand It," *Prospect*, April 5, 2023, prospectmagazine .co.uk/society/cities/60923/what-is-freedom-15-minute-city-conspiracies-show-just-how -little-some-understand-it.

131 **Ari Weil, a PhD candidate:** Ari Weil, "Protesters Hit by Cars Recently Highlight a Dangerous Far-Right Trend in America," NBC News, July 12, 2020, nbcnews.com/think /opinion/seattle-protester-hit-car-latest-casualty-dangerous-far-right-trend-ncna1233525.

132 **"I worry that that then":** Sarah Goodyear, host, *The War on Cars*, podcast, episode 47, "Vehicles as Weapons," August 3, 2020, thewaroncars.org/2020/08/03/vehicles-as-weapons.

132 **"moving with other people":** Sarah Goodyear, host, *The War on Cars*, podcast, episode 94, "Walking the Walk with Jonathon Stalls," November 1, 2022, thewaroncars.org/2022 /11/01/walking-the-walk-with-jonathon-stalls.

135 **"Look, I'm sure in every other context":** Goodyear et al., *The War on Cars*, episode 99, "Car Brain."

CHAPTER SEVEN: CARS ARE UNJUST

138 **We talked with historian:** Gretchen Sorin, *Driving While Black: African American Travel and the Road to Civil Rights* (Liveright, 2020).

138 **"the decency of someone else":** Sarah Goodyear, host, *The War on Cars*, podcast, episode 42, "Driving While Black with Gretchen Sorin," May 8, 2020, thewaroncars.org/2020/05 /08/driving-while-black-with-gretchen-sorin.

139 **An essential tool in a Black road tripper's kit:** Victor H. Green, *The Negro Motorist Green Book: An International Travel Guide* (Victor H. Green, 1949), 1.

139 **Driving a personal motor vehicle:** "Jim Crow Segregated Car," B&O Railroad Museum, accessed March 4, 2025, borail.org/explore-learn/exhibitions/jim-crow-segregated-car.

140 **In 2024, the US Justice Department brought charges:** Nick Judin, "Mississippi Town

Ran 'Kinds of Debtors' Prisons Charles Dickens Described,' Justice Department Alleges," *Mississippi Free Press*, September 26, 2024, mississippifreepress.org/mississippi-town -ran-kinds-of-debtors-prisons-charles-dickens-described-justice-department-alleges.

141 **Legal scholar Sarah Seo, in her book:** Sarah A. Seo, *Policing the Open Road: How Cars Transformed American Freedom* (Harvard University Press, 2020).

141 **"The traffic code became":** Aaron Naparstek, host, *The War on Cars*, podcast, episode 30, "The Automotive Police State," October 31, 2019, thewaroncars.org/2019/10/31/the -automotive-police-state.

143 **"The law's accommodation,"** Seo, *Policing the Open Road*, 8.

144 **analysis of one hundred million traffic stops:** Emma Pierson, Camelia Simoiu, Jan Overgoor, Sam Corbett-Davies, Daniel Jenson, Amy Shoemaker et al., "A Large-Scale Analysis of Racial Disparities in Police Stops Across the United States," *Nature Human Behavior* 4 (May 2020): 736–45, doi.org/10.1038/s41562-020-0858-1.

144 **"the automobile stood":** Seo, *Policing the Open Road*, 5.

146 **"long-standing issue of [B]lack mobility":** Rod Clare, "Black Lives Matter: The Black Lives Matter Movement in the National Museum of African American History and Culture," *Transfers: Interdisciplinary Journal of Mobility Studies* 6, no. 1 (Spring 2016): 122, doi.org/10.3167/TRANS.2016.060112.

147 **Nelson, then twenty-nine:** Angie Schmitt, *Right of Way: Race, Class, and the Silent Epidemic of Pedestrian Deaths in America* (Island Press, 2020), 47.

148 **"a scary situation like that":** David Goldberg, "Protect, Don't Prosecute, Pedestrians— Raquel Nelson Seeking a New Trial," *T4America* (blog), August 5, 2011, t4america.org /2011/08/05/protect-dont-prosecute-pedestrians-raquel-nelson-seeking-a-new-trial.

150 **"It causes people to travel less":** Sarah Goodyear, host, *The War on Cars*, podcast, episode 128, "Women's Freedom to Ride," June 11, 2024, thewaroncars.org/2024/06/11/128 -womens-freedom-to-ride.

151 **In the United States, according to a 2019 survey:** Jodi Godfrey and Robert L. Bertini, "Attracting and Retaining Women in the Transportation Industry" (Mineta Transportation Institute, February 2019), transweb.sjsu.edu/sites/default/files/1893-Godfrey-Attract-Retain -Women-Transportation.pdf.

152 **The boy driving the Ford F-250:** Ian Dille, "The Horrific Coal-Rolling Incident That Nearly Killed 6 Cyclists," *Bicycling*, May 23, 2024, bicycling.com/news/a60747401/waller -texas-coal-rolling-cyclist-crash.

152 **Scholar Cara Daggett wrote about rolling coal:** Cara Daggett, "Petro-Masculinity: Fossil Fuels and Authoritarian Desire," *Millennium: Journal of International Studies* 47, no. 1 (2018), doi.org/10.1177/0305829818775817.

CHAPTER EIGHT: DESIGNING A BETTER WORLD

157 **"First, we shape the cities":** Jan Gehl, *Cities for People* (Island Press, 2010), 6.

158 **"We had a Wednesday-night":** Frank Greve, "Curb Ramps Liberate Americans with Disabilities—and Everyone Else," *McClatchy DC*, June 11, 2007, mcclatchydc.com/news /article24460762.html.

159 **calls it the "curb-cut effect":** Angela Glover Blackwell, "The Curb-Cut Effect," *Stanford Social Innovation Review*, Winter 2017, ssir.org/articles/entry/the_curb_cut_effect.

160 **Nearly one in three:** US Department of Transportation, Policy and Governmental Affairs, Office of Highway Policy Information, accessed March 5, 2025, https://www.fhwa.dot .gov/policyinformation/statistics/2020/dl1c.cfm.

161 **When President Biden was under pressure:** Franklin Foer, "Someone Needs to Take Biden's Keys," *The Atlantic*, June 28, 2024, theatlantic.com/politics/archive/2024/06/democrat-biden-trump-debate/678823.

161 **"talk about life without driving":** Sarah Goodyear and Doug Gordon, hosts, *The War on Cars*, podcast, episode 125, "When Driving Is Not an Option with Anna Zivarts," May 7, 2024, thewaroncars.org/2024/05/07/125-when-driving-is-not-an-option-with-anna-zivarts.

162 **the "kinetic elite":** Mimi Sheller, "Mobility Justice, Climate Migration and the Lessons of Pandemic (Im)mobilities," online talk at the University of British Columbia Centre for Migration Studies, September 25, 2020, posted September 28, 2020, by UBC Centre for Migration Studies, YouTube, 40 min., 36 sec., migration.ubc.ca/events/event/mimi-sheller-mobility-justice-climate-migration-pandemic-immobilities.

162 **"I think that parking":** Doug Gordon, host, *The War on Cars*, podcast, episode 98, "The High Cost of Free Parking," January 17, 2023, thewaroncars.org/2023/01/17/the-high-cost-of-free-parking-with-donald-shoup.

162 **Shoup, an engineer:** Donald Shoup, *The High Cost of Free Parking* (Planners Press, 2005), 7.

164 **"Cities require off-street parking":** Shoup, *The High Cost of Free Parking*, 8.

165 **In 2023, journalist Henry Grabar published:** Henry Grabar, *Paved Paradise: How Parking Explains the World* (Penguin Books, 2024).

166 **"permitted on the parking lot":** Doug Gordon, host, *The War on Cars*, podcast, episode 105, "Paved Paradise with Henry Grabar," May 23, 2023, thewaroncars.org/2023/05/23/105-paved-paradise-with-henry-grabar.

167 **But the Parking Reform Network:** Sarah Stuetz, "The Diffusion of Parking Reform in the US: How and Why Now?," Parking Reform Network, July 18, 2024, parkingreform.org/2024/07/18/the-diffusion-of-parking-reform-in-the-us-how-and-why-now.

167 **"until only a few lagging":** Stuetz, Parking Reform Network.

169 **To even buy a car in Japan:** Paul Barter, "Japan's Proof-of-Parking Rule Has an Essential Twin Policy," Reinventing Parking, June 4, 2014, www.reinventingparking.org/2014/06/japans-proof-of-parking-rule-has.html.

169 **Parking on the street overnight:** Christopher Gray, "Streetscapes/Cars: When Streets Were Vehicles for Traffic, Not Parking," *New York Times*, March 17, 1996, nytimes.com/1996/03/17/realestate/streetscapes-cars-when-streets-were-vehicles-for-traffic-not-parking.html.

170 **"Parents we met on our trip":** Margo Pedroso, "SRTS Lessons and Inspirations from Japan," Safe Routes Partnership, 2011, saferoutespartnership.org/resourcecenter/japan.

173 **Seattle architect Paul Thiry had this to say:** Dana Behar, "Seattle I-5 History," Lid I-5, accessed March 5, 2025, lidi5.org/wp-content/uploads/2016/06/seattle-i-5-history.pdf.

173 **A group called Lid I-5:** "Local Freeway Lid History," Lid I-5, accessed March 5, 2025, lidi5.org/history.

174 **During peak travel hours:** Mike Lindblom, "It's Worse Than You Think: Everett Leads the Nation in Traffic Congestion, Report Says," *Seattle Times*, February 5, 2018, seattletimes.com/seattle-news/transportation/its-worse-than-you-think-everett-leads-the-nation-in-traffic-congestion-report-says.

175 **Janno Lieber, the chair:** Emma G. Fitzsimmons, "The Power Broker at 50," *New York Times*, September 3, 2024, nytimes.com/2024/09/03/nyregion/the-power-broker-at-50.html.

175 **something called "induced demand":** Robert A. Caro, *The Power Broker: Robert Moses and the Fall of New York* (Vintage Books, 1975), 515.

176 **The Inflation Reduction Act of 2022:** Ashley Stimpson, "Will the Inflation Reduction

Act Finally Tear Down Baltimore's Highway to Nowhere?," *Next City*, October 5, 2022, nextcity.org/urbanist-news/inflation-reduction-act-baltimore-highway-to-nowhere -removal.

176 **Texas journalist Megan Kimble details:** Megan Kimble, *City Limits: Infrastructure, Inequality, and the Future of America's Highways* (Crown, 2024).

176 **"Seventy years of evidence":** Sarah Goodyear, Doug Gordon, and Aaron Naparstek, hosts, *The War on Cars*, podcast, episode 123, "The Texas Freeway Fight with Megan Kimble," April 2, 2024, thewaroncars.org/2024/04/02/123-the-texas-freeway-fight-with-megan-kimble.

177 **"we're never going to be heard":** Kimble, *City Limits*, 216.

CHAPTER NINE: POLITICAL WILL

180 **In 2017, Filip Watteeuw:** Filip Watteeuw, interview with Doug Gordon, June 18, 2024, Ghent.

180 **After all, the last time this small Belgian city:** Stephen Scourfield, "A Proper Ghent," *West Australian*, July 19, 2020, thewest.com.au/travel/europe/a-proper-ghent-ng-b881613941z.

181 **He was under police protection for three weeks:** Tamsin Rutter, "Car-Free Belgium: Why Can't Brussels Match Ghent's Pedestrianised Vision?," *The Guardian*, November 28, 2016, theguardian.com/cities/2016/nov/28/car-free-belgium-why-cant-brussels-match-ghents -pedestrianised-vision.

182 **Cédéric De Clercq, a mobility:** Cédéric De Clerq, interview with Doug Gordon, June 18, 2024, Ghent.

183 **"The most important part":** Doug Gordon, host, *The War on Cars*, podcast, episode 77, "Curbing Traffic with Melissa and Chris Bruntlett," December 27, 2021, thewaroncars .org/2021/12/27/curbing-traffic-with-melissa-and-chris-bruntlett.

183 **It's pleasant and safe, too:** Renate van der Zee, "How Groningen Invented a Cycling Template for Cities All Over the World," *The Guardian*, July 29, 2015, theguardian.com/cities /2015/jul/29/how-groningen-invented-a-cycling-template-for-cities-all-over-the-world.

184 **60 percent of all trips were now made by bike:** Mark Wagenbuur, "Groningen; Cycling City of the Netherlands?," *Bicycle Dutch*, March 8, 2016, bicycledutch.wordpress.com /2016/03/08/groningen-cycling-city-of-the-netherlands; and "Groningen Has Cleanest Air of Dutch Cities; A'dam Most Polluted," *NL Times*, June 17, 2021, nltimes.nl/2021/06 /17/groningen-cleanest-air-dutch-cities-adam-polluted.

185 **Public parking would not be allowed at all:** "Parking in Ghent: Paid Parking in the City," Visit Ghent, accessed April 21, 2025, visit.gent.be/en/good-know/practical-information /how-reach-ghent/ghent-car/parking-ghent.

187 **Workers removed or erected:** "Cycling Policy," accessed February 27, 2025, stad.gent/en /mobility-ghent/cycling-policy.

189 **The impacts of Ghent's traffic circulation plan:** CoMoUK, "Shared Mobility and a Car-Free Centre in Ghent—a People Focussed Approach," CoMoUK, January 2021, cdn.prod .website-files.com/6102564995f71c83fba14d54/618d2b5889c4361b1d79f42a_CoMoUK %20Mobility%20hubs_Ghent%20case%20study_Jan%202021.pdf; and "The Ghent Circulation Plan," Samen voor Zuivere Luct, accessed February 28, 2025, samenvoorzuivereluct. eu/en/inspiratie/ghent-circulation-plan.

189 **Ghent met its goal by the fall of 2018:** Froso Christofides, "Ghent's History and Future with Cycling," European Cycling Federation, August 29, 2022, ecf.com/en/news/ghents -history-and-future-with-cycling; and "Mobility Policy Ghent," Stad Gent, February 9, 2024, stad.gent/sites/default/files/media/documents/20230905_PR_Mobility%20policy %20Ghent_Focus%20Bicycle_EN.pdf.

189 **All this for a plan that cost only:** Watteeuw, interview.

189 **The data bear this out:** "Mobility Policy Ghent," Stad Gent.

189 **About 450 on-street parking:** "Mobility Policy Ghent," Stad Gent.

190 **And while the city has built:** Mark Wagenbuur, "Ghent (Belgium) Improved Cycling by Diverting Through Traffic," *Bicycle Dutch*, July 3, 2024, bicycledutch.wordpress.com /2024/07/03/ghent-belgium-improved-cycling-by-diverting-through-traffic.

190 **"the best orchestral composer":** Carlton Reid, "How a Belgian Port City Inspired Birmingham's Car-Free Ambitions," *The Guardian*, January 20, 2020, theguardian.com/environment/2020/jan/20/how-a-belgian-port-city-inspired-birminghams-car-free-ambitions.

190 **"The dominant paradigm of our streets":** Meredith Glaser, interview with Doug Gordon, June 18, 2024, Ghent.

192 **"If you're an international star":** Velo Team, "Olympic Gold Medalist and NBA Star Devin Booker Rides Lime Bike Share in Paris," *Velo*, August 13, 2024, velo.outsideonline .com/olympics/olympic-gold-medalist-and-nba-star-devin-booker-rides-lime-bike -share-in-paris.

192 **A recent study found that in central Paris:** Rosie Frost, "Cycling Is Now More Popular Than Driving in the Centre of Paris, Study Finds," Euronews, April 12, 2024, euronews .com/green/2024/04/12/cycling-is-now-more-popular-than-driving-in-the-centre -of-paris-study-finds.

193 **In late 2020 we talked with Christophe Najdovski:** Sarah Goodyear, host, *The War on Cars*, podcast, episode 54, "The French Connection," December 10, 2020, thewaroncars .org/2020/12/10/the-french-connection.

193 **A drivers' advocacy organization:** Salome Gongadze and Anne Maassen, "Paris' Vision for a '15-Minute City' Sparks a Global Movement," World Resources Institute, January 25, 2023, wri.org/insights/paris-15-minute-city.

193 **It's true that the mayor's approval ratings:** Marie Pouzadoux, "Anne Hidalgo Obtains the Worst Presidential Election Result in the History of the Parti Socialiste," *Le Monde*, April 11, 2022, lemonde.fr/en/2022-presidential-election/article/2022/04/11/anne-hidalgo-obtains -the-worst-presidential-election-result-in-the-history-of-the-parti-socialiste-ps_5980262 _16.html.

193 **"They are philistines":** Clea Caulcutt, "Anne Hidalgo's Sack of Paris," *Politico Europe*, December 15, 2021, politico.eu/article/anne-hidalgo-paris-mayor-urban-revolution.

194 **Hidalgo's deputy Najdovski:** Goodyear, "The French Connection."

194 **In an early 2024 referendum:** Chris Liakos and Laura Paddison, "SUV, Non Merci! Paris Votes to Triple Parking Charges for Hefty Cars," CNN, February 5, 2024, edition.cnn .com/2024/02/05/climate/paris-suvs-parking-charges-triple-climate-intl/index.html.

194 **That road itself became a target:** France 24, "Speed Limit on Vital Paris Ring Road Falls to 50km Per Hour on October 1," September 9, 2024, france24.com/en/france/20240909 -speed-limit-on-vital-paris-ring-road-peripherique-lowered-50km-per-hour.

195 **As is customary in France:** "Les riverains les plus exposés ne sont pas convaincus par le périphérique à 50 km/h," *Auto Moto*, September 18, 2024, auto-moto.com/en-bref/les -riverains-les-plus-exposes-ne-sont-pas-convaincus-par-le-peripherique-a-50-km-h -45903.

195 **But Hidalgo and her administration:** "La Zone à Trafic Limité entre en vigueur dans le centre de Paris: Comment ça marche?," City of Paris website, November 13, 2024, paris.fr /pages/paris-cree-une-zone-apaisee-dans-le-centre-de-la-capitale-20426.

197 **"There is a desire for this":** Sarah Goodyear, host, *The War on Cars*, podcast, episode

114, "John Bauters, America's Bike Mayor," November 7, 2023, thewaroncars.org/2023 /11/07/1808.

198 **"You won't even get":** Email from John Bauters to Sarah Goodyear, November 30, 2024.

198 **"I think political will":** Goodyear, "John Bauters, America's Bike Mayor."

CHAPTER TEN: DO IT YOURSELF

200 **The producer snapped a photo:** SUGARPOND (@sugarpond), "Wow! @NYC_DOT is really getting radical!," Twitter (now X), October 1, 2019, x.com/sugarpond/status /1178978613863038976.

200 **Nevertheless, the mysterious hacker:** Aaron Gordon, "'Cars Are Death Machines': Someone Keeps Hacking Road Signs in Brooklyn," *Jalopnik*, October 8, 2019, jalopnik .com/cars-are-death-machines-someone-keeps-hacking-road-sig-1838874851.

203 **On June 11, 2023, a tanker truck:** Mark Scolforo, "Crash That Destroyed I-95 Bridge in Philly Caused by Unsecured Tanker Hatch Spilling Gas, Report Says," PBS News, June 13, 2024, pbs.org/newshour/nation/crash-that-destroyed-i-95-bridge-in-philly-caused-by -unsecured-tanker-hatch-spilling-gas-report-says.

203 **As a result, a temporary six-lane roadway:** Maggie Kent and Briana Smith, "I-95 Re-opens to Traffic with Temporary Lanes 12 Days After Collapse, Tanker Fire," 6abc, June 23, 2023, 6abc.com/i-95-bridge-collapse-live-stream-philadelphia-repair/13417623.

204 **Proposals to improve bus service:** Jesse Coburn and Dave Colon, "'Betrayal': Adams Caves to Opposition, Abandons Bus Improvement Plan on Fordham Road," *Streetsblog NYC*, September 22, 2023, nyc.streetsblog.org/2023/09/22/adams-administration-caves-to -opposition-abandons-bus-improvement-plan-on-fordham-road.

204 **The entire process, from idea to installation:** Clarence Eckerson, Jr., "Go Fourth and Ride: Families Celebrate Brooklyn's 4th Ave Protected Bike Lane," posted Jun 17, 2019, by Streetfilms, 2 min., 22 sec., youtube.com/watch?v=BcaQkeep9vs.

204 **Granted, the short section of highway:** Amanda Holpuch, "I-95 Overpass Collapses in Philadelphia After a Tanker Fire," *New York Times*, June 11, 2023. nytimes.com/2023/06 /11/us/philadelphia-i-95-collapse-vehicle-fire.html.

205 **"employs short-term actions for long-term change":** Mike Lydon and Anthony Garcia, *Tactical Urbanism* (Island Press, 2015), 2; and Robert Steuteville, "Tactical Urbanism Comes of Age," *Public Square*, June 23, 2021, cnu.org/publicsquare/2021/06/23/tactical -urbanism-comes-age.

206 **On the morning of Friday, August 7, 2015:** John R. Ellement, "What the Police Report Shows on the Tragic Crash in Back Bay That Left Bicyclist Dead," *Boston Globe*, February 1, 2018, bostonglobe.com/metro/2018/02/01/what-police-report-shows-tragic-crash-back -bay-that-left-bicyclist-dead/PsSDSt4eyMy4K5tXeC1yCL/story.html.

206 **In all, he spent about forty dollars:** Steve Annear, "Cyclist Creates Temporary Mass. Ave. Bike Lane with Plants," *Boston Globe*, September 9, 2015, bostonglobe.com/metro/2015 /09/09/cyclist-places-potted-plants-mass-ave-create-temporary-bike-lane-plans-install -more/rhH0HV94d1mpImKPy8vfJO/story.html.

207 **"complete lack of will to do what is required":** Jonathan Fertig, GoFundMe, September 9, 2015, gofundme.com/f/flowerlanes.

207 **Fertig raised $1,100 in just two days:** Geffen Semach, "A Commuter Created a Protected Bike Lane with Potted Plants," *Momentum Mag*, September 9, 2015, momentummag.com /a-commuter-created-a-protected-bike-lane-with-potted-plants.

208 **the Department of Transformation:** Stephen Miller, "Eyes on the Street: A Flower-Protected

Chrystie Street Bike Lane," *Streetsblog NYC*, October 7, 2015, nyc.streetsblog.org/2015/10/07/eyes-on-the-street-a-flower-protected-chrystie-street-bike-lane.

208 **A group calling itself:** Chris Cassidy, "Going Rogue: SFMTRA Improving SF Streets," San Francisco Bicycle Coalition, January 21, 2017, sfbike.org/news/going-rogue-sfmtra-improving-sf-streets.

208 **A group of activists in Wichita, Kansas:** Shaunacy Ferro, "Wichita Gets Safer Bike Lanes Thanks to Toilet Plungers," Mental Floss, March 2, 2017, mentalfloss.com/article/92874/wichita-gets-safer-bike-lanes-thanks-to-toilet-plungers.

208 **a bike commuter named Jeffrey Leary:** Lynn Arditi, "Plunger Protest Aims to Help Unclog Bike Lanes," *Providence Journal*, May 11, 2017, providencejournal.com/story/news/politics/county/2017/05/11/toilet-plunger-protest-aims-to-help-unclog-providence-bike-lanes/21053653007.

209 **"The city of Los Angeles doesn't keep us safe":** Crosswalk Collective, accessed March 2, 2025, crosswalksla.org.

209 **"One thing about which fish":** Marshall McLuhan and Quentin Fiore, *War and Peace in the Global Village* (Bantam, 1968), 175.

210 **On a crisp fall morning:** John Bela, interview with Aaron Naparstek, October 2023.

212 **"Improve your neighborhood":** "How-To Manual," Park(ing) Day, accessed February 28, 2025, myparkingday.org/how-to; and Rebar, *The Park(ing) Day Manual* (Rebar Group, Inc., 2009–11), asla.org/uploadedFiles/CMS/Events/Parking_Day_Manual_Consecutive.pdf.

213 **The first official Park(ing) Day:** Rebar, "Park(ing) Day 2006 Trailer," posted July 16, 2007, by rebargroup, YouTube, 4 min., 5 sec., youtube.com/watch?v=6zvG-ay7k5c.

215 **In Los Angeles, 81 percent of businesses:** "L.A. Al Fresco," City of Los Angeles Department of Transportation, accessed February 28, 2025, ladot.lacity.gov/al-fresco.

215 **A New York City Department of Transportation survey:** RSG, "Citywide Mobility Survey: Transportation Impacts of COVID-19—October 2020 Panel Results," New York City Department of Transportation, nyc.gov/html/dot/downloads/pdf/2020_cms_covid_october_summary_report.pdf.

215 **In Iowa, the owner of a:** Katie Akin, Patrick Cooley, Tom Daykin, Mark Kurlyandchik, and Brett Molina, "As Winter Weather Approaches, Restaurants Get Creative with Outdoor Dining," *USA Today*, October 8, 2020, usatoday.com/story/money/2020/10/08/colder-weather-nears-restaurants-rethink-outdoor-dining/5896451002.

216 **On the windshield of each:** "Leaflet," Tyre Extinguishers, accessed February 28, 2025, tyreextinguishers.com/leaflet.

217 **The Tyre Extinguishers went on:** Damien Gayle, "Tyre Extinguishers—Deflating SUV Tyres as a Form of Climate Action," *The Guardian*, March 18, 2022, theguardian.com/environment/2022/mar/18/tyre-extinguishers-deflating-suv-tyres-as-a-form-of-climate-action.

218 **the International Energy Agency:** Laura Cozzi and Apostolos Petropoulos, "SUVs Are Setting New Sales Records Each Year—and So Are Their Emissions," International Energy Agency, May 28, 2024, iea.org/commentaries/suvs-are-setting-new-sales-records-each-year-and-so-are-their-emissions.

CONCLUSION: MOVING TOWARD A LIFE AFTER CARS

223 **In his 1951 short story, "The Pedestrian":** Ray Bradbury, "The Pedestrian," in *The Golden Apples of the Sun* (Doubleday, 1953), 25–30.

225 **"A police car pulled up":** "Ray Bradbury on an Encounter with the Police," undated in-

terview, posted March 19, 2015, by Caryn Brooks, YouTube, 1 min., 45 sec., youtube
.com/watch?v=f-PSXTd3yP0.

226 **That of course means accepting:** "Road Traffic Injuries," World Health Organization,
December 13, 2023, who.int/news-room/fact-sheets/detail/road-traffic-injuries.

227 **not to mention the ocean floor:** Alexandra Gillespie, "Your Next Car May Be Built with
Ocean Rocks. Scientists Can't Agree If That's Good," NPR, September 3, 2021, npr.org
/2021/09/03/1031434711/your-next-car-may-be-built-with-ocean-rocks-scientists-cant
-agree-if-thats-good.

228 **Just ask the San Francisco neighbors:** Wes Davis, "Waymo's Robotaxi Depot Is Still
Honking Its San Francisco Neighbors Awake," *The Verge*, August 18, 2024, theverge
.com/2024/8/18/24223160/waymo-honking-san-francisco-parking-lot-depot-fix-not
-working.

229 **Melissa and Chris Bruntlett, authors:** Melissa & Chris Bruntlett (@modacitylife), "20th
century urban planning changed the concept of a street from a place to pass time to a place
to pass through. 21st century planning is about reversing that mindset and prioritizing people living in a city over cars driving through it. Ferenciek tere, Budapest:2011 vs. 2024," X,
September 21, 2024, x.com/modacitylife/status/1837380600996462969.

229 **offering the Deutschland-Ticket:** "Deutschland-Ticket," Deutsche Bahn, accessed February 27, 2025, int.bahn.de/en/offers/regional/deutschland-ticket.

233 **"I think this is the most important thing":** Jan Gehl, "Jan Gehl: Architects Know
Very Little About People," interview by Matthias Oppliger, *TagesWoche*, March 17, 2015,
tageswoche.ch/politik/jan-gehl-architects-know-very-little-about-people/index.html.

Bibliography

Abbey, Edward. *Desert Solitaire: A Season in the Wilderness.* Touchstone Books, 1990.

Appleyard, Donald. *Livable Streets.* University of California Press, 1981.

Bruntlett, Melissa, and Chris Bruntlett. *Building the Cycling City: The Dutch Blueprint for Urban Vitality.* Island Press, 2018.

Bruntlett, Melissa, and Chris Bruntlett. *Curbing Traffic: The Human Case for Fewer Cars in Our Lives.* Island Press, 2021.

Caro, Robert A. *The Power Broker: Robert Moses and the Fall of New York.* Vintage Books, 1975.

Clarsen, Georgine. *Eat My Dust: Early Women Motorists.* Johns Hopkins University Press, 2008.

Cuomo, Chris J. *Feminism and Ecological Communities: An Ethic of Flourishing.* Routledge, 1998.

Davis, Veronica O. *Inclusive Transportation: A Manifesto for Repairing Divided Communities.* Island Press, 2023.

Doolittle, James Rood, ed. *The Romance of the Automobile Industry: Being the Story of Its Development—Its Contribution to Health and Prosperity—Its Influence on Eugenics—Its Effect on Personal Efficiency—and Its Service and Mission to Humanity as the Latest and Greatest Phase of Transportation.* Klebold Press, 1916.

Ennis, Grant. *Dark PR: How Corporate Disinformation Undermines Our Health and the Environment.* Daraja Press, 2023.

Forman, Richard T. T. *Road Ecology: Science and Solutions.* Island Press, 2003.

Gehl, Jan. *Cities for People.* Island Press, 2010.

Gorz, André. *Ecologica.* Translated by Chris Turner. Seagull Books, 2018.

Grabar, Henry. *Paved Paradise: How Parking Explains the World.* Penguin Books, 2024.

Green, Victor H. *The Negro Motorist Green Book: An International Travel Guide.* Victor H. Green, 1949.

The Holy Bible: Containing the Old and New Testaments, Translated out of the Original Tongues and with the Former Translations diligently compared, Commonly Known as the King James Version. National Bible Press, 1958.

Illich, Ivan D. *Energy and Equity.* Calder & Boyars, 1974.

Jordan, Pete. *In the City of Bikes: The Story of the Amsterdam Cyclist.* Harper Perennial, 2013.

Kay, Jane Holtz. *Asphalt Nation: How the Automobile Took Over America and How We Can Take It Back.* University of California Press, 1997.

Keats, John. *The Insolent Chariots.* J. B. Lippincott Company, 1958.

Kimble, Megan. *City Limits: Infrastructure, Inequality, and the Future of America's Highways.* Crown, 2024.

Lange, Alexandra. *The Design of Childhood: How the Material World Shapes Independent Kids.* Bloomsbury Publishing, 2018.

Longhurst, James. *Bike Battles: A History of Sharing the American Road.* University of Washington Press, 2015.

Lydon, Mike, and Anthony Garcia. *Tactical Urbanism: Short-Term Action for Long-Term Change.* Island Press, 2015.

Malm, Andreas. *How to Blow Up a Pipeline: Learning to Fight in a World on Fire.* Verso, 2021.

Marshall, Wes. *Killed by a Traffic Engineer: Shattering the Delusion That Science Underlies Our Transportation System.* Island Press, 2024.

Mumford, Lewis. *The Highway and the City.* Harcourt, Brace & World, 1963.

Nader, Ralph. *Unsafe at Any Speed: The Designed-In Dangers of the American Automobile.* Grossman, 1965.

Norton, Peter D. *Fighting Traffic: The Dawn of the Motor Age in the American City.* MIT Press, 2008.

Norton, Peter D. *Autonorama: The Illusory Promise of High-Tech Driving.* Island Press, 2021.

Odell, Jenny. *How to Do Nothing: Resisting the Attention Economy.* Melville House, 2019.

Purdy, Jedediah. *After Nature: A Politics for the Anthropocene.* Harvard University Press, 2015.

Putnam, Robert D. *Bowling Alone: The Collapse and Revival of American Community.* Simon & Schuster, 2000.

Rajput, Swati, Kavita Arora, and Rachna Mathur. *Urban Green Space, Health Economics and Air Pollution in Delhi.* Routledge, 2021.

Rutherford, Markella B. *Adult Supervision Required: Private Freedom and Public Constraints for Parents and Children.* Rutgers University Press, 2011.

Sadik-Khan, Janette, and Seth Solomonow. *Streetfight: Handbook for an Urban Revolution.* Viking, 2016.

Schmitt, Angie. *Right of Way: Race, Class, and the Silent Epidemic of Pedestrian Deaths in America.* Island Press, 2020.

Schneider, Kenneth R. *Autokind vs. Mankind: An Analysis of Tyranny, A Proposal for Rebellion, A Plan for Reconstruction.* Authors Choice Press, 1971.

Seo, Sarah A. *Policing the Open Road: How Cars Transformed American Freedom.* Harvard University Press, 2019.

Sheller, Mimi. *Mobility Justice: The Politics of Movement in an Age of Extremes.* Verso, 2018.

Shoup, Donald. *The High Cost of Free Parking.* Planners Press, 2005.

Singer, Jessie. *There Are No Accidents: The Deadly Rise of Injury and Disaster—Who Profits and Who Pays the Price.* Simon & Schuster, 2023.

Slack, Charles. *Noble Obsession: Charles Goodyear, Thomas Hancock, and the Race to Unlock the Greatest Industrial Secret of the Nineteenth Century.* Hyperion, 2002.

Sorin, Gretchen. *Driving While Black: African American Travel and the Road to Civil Rights.* Liveright, 2020.

Stalls, Jonathon. *Walk: Slow Down, Wake Up, and Connect at 1–3 Miles Per Hour.* North Atlantic Books, 2022.

Vanderbilt, Tom. *Traffic: Why We Drive the Way We Do (and What It Says About Us).* Alfred A. Knopf, 2008.

Verkade, Thalia, and Marco Te Brömmelstroet. *Movement: How to Take Back Our Streets and Transform Our Lives.* Scribe Publications, 2022.

Walker, Peter. *How Cycling Can Save the World*. TarcherPerigree, 2017.

Watson, Ann Y., Richard R. Bates, and Donald Kennedy, eds. *Air Pollution, the Automobile, and Public Health*. National Academy Press, 1988.

Yeomans, Matthew. *Oil: Anatomy of an Industry*. New Press, 2004.

Zivarts, Anna Letitia. *When Driving Is Not an Option: Steering Away from Car Dependency*. Island Press, 2024.

Index

Italicized page numbers indicate material in photographs or illustrations.